# ENEMIES OF THE STATE

Teresa Radomska

for an incredible family who survived the labour camps,
their body and spirit sorely tested in the Russian wilderness.
They never gave in to Stalin, they fought for their freedom
over the many stages of their escape.
They will not be forgotten nor will 'those we left behind,
too starved to lift themselves off the ground,
we remember our Sybiraks'

**Please note:**
*'A Family Exiled'* has now been amended and split into two separate shorter books; *'Enemies of the State'* (the prequel) and *'Hurricanes of Polish Fury'* (the sequel – due for publication by end of 2024). This is to allow for an easier read of substantial volume of historical information.

ISBN: 978-1-917425-51-3

# CONTENTS

## The Uninvited Visitors 10th February 1940

*In honour of my family, let me tell their story as victims of the Russian dictator Stalin, who brutally suppressed anyone or any country that got in his way. Even Lenin thought he could be dangerous, if he had more power than he could handle and so it proved!*

The Bolsheviks were everywhere, Stalin had a plan for the Polish Military settlers in the Kresy Kazia thought as she sat by the window watching events unfold, waiting. She had seen German planes pounding her country into submission, many of her friends had already been arrested and she now waited for the knock on her door.

Refugees were escaping from the German invasion in the west, their carts loaded with belongings and there were tanks full of Russian soldiers advancing into Poland from the east. Hitler and Stalin were meeting the terms of their 1939 agreement, the Molotov-Ribbentrop pact, the eradication of the entire Polish nation, its people and culture.

The long awaited knock on the door, or rather, the aggressive entrance into their home, came in the early hours of 10th February 1940 when the NKVD entered. Waving their pistols and shouting, 'you are an enemy of the people a threat to public order.' 'You are under arrest, pack your things, you have one hour, be ready,' the leader screamed at her.

Many would be stunned into terror and shock but Kazia was ready, had been for weeks, her first thought, how would she get word to her husband who was in hiding from these very Bolsheviks?

She gathered her frightened children together, Alicja, Jasia and Janusz and told them to dress quickly, put as many clothes on as they could and as many as would go into bags. She knew where they were being taken. Memories of her Dziadek and his arrest by the Tzarist Security Police came to mind.

Alicja the eldest headed for the cellar to gather as much food as she could. The children were terrified but did as Kazia asked. She meanwhile got together as much as she thought would be good to barter for what they might later need. She also put the family photographs into a pillow case, covered with towels.

Those photographs travelled over 20,000 kms, protected for future generations and are featured in this memoir.

*My Babcia, was incredible, to have such foresight in a most terrifying moment. – With my Mother Alicja, an inspiration to write this story.*

After about an hour the Bolsheviks returned and led the family, Kazia, Alicja, Jasia and Janusz outside and under very heavy snowfall bundled them onto a sleigh where some of their neighbours already sat, shivering and so very scared.

They were all terrified and held onto each other tightly and as Kazia looked back to their home she noticed the heavy snow was covering their very existence and saw Cezar their dog lying in the snow, shot by the Soviets. She took a deep breath and kept the sobs at bay.

After about an hour they were met at Lubomyrka station with many goods wagons surrounded by large numbers of Soviet soldiers and many families gathered, cold, frightened, in tears and shock. The Trains stretched as far as the eye could see. Where was Adam. There had been no time to get word to him, would he find them before the trains left Poland?

So began an ordeal for my family and 1.7 million other Polish citizens, exiled by Stalin to the gulags spread over the USSR, There were over 30,000. It was the beginning of many journeys of more than 22,000 km's over several years. There's more detail in Chapter 10.

The Polish exiles travelled through Poland to Arctic Russia and other remote parts of the USSR. My family and the military settlers were sent to the Arkhangelsk Oblast.

After the so called 'amnesty' in 1941 the family, with others who were just fit enough physically and mentally, escaped from Russia, taking on the most demanding journeys through the Ural mountains, the Kurdistan Steppes, Kazakhstan, Uzbekistan and eventually into Pahlevi in Persia and freedom. Numerous journeys amounting to about 4,000 kms.

The journeys were long and exhausting with little medical attention along the many stops and a large number didn't make it, the labour camp conditions taking a toll. The NKVD were also disrupting access to the trains and generally making things difficult.

When they arrived at Tashkent about 30 of the escapees were taken into a field and told to wait. Two days and nights without food or water, no Polish officials there to help them, they were terrified. Then the Uzbeks came and they were put onto a train to Bukhara, then to Vobkent in a yak to work in the fields for the Uzbeks. They were distraught, and still prisoners of Stalin.

*Read how Kazia got her daughters Alicja and Jasia, out of the grip of the Uzbeks and the NKVD and into the eventual warm embrace and hospitality of the Persian people. She and my Wujek Janusz were now separated from the girls staying behind in Vobkent, did they ever find each other? Read on....*

In Pahlevi, Isfahan and Tehran the refugees were very warmly welcomed by the Persian people who offered them safety and helped them with recovery together with English and Polish Nursing units based there.

This story is one of daily struggles with physical and mental efforts to survive the unspeakable hardship they had gone through. The winters had been icy, mostly -30 and even children were sent into the forests to work in those conditions, my Mum Alicja was just 16, spending that birthday on the train to Russia.

There had been rampant disease and starvation then the despair of losing their country to the Communists, betrayed at Yalta.

Yet the Polish exiles, when eventually recovered, fought on with the Allies to the very end. Their many achievements as an Ally are listed in the Sequel – 'Hurricanes of Polish Fury' of this memoir.

*I hope I've captured your interest to read on and become familiar with a little known episode of WW2.*

Teresa Radomska,
Córka i Wnuczka Sybiraczek – 2024

My family and the many other Sybiraks will not be a forgotten part of WW2 history.

*'If you don't recount your family history*
*it will be lost.*
*Honor your own stories and tell them too,*
*they may not seem very important*
*but they are what binds families and*
*makes each of us who we are.'*

**Madelaine L'Engle**

## The Family Radomski – Góral

My grandparents, Kazia and Adam my mother Alicja, Aunt Janina and Janusz my Uncle at the time of the invasions lived in Równe. Kazia's brother Walery and his wife Ziuta, sons Włodek and Zbigniew and daughter Marysia were living on their Osada Krechowiecka (named after Adam and Walery's regiment the 1st Lancers Krechowiecki) just outside Równe and near to the Ukrainian Russian border in the eastern borderlands of Poland. My Grandfather Adam and Great Uncle Walery had been awarded Osadas on the borderlands after the Bolshevik war of 1920 as reward for the success of Poland regaining territory lost in previous partitions.

On the 10th February 1940 on a bitterly cold day at 5am Stalin's Secret Police, the NKVD, burst into my grandparent's home waving guns and screaming at them. They were arrested as 'anti Soviet elements,' told they were to be exiled to Siberia, stripped of their land and home and given half an hour to pack some belongings. They were then taken to an assembly point outside Równe in a horse drawn sledge passing many of their neighbours awaiting the same fate. Stalin viewed these Military settlers as a danger to his plans to Sovietise parts of Europe as this was the most likely group of people to stand up to him and his plans.

There were 5 mass deportations of the military and civilian populations of eastern Poland in 1939-41 with a clear distinction made between the February 1940 deportation and the April one. The February military deportees were targeted as 'special settlers' and sent to zones selected in isolated areas and administered by a special branch of the NKVD. They were sent to 13 Oblasts, Arkhangelsk, Yekaterinburg, Irkulsk, Molotov, Vologda, Omsk, Novosibirsk, Chelysbinsk, Gorki, Czkalovsk, Kirov, Ivanovo and Yaroslavi. Other deportees were sent mainly to Kraij-Altai, and Krasnoyarsk, Komi, Mari, Yakut and Bashkiv.

From their home in Równe they were transported in cattle wagons towards the deep snows of Siberia and the Arctic regions, the train stopping at Gorki after 17 days then onto Sharya from where they had to walk many miles in very deep snow to the labour camp, Poldniewica, the first of 3 camps, later to Duraszewo and finally to Derewalka. Their only crime was being Polish and being 'an enemy of the people.'

They were expected to work for their communist masters, clearing forests to lay tracks for a railway line, from dawn to dusk on the most meagre rations. Many perished through malnutrition, disease and the cold.

Used as slave labourers they were worked until they dropped. A deportee was a 'nonperson,' a slave of the Soviet penal system. Upon arrival at the prison, labour camp or penal colony they were told by the Commandant: 'Here you will live and here you will die, niechevo, hairs will grow on my palms before you are free.'

By the middle of 1941 most of those Polish citizens had been imprisoned in subhuman conditions throughout Russia, from the Caucasus to the White Sea, in Steppe, Tundra and Taiga, from the Urals, Kazakhstan and onto the mountains of Russian Asia. At the same time 222,000 Polish servicemen arrested in 1940, were imprisoned in Siberian Gulags.

Life was awful from the very beginning but their spirit and determination was so strong, it saw them through the hell of the labour camp, the towers, barbed wire fences, searchlights and the routine aggression towards them. Every day they prayed, 'do not despair, have faith the Bolsheviks will not break you.' They suffered incredible hardship and many starved. Survival was of the utmost importance and attitude was a crucial factor and I put their survival down to their faith and love for each other and their spirit, the spirit that Stalin wouldn't break.

They also had good luck on their side and the kindness of the friends they had made, including the generous acts from the Russians deported there after the Revolution in 1917 which added towards their survival. The Russian people gave shelter when needed and shared what little food they had. The conditions were brutal, lone women were forced to give up their children to Soviet orphanages or watch as they starved to death. It was heart breaking.

Upon Hitler's attack on the USSR in June 1941 Stalin, unable to withstand Hitler's forces on his own, had no choice but to enter into an alliance with the West and turned to Churchill and Roosevelt for help. Their condition was the release of his Polish prisoners and the formation of a Polish army. The Soviet Ambassador to the UK Ivan Maisky and General Sikorski on behalf of the Polish Government signed the first diplomatic agreement on 30th July 1941. Maisky then announced that the Soviet-German treaty of August 1939 relating to the territorial division of Poland along the Ribbentrop-Molotov line was no longer valid.

General Anders had been nominated as Commander of the new Polish Army by Genera Sikorski and it was his intention to get as many Poles out of Russia as he could and he did his utmost against a belligerent Stalin. Polish soldiers had been commissioned to travel to the various camps and Kolkhozes across the USSR to gather as many isolated families as they could. The area was vast and the terrain, mountains, forests the sub-arctic climate made it extremely difficult to reach those spread so widely.

Stalin agreed an 'amnesty' which assured the release of Polish POWs and civilian deportees which took considerable time to get through to the Poles across the vastness of the USSR. Many were never informed that they were free to leave, the 'amnesty' deliberately kept from them to retain their labour. However, by late 1941 25,000 Polish recruits had joined Anders' Army from the gulags (Buzuluk RU) with civilians joining them and they all headed towards Tehran.

Although Stalin officially complied he made things very difficult with inadequate rations, medical aid and equipment so General Anders demanded that his army be evacuated from the USSR to the Middle East to fight under British command. He also demanded that all Polish civilians leave with him. An invitation to the many Poles incarcerated in labour camps and gulags that they couldn't refuse despite their hatred for the Bolsheviks, they just wanted to fight the Germans.

In March/April 1942 33,069 Soldiers and 10,879 civilians including 3,100 children were evacuated from USSR and Anders' army operations moved to Tashkent in Uzbekistan. Civilian Poles from the labour camps also headed there and in August-September 1942 43,746

Soldiers from the Gulags and 25,501 civilians including 9,633 children were evacuated to Persia.

The Polish Embassy in Kubyshev in the meantime was struggling to help the many thousands of refugees moving south, fleeing their mistreatment and imprisonment, they were exhausted and suffering from malaria, dysentery, typhus and other ailments, especially the effects of starvation. Their physical condition not able to sustain them through about 4,000 km of Soviet terrain and they had to contend with the NKVD disrupting their journeys and intercepting them for their labour despite the safety to travel towards the Polish army assured them by the 'amnesty.'

Once discharge papers had been issued my family were faced with the arduous journey from Siberia to Uzbekistan. Like many Poles who made their escape from imprisonment in Russia, they were determined to join the Polish Army gathering in Tashkent. They had no other option and another struggle for survival began. With very little food to sustain them, often ill with dysentery and typhus, they weren't fit to fight and were separated at times but with great determination they journeyed on towards the Polish army. That was the only thing on their mind, to link up with the Polish army however long it took and they barely survived their ordeal.

The journeys from the labour camp took the family on the Trans Aral, Trans Siberian railways and into five time zones. Briefly, they travelled through the Ural Mountains, skirting the Kurgistan Steppes, through Kazakstan and into Uzbekistan. From Bukhara they were taken to Vobkent and forced by the Soviets, determined to delay them reaching freedom, into hard labour for the Uzbeks. Their physical condition was desperate.

They were only able to leave Vobkent when reunited with Walery who had been searching for them. He had been posted to nearby Tashkent and advised Kazia to enlist my mother and aunt in the Polish cadets in Guzor. The girls set off to Guzor and my grandfather was posted to Iraq whilst Kazia stayed with my uncle Janusz in Vobkent. They were reunited with the girls in Pahlevi sometime later as Kazia had finally managed to enlist Janusz in the cadets. She was now desperately ill in hospital in Tehran.

Once in the safety of Pahlevi in Persia they were out of Stalin's reach and able to begin their recovery. By this stage they had other journeys to make, to Refugee camps from Pahlevi to Tehran and Isfahan then onto

Ghazir and Beirut in Lebanon, where my mother married in 1946 an Englishman serving in the RAF. The family would eventually find a home in England, my Mother and her husband William and Aunt in 1946 and my grandparents and uncle in 1948.

On their arrival at Liverpool docks from Lebanon on 19.2.1948, Kazia Góral nee Radomska, born in Wróblewo on 23.2.1899 presented her Paszport 11445/43c issued in Beirut on 25.2.1943 and was presented with Alien Order A128294.

Adam Góral born Daleszewicze on 26.5.1894, presented his Paszport 11446/43c and was issued his Alien Order A128295.

'Permission to land at Liverpool was granted on condition that the holder registered at once with the Police'. They were not exempt from restrictions of the Alien Orders until 29.5.1961.

From Liverpool my grandparents and Uncle were assigned to Resettlement Camps in Pulborough, Horsham, Helstem and Ely over a period of time. They had clothing issued to them on 1.3.1948 as they had arrived in England with very little as had many refugees arriving in England after the war. Many of the refugees from Poland were initially subsidised by the Polish Government as they had been in the refugee camps in Persia and Lebanon.

My parents were there to meet them at Liverpool and it was a joyous and emotional day, I was 6 months old, the first born to a free family and it was my Mother's birthday. Very many tears were shed.

Some thoughts from my Mother, Alicja, regarding refugee families in England. – 'we made up small pockets of Poland, holding onto whatever fragments remained of our once normal lives. We spoke Polish, German, Russian, Hungarian, Czechoslovakian and Yiddish. We all felt out of place, we knew we were new to this country and that we belonged somewhere else... We were survivors and children of survivors and many of us had lost family members. Marriages were made in haste and some out of desperation, there was a deep need to have someone to hold and love. Most of us were still in shock and grieving for a lost Poland.'

Life in England as a refugee was difficult and my grandparents especially didn't tell many people of their past, they hid it and somehow dealt with their demons. Physically, the family gradually recovered, yet the mental scars were more difficult to heal. The family had lost absolutely everything, their home, livelihood and liberty and gone through a life threatening experience. There were times when something would trigger a memory and transport them back to the camp and they would feel the fear. I sometimes saw it in my Mother's eyes and manner and the way she would regularly walk up and down the long lounge struggling with her emotions, walking the memories away.

They would hoard food, treasure it, remembering the starvation in the camps. They always had to have enough food and my Mother's cupboards were crammed full of tins and packets and jars from the Deli. She and my grandparents never returned to Poland, they didn't take the opportunity to see their homeland again, the Kresy, it was now part of the Ukraine with the border changes made by Stalin.

I am but one voice, a grandaughter and daughter of an extremely brave family and I have gone through an emotional journey of my own to unravel their past, their suffering which was buried very deep, their stubborn resilience, belief and determination. The Radomski's were never far behind or ahead of the Góral's in any of the many routes covered from Poland to the USSR to Persia to Lebanon and finally to England where they were all reunited. They seemed to be connected by a very strong radar of their own, a very lucky family and their defiant spirit shines out still.

I dedicate this memoir specifically to my dahlink Mamusia Alicja, who at 97 still remembers the labour camp in Siberia despite suffering from Alzheimers and to the memory of my beloved grandparents, Kazia and Adam and the other members of the Góral and Radomski family's who have been my inspiration. My reason for looking into their history, which is my history, a big part of who I am.

There is an irony in the telling of this episode of WW2. Had my family not been deported to Siberia they would most likely have fallen victim to the massacre of Poles in Wołyn and Eastern Galicia, by the Ukrainian Nationalists who razed their town Równe, to the ground and murdered those settlers who had escaped Stalin's deportations. Between 76,000 and 106,000 were victims of this barbarism, mostly women and children over the entire region, my Babcia's cousin Toscia and her two infant sons were burned alive. In 2016 the Parliament of Poland passed a resolution recognising the massacres as a Genocide and in the Ukraine to this day the UPA members are celebrated as heroes.

*A person is only forgotten*
*if their name is forgotten,*
*the Góral - Radomski's are not forgotten,*
*their name is written into memory*
*in this biography.*

Teresa Radomska 2021

Alec, Alicja and Teresa

## Hitler, Stalin and Roosevelt

In September 1939, in the signing of the Molotov-Ribentrop pact, Stalin with Hitler partitioned Poland in two. I am concentrating mainly on the Russians in this memoir as Stalin was the guilty warmonger who caused huge misery and terror to my family. Millions of Poles, Kulaks, Cossacks, Ukrainians, Kazakhs, Soviet veterans and Orthodox Christians died or were executed and many others suffered similar fates. Stalin had seen an opportunity when signing the Pact with Hitler to take revenge on the Polish Military settlers of the Kresy whom he considered 'enemies of the state.'

I will call this action a Holocaust because it was, without doubt, the deliberate and systematic destruction of a group of people because of their ethnicity – and this Holocaust of the Polish people and their country is ignored by the West and neither of the perpetrators have made sufficient if any restitution to Poland.

They both inflicted horrors on the Polish people who in 1939 numbered 35 ml and by 1945 were 24 ml. As well as the two main protagonists there was the Ukrainian UPA an ally of Germany who murdered over 100,000 Poles, mostly women and children in Wołyn, Polesia, Galicia, Podilia and Carpathia. Poland had suffered the most awful barbarism inflicted on any nation and unlike the Jewish Holocaust which quite rightly has world wide support the Polish Holocaust appears to have none.

Stalin's hatred of the Poles was based on class and was the motivation for his first act on entering Poland in 1939 to focus on the bourgeoise of Poland, the elements of Polish society who would most likely oppose Communist rule and this included the military men who had settled the Kresy after the Polish - Russian war of 1920 – men like my grandfather Adam and Great Uncle Walery.

Stalin's aim was to crush the military families, there was no place for this 'clique' in the Soviet order, he had not forgotten the defeat of the 1920 war and he wasted no time in deporting them en masse to the frozen wastelands of Siberia. These Poles were damned in the eyes of the Soviets who hated them. Aristocrats, Military Officers, Judges, writers, teachers, forest workers, land owners, the bourgeoise of Poland, Stalin's reason for wanting to eliminate them as they posed a threat in being more likely to stand up to him.

Hitler's plan meanwhile was to establish the supremacy of the Aryan race which meant not just the elimination of Polish Jews but also of Polish Christians, who were referred to by Hitler as 'subhuman'

(Untermenschen). His hatred for the Polish people in general, was so intense he intended to eliminate them from the face of the earth. One of his initial commands was 'to send to death mercilessly and without compassion men, women and children of Polish derivation and language.' His attitude towards the citizens of Warsaw was 'Every inhabitant of Warsaw has to be killed, including men, women and children and all traces of their existence have to be removed. Do not take any prisoners! Every building has to be razed, Warsaw must be levelled to the ground in order to set a terrifying example to the rest of Europe.' Adolf Hitler 1944. The Warsaw Uprising had infuriated the German leaders who decided to make an example of the city and its people.

The night time arrests by Stalin's Secret Police began in 1940 without explanation or warning when they arrested over 250,000 civilians, 'anti-Soviet elements' and took them to already waiting transport, – cattle wagons primed for the journey to exile. Without adequate clothing in the bitterly cold winter and very little food, it would lead to the starvation of hundreds of thousands who were faced with the ever present stench of death, gnawing hunger and oppression by the NKVD.

Poles were also to suffer the first of many deaths at Auschwitz for which the camp had initially been built in 1940, to hold Polish political prisoners, the first group arriving in June 1940. By October 1941 20,000 Polish Catholics and 10,000 Soviet prisoners of war had been 'processed' at Auschwitz. The Germans forcibly deported approximately 2.8 ml Polish gentiles into labour for the Third Reich and the Russians had deported almost 1.7 ml Poles to Siberia by June 1941. An innocent people terrorised by two tyrants who then suffered massacres at the hands of the UPA.

There is no argument that Hitler abhorred Jews and caused so many ruthless deaths, I do not wish to lessen the enormity of the murders in the Holocaust but there were others, non-Jewish victims who are forgotten from Remembrances. So many precious lives were lost, over 3,000,000 were Polish Christians.

Despite being under constant surveillance, many Poles risked their lives to help Jews during the occupations and many were murdered for helping Jews. Poland was the only country in Europe with the death penalty imposed ruthlessly by German death squads for helping their brother Poles. They were also terrorized into transporting Jews to the Concentration camps and not to comply would have meant death to them and their family. Many Polish railway workers were also forced into transporting their countrymen to the prison camps and gulags across the Soviet Union.

In June 1941 Hitler declared war on the USSR, in Operation Barbarossa and a Polish-Soviet agreement was signed, the Sikorski-Maiski, after the reinstatement of Polish-Soviet diplomatic relations. On the signing of that agreement in August 1941 Stalin had agreed to revoke the Poland related aspects of the Molotov-Ribbentrop pact of 1939 and an 'amnesty' was declared for the Polish citizens in the labour camps and gulags across Russia. This prompted a massive exodus of Poles fleeing the USSR to join the Polish Army in Iran.

Stories like this are unknown to many westerners and when told they find it difficult to comprehend the depravation of what 1.7 ml Polish deportees went through. Not many Western history books record this episode and few politicians honour these victims in speeches commemorating World War II. From a personal view accounts of the war are incomplete without this neglected historical tragedy which is also mostly unknown of in Poland's communist era, not taught in schools and forbidden to be spoken of.

There are many photographs in the public domain showing victims from German extermination camps and scenes of German atrocities but not a single photo of a Polish adult prisoner of the Soviet gulag! Or of a Polish Mother and child as they really looked after escaping out of Russia, starved, skeletal and in rags. The legacy of silence and disinformation and deception to which the Roosevelt administration went to during the war remains to this day unchallenged and is an affront to historical truth.

The US propaganda machine, the OWI, (Office of War Information) held back photos of skeletal Polish children, taken in August 1942 by Lieutenant Colonel Henry Szymanski of the US army, publishing instead those of healthy children. Szymanski's photograph's and report of his observations on the deplorable condition of the refugees was classified as 'secret' and not published until 1952. Such was Roosevelt's fear that Americans, especially Polish Americans would learn the truth about Stalin's crimes against Poland and her people, his brutality was ignored so as not to upset the alliance with him! – although this is hugely questionable.

Roosevelt hid the Soviet mass murder of Polish POWs in Katyn and supressed an official US Government report of it as well as ignoring a British report from Churchill. A Polish Officer, Intelligence agent & Resistance leader, Witold Pilecki presented his report on the mass murder of Jews in German occupied Poland to the Allies which was ignored. Jan Karski, a Polish Diplomat, Underground courier for the Polish Government in Exile and Resistance member, relayed his eyewitness evidence of the Holocaust to US Supreme Court Justice, Felix Frankfurter, it too was ignored. They both risked their lives gathering information in Auschwitz and the Warsaw Ghetto and were not believed by Roosevelt or Churchill.

The mistreatment of Polish deportees was ignored, there was a total blackout, instead, Soviet propaganda of these events was spread in radio broadcasts by the OWI and the VOA (Voice of America) agencies headed by Communist sympathisers. Roosevelt refused to admit one Polish orphan during the war despite official representatives from the British Government to take 30,000 of the Polish refugees left in Persia who were the dependants of the 44,000 Poles who had joined the Polish Army. Persia at that time had already taken in large numbers of Polish war refugees.

The State Department advised the British Government 'that the US would not accede to its request' but the British representatives asked a second time and in reply the State Department declared 'that the US immigration laws would not permit these people to enter the US' and furthermore the US State Department advised the British representatives 'to take the Polish refugees to South Africa' a country that had already taken in large numbers.

The State Department then informed the British representatives that if they could find some country to take the Polish refugees then the US Government and the American Red Cross would help with aid. General Sikorski met with Mexican President Manual Camacho who in December 1942 agreed to take 28,000 refugees on quite restrictive conditions and Roosevelt agreed to make $3ml available for the transportation of the Poles to Mexico and for their first year there.

The whole episode was shrouded in secrecy, the refugees were kept in internment camps with Japanese Americans and travelled from Los Angeles to Santa Rosa in Mexico in a sealed train guarded by US army officials. Some of these refugees and orphans were on the Windrush with the West Indians after the war, hidden from view and not allowed to mix freely.

The end of the war brought about the complete betrayal of Poland to Russian oppression at the Yalta meeting on 11th February 1945 between Roosevelt, Churchill, and Stalin. It was a most unexpected blow to the many Poles dispersed throughout the world, who had fought, bled and died for the Allied cause. An agreement had been reached, with no resistance from Roosevelt or Churchill and no representation from the Polish Government, that Poland would fall into the Soviet sphere post WW2. The matter of returning home suddenly ceased to be taken for granted. How could my grandparents return to a communist Poland, a dictatorship? Unless you were a communist there was no future in Poland and my Dziadek abhorred Communism.

Or as Witold Gombrowicz Polish novelist and dramatist put it, 'The end of the war did not bring liberation to the Polish people, in the battlegrounds of central Europe it just meant swapping one form of evil for another, Hitler's henchmen for Stalin's. While sycophants cheered and rejoiced at the 'emancipation of the Polish people from the feudal yoke' the same lit cigarette was simply passed from hand to hand in Poland and continued to burn the skin of the people'. I think Dziadek would have agreed with those sentiments.

Poland had become a forgotten backwater trapped behind the Iron Curtain and largely ignored by the world until the rise of Solidarność in the late 1970's and early 1980's. My grandparents died in 1983 and 1984 and lived to see the beginnings of revolution but not the eventual outcome.

The Germans destroyed 43% of Poland's educational, scientific and research institutions, over 50% of transportation and telecommunication infrastructure, 55% of the health infrastructure (352 hospitals) 60% of industry and nearly 1 ml acres of forest. They destroyed 40% of Poland's cultural goods (25 museums). They looted and transported to Germany, 2,800 European School paintings, 11,000 paintings by Polish masters, 1,400 sculptures, 172,000 old manuscripts, maps and gravures, 300,000 graphic art items, 15,000 rare books, 22 ml books from library collections and many other rare and valuable objects including priceless furniture, tapestries, even 5,000 church bells.

War damages have been estimated by successive Polish Government commissions from $750 to $1,000 billion (2017). The material damages to Warsaw alone were assessed by a special commission in 2005 at $54 billion. Warsaw was 85% destroyed and the loss of life was over 200,000, the damage to the health of the survivors is beyond valuation but the Poles began rebuilding their capital almost before the dust of the Wermarcht bombings had blown away.

It is very hard to understand why the West ignored the Soviet attack and occupation of Poland, the indifference politicians and journalists showed to the suffering of the Poles. Survivors were much affected by this painful indifference to the Soviet atrocities and it is a mainly untold story to this day. My family adapted to a new life in a new country but it was a largely unsympathetic one.

I am hugely conscious and proud of my roots, as a daughter of Kresy survivors, and I continue the story on the theme of the prequel, Midnight Train to Siberia with the homage it deserves. I feel it is important to show where a complete disregard of common rights can lead especially today when anti-Polonism is on the rise again.

Polish people surely deserve that their Holocaust merits the same as the Jewish Holocaust and that Germany in particular makes the proper restitution, as it is Israeli political and media activists are demanding restitution from Poland and actively spreading anti Polonism.

**All Polish people suffered hugely during WW2
and we must remember them all.**

'I eventually started writing my biography after the gentle encouragement of my daughter Tereska, who urged me to start writing my family history in 2003 but I just didn't know how to start, where to begin and then one day at the age of 79 it came to me. I started and I looked forward to writing every day.'

Alicja Góral – Sybiraczka

*– my Mother, who embodies the spirit, passion and soul of the Polish people.*

CHAPTER 1

# Childhood in The Kresy

My Babcia Kazimiera Radomska was born on 23rd February 1899 in Wróblew a village in Sieradz County, Lodz, in Central Poland. Her father, Władyslaw Radomski was the son of nobleman Walerian, whose coat of arms in official papers of that time identified him as Bielawski. He had lost his estates after taking part in the Uprising against the Russian occupation in 1863.

The Uprising had begun on 22nd January 1863 as a spontaneous protest by young Poles against conscription into the Lithuanian Russian army and they were joined by Officers of the army and various politicians. The insurrection was unsuccessful, they were severely outnumbered and lacked any real support forced instead to resort to guerrilla tactics. Public executions and deportations to Siberia led many Poles to abandon the armed struggle and it resulted in even stricter Russian control over Poland.

Walerian Bielawski, my grand mother's grandfather, was one of many insurgents to be captured and imprisoned at Częstochowa in southern Poland for his part in the Uprising, he was charged and sentenced with expulsion to Siberia but escaped from the prison with the help of a relative Cardinal Bielawski and made his way with his wife and children to eastern Poland to a friend who owned the Rozienek estate where they would be safe. Dates are very difficult to pinpoint as the family has very little detail on Walerian, and I am assuming his son Władysław born in 1863 continued to live on the Rozienek estate later working as the manager. He met and married Sofia and had children Walery, Kazia, Bronia, Antoni and Eugenia and although I am short of detail on Walerian and Sofia there are photographs of the family included here.

My Dziadek Adam Góral was born on 26th May 1894 in Daleszewo, a village in Gmina Gryfino in the Gryfino county in north western Poland, quite close to the German border, where his Mother Konstancja worked on the estate of Count Erazma Rupniewski. She and the Count fell in love, had an affair and she became pregnant with Adam. The Count refused to acknowledge his son or to support Konstancja and she had to leave the estate to find work elsewhere. The stigma of illegitimacy was something to be greatly ashamed of in those days and Adam never forgave the Count for the way he had treated his Mother.

Konstancja later married Bolesław Góral who was working on the estate of Count Szczerbek. He accepted Adam and gave him a home in his cottage on the estate and brought him up with his half brother and sisters. Adam worked on the estate until he was about 17 and in an effort to do something with his life he enlisted in the Krechowiecki Lancers, to train and fight for his beloved country to help free Poland from Russia's oppression. It was on one of his visits to his family back on the estate of Count Szczerbek that he met Kazia who was visiting friends. This was in 1914 on the eve of WW1 he was almost 20 and Kazia was 15.

They obviously got on very well and Adam fell in love with the 'beautiful Kazia' very quickly. After a customary courtship, in those days there were formalities to follow, Adam proposed to Kazia who accepted and he then left to join his regiment. He promised Kazia with the bravado of a young cavalryman, 'that the enemy bullets would not get him' and he would come back safely from war. However, following WW1 there was another war to fight, the Bolshevik War from 1919-1920 that both Walery, Kazia's brother and Adam fought in for Poland's independence until September 1920 when they returned victorious.

In the Spring of 1921 a group of Soldiers from a small village in eastern Poland, in the area of Gmina Łyse in Ostrołęka County set off towards Wołyn by train with their horses, sabres and saddles to take up residence on land of the eastern frontier recently reclaimed from the Bolsheviks. Adam and Walery had been granted the land on the eastern borderlands by the Polish Government as a reward for their war service.

Many military settlers had been given land and were to build their homes there. Having fought in the 1914-18 war and also in the Polish-Russian uprising in 1920 they had earned the right to the land which was in a terrible state and needed incredible planning and work to make it habitable and there were very few tools to do the job.

Progress was generally good and by 1921-22 the land had been mapped out into individual plots and Adam was busy building his own bungalow to be ready before he could marry Kazia. The military settlers lived in groups and worked together helping each other digging wells and building houses so they could start living on their own plots although to begin with they would live in dugouts.

Beginnings were very hard and there was unpleasantness from the neighbouring villages populated by indigenous Russians and Ukrainians who were hostile to the Military settlers but as time went on relations developed and cooperation and respect became mutual although at the outbreak of the Soviet invasion to come, the Ukrainians became extremely hostile.

By Autumn the settlement covered about 1500 hectares with 2 instruction farms of 45 hectares and 85 ordinary farms of 11-13 hectares with 2 hectares of meadows. The veterans had worked hard and Adam was almost ready to make arrangements with Kazia and their families for a wedding and they married in 1923 in the church on Count Rozienek's estate.

He and Kazia moved to Lipniki, a small village in the area of Gmina Łyse in Ostrołęka County shortly after their wedding and my Mother Alicja was born there on 19th February 1924. I haven't been able to find out why they moved there when Adam had his land on the Osada. The name Lipnicki is thought to come from the Lipa or Linden trees which grew in abundance in the village and surrounding areas. They then moved onto their newly built Osada and were happily settled there, almost carefree after the disruption and horrors of WW1 and the Bolshevik War. With the many other Polish soldiers and their families they worked the small plots of land to help re-establish Polish claims to the area previously lost in the partitions of Poland.

**Wołyn, Powiat Rowne, Gmina Aleksandria**
**Osada Krechowiecka**
**– settled by the families Góral and Radomski**

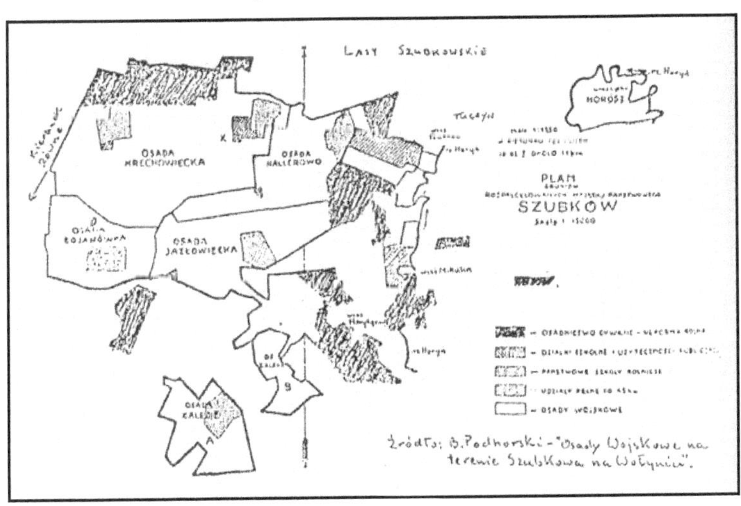


*The Osada Krechowiecka is now called Nova Ukrainka and belongs to the Ukrainian republic. All towns and villages have been renamed since the Yalta Convention in 1945.*

Although the family were happy with life on the Osada, Adam was not a natural man of the soil like his brother in law Walery and wasn't able to make the farm pay. He found work in the town and made arrangements to move the family into an apartment in Równe. By this time Jasia born in 1926 and Janusz born in 1930 had been added to the family. Adam rented his settlement on the Osada to a German family who were very grateful for the work and home and were better fitted to work the land. Adam only asked them as a favour to plant as many fruit trees as they could.

When Hitler recalled all Germans across Europe into his army, the German family visited Adam to thank him for his kindness and to say goodbye, they had brought baskets of fruit for him in gratitude. When the German family left Równe and before my family were loaded onto the trains to exile in Siberia the Ukrainians had taken over their Osada for 'safekeeping'.

Kazia made clothes, she was an excellent tailor and their finances began to improve. Life was better, the family lived by the river and the children went to a school named after the Polish Queen, Jadwiga. They were happy but there was always a worry about Kazia's health as she had a heart condition and suffered very frequent attacks which caused worry to the family, especially the children.

On summer vacations the family would visit Walery's Osada and they had wonderful happy, carefree times with their cousins, Włodek born in 1925, Zbigniew in 1927 and Marysia in 1930, they slept in the barn in the hay and enjoyed the beautiful fields, the forests and the river, picking mushrooms. It was an ordinary, simple life and the families were very close.

Kazia and Adam continued getting on with their lives day to day, as did most of the settlers and residents of Równe who were aware of some unrest but totally unprepared for the horrors soon to be unleashed upon them.

When that came on 1st September 1939 with the Germans invading their country and then on the 17th September the invasion by the Soviets it was still a huge shock to everyone and 'destroyed our life's work.' Then in February 1940 came the expulsions to forced relocation of all the military settlers to the forests of Northern European Siberia the Steppes of Kazakhstan, and as far as the frontier of Mongolia. 'We had no idea what lay in store for us and were extremely frightened'. Exile to remote regions of the Russian empire was not unknown to the Poles, after uprisings against the Russians in the 19th century many Poles had been exiled to Siberia. Those earlier exiles knew the reason for their expulsion, the new deportees of 1940-41 did not know where they were going or why. 'We would never see our beloved homes again, our lives had been ripped apart, changed for ever.'

'Without any warning in the early morning of 10th February 1940 armed Russian soldiers crashed through our door and ordered us to dress and pack. They would come back in half an hour and told us to be ready.'

This is the story of the deportation of my family by Stalin's secret Police, the NKVD, and the partitioning of Poland into the hands of the Soviet Union and Germany after the Molotov-Ribbentrop pact of 1939. Yet another example of German and Soviet plundering of Polish territories. The German terror in Europe from 1939 to 1945 was based on a primitive theory of race and the level of killing was without pity or mercy and unprecedented in the history of Poland and indeed the world. The Polish people were essentially in a state of slavery to both Hitler and Stalin.

Between five and six million Polish citizens fell victim to the Germans. Stalin's 'Eastern Plan', was based purely on class, of ridding the 'bourgeoise of the eastern borderlands' and spreading communism through the rest of Europe. It included a scheme to deport these 'enemies of the people' to Siberia and other remote Russian territories, and this was accomplished with the further loss of life to the Poles of over 2 ml.

I've included some personal testimonies from survivors with more detail expressing their own views on what happened to their country and people. Poland's history is a partly sad one, invaded by many of its neighbours, especially the Russians.

I'll begin with my dahlink Ciocia Jasia's remembrance of a reunion dinner at the White Eagle Club in Balham in 1991 and Danuta Mączka-Gradosielska's memories from home and a few others which basically tell a similar story in their own words. I've also included some notes from my Dziadek and Wujek Walery.

### Janina Góral

*'I am still under the spell of our reunion dinner on 23rd February 1991 in the White Eagle Club in Balham, London. For me my sister Ala and brother Janusz it was a deeply emotional reliving of the past. Before my eyes I could picture beautiful Wołyn, the Krechowiecka settlement and Równe. In a word, the land of my childhood, idealized through the prism of time. I remember Horyn, that dark and horrendous river, where we used to go swimming with Włodek and Zbyszek Radomski, when we used to come for vacation from Równe to stay at our Aunt and Uncle's at the settlement. I remember beautiful fields on the outskirts of Równe, covered in marigolds and the bewitching strong smell of 'sweet rush' and 'bird cherry' which I have never smelt or come across since in the rest of my days. I remember the forests surrounding the settlement, towards the Ukrainian village of Kozlin. I used to go to this village with my sister Ala and our Mamusia or sometimes our Babcia to pick mushrooms. It was also here in the woodland that the family Ławicki lived. They had four daughters and we befriended the girls. Their house was surrounded by fields of wild flowers. One field was white and the second purple. A tiny stream flowed through the forest, the water was crystal clear and the bottom was covered in golden sand and here lived tiny frogs. As children we sat on the bank of the stream catching the little frogs so we could touch them and examine them and later throw them back into the stream. I also remembered the road to Aleksandria which we used to walk with Ala and Babcia on Sundays to church. The views were beautiful from here leading through woodland. I relived these memories so strongly in my mind that it left me with a great desire to share them, because they underline the magic and the beauty of Osada Krechowiecka and the region of Wołyn.'*

### Selected excerpts by Danuta Mączka-Gradosielska – *family friend*

'Poland regained her independence in 1918 but our fathers had to fight with Soviet Russia for the eastern territories until September 1920. On

17th November 1920 an Act was adopted awarding land ownership to soldiers of the Polish army. The Riga Treaty was signed on 18th March 1921 and it was then that Poland's eastern borders were defined. The soldiers who qualified to receive land on the eastern frontiers of the Republic of Poland were soon demobilized.

In the spring of 1921 102 soldiers of the Krechowiecy Ułans Regiment were festively celebrating their last Easter in the home Regiment. A week later they set off from Hrubieszowto Wołyn, going by train, as military custom had it, each travelling in the same car as his horse, sabre, saddle and in uniform, by then quite badly worn.

The Regiment assigned them a few supply carts, two field kitchens, some equipment but no tools or farming utensils. For the first two months the veterans were provided with provisions for the people, and fodder for horses for 6 months from the garrison in Równe some 16 km away. The veterans travelled to Wołyn to start a new life on land of their own. They had hard pioneering work to do on land plots awarded them free 'for defending Homeland borders'.

The assigned terrain had no buildings, it was utterly desolated, so the veterans billeted themselves in the village of Horyngrod and immediately started by nominating a board of the 'work column' chief, warehouse manager, head of chancery and treasurer. The veterans eventually moved closer to villages Szubkow and Remel.

The veterans lived in groups and worked jointly, helping each other operating communal kitchens and building dug-outs and from September 1921 had to arrange everything for themselves. Some were helped by their families and those who were married were helped by their wives' dowries. Soon the land was mapped out into individual lots which took some time. By the autumn the settlement covered approximately 1500 hectares and consisted of 2 instruction farms of 45 hectares and 85 ordinary farms of 11-13 hectares plus 2 hectares of meadows. The Karlowszczyzna woods covered 200 hectares with a plot for a community house and a school of 4 hectares.

The settlement was shielded from the north by state owned forest over the entire length of 5 km. Through the middle ran a wide road from Równe to Tuczyn cut through with local lanes leading to neighbouring villages, Zytynia, Aleksandria, Remel, Azubkow, Kozlin and several others. These were large villages populated by indigenous Russian and Ukrainian people and in the early years there were unpleasant incidents. They were hostile and mistrustful of the Polish military settlers but as the years went by reciprocally correct neighbourly relations developed and in some cases there was even good cooperation and mutual respect.

Beginnings were very hard and many lived in dugouts. They started digging wells and building houses and they worked together so they could start living on their own plots as soon as possible. By 1923 almost all the settlers were married and the settlement flourished, much was achieved by joint efforts. A dairy operated in a rented house and in another house a school was set up. In 1929 a community hall was started and finished in the same year. Classes were being added, there were 7 and 240 children and the teaching staff also grew.

From 1930 the settlement was financially secure with a post office, a telephone operator and a cooperative shop. Scouts, guides and brownies and a farmer's association flourished and there was a bus route into Równe. There were orchards, plantations of sugar beets and tobacco the ponds were full of fish and there were herds of cattle, flocks of fowl and all the common effort of the settlers was bringing prosperity.

The local populations also benefitted from the settlers, they found work on the farms and there was access to better and improved breeds of cattle and fowl, better types of grains and seeds. The crowning glory was the building of the church in the Karowszczyzna Range in 1937.

The settlers worked as a group for their ideals and the common good and on a social level there were dances and social meetings, child raising courses and a health centre. A friendly atmosphere of solidarity prevailed where help was available for every need.

In 1931 the settlement celebrated its 10th anniversary with a community dinner for several hundred guests and cavalry veterans were present.'

## Memories of Walery Radomski, brother of Kazia

'Adam and I and our fellow cavalry colleagues, were not only given the land as a reward by the new Polish state, it was also to increase the number of Poles in those territories where the Ukrainian and Byelorussian population prevailed. We were expected to take part in the economic and cultural life of these backward provinces and boost modern methods of farming.

The beginnings of the settlement were very difficult, there were a number of unpleasant incidents with the local populations in surrounding villages of Ruthernian and Ukrainian culture. There was an attitude of hostility and distrust on the part of the locals towards the military settlers although over time relations improved.

We settled the land and made a life for ourselves and the early years were extremely hard as the land was pitted with shell holes, trenches and other debris of war. We worked hard and made the land habitable and plentiful and our families lived a fairly happy and prosperous life. We managed to draw our Ukrainian and Byelorussian neighbours closer, removing the initial prejudice we had found as our neighbours had themselves hoped to acquire this land. Large parts of the land however were no man's land which had belonged previously to the Tsar's family, the Russian government and Russian landlords.

Our regiment the Krechowiecka Lancers, was allocated an area near Szubkow on the left bank of the river Horyn, in the county of Równe. The land Adam and I had chosen was part of a settlement peopled by couples very much like ourselves with a short walking distance between the farms and quite close to the local village. Living in groups like this and working as teams we helped each other to build our homes together. The Osada was comprised of two training farms of 45 hectares each, 85 regular farms of 11 to 13 hectares each and two meadows of 2 hectares each. There were also plots for public use, the Karowszczyzna Wood of 200 hectares and 4 hectares for the settlement community centre and school.

The Osada was bisected by the wide well travelled road from Równe to Tuczyn with many country roads leading to various villages. Aleksandria, Remel, Szubkow amongst them, whose inhabitants were assimilated into the prevailing Ruthenian and Ukrainian culture and with the passing of years relations improved and cooperation and respect developed between us.

By 1923 most of us settlers were married, and the settlement was developing well. A dairy operated and a school was established. A great deal had been established by common effort and by the 1930's the settlement was in full bloom economically. Our families lived well and happily. As well as the school and dairy, there was a post office and telephone operator, a co-operative shop, a warehouse for grain and the offices of all executives of the farmers' association, the brownies, guides and scouts.

There were orchards, plantations of sugar beet, tobacco, the ponds were full of fish and the herds of cattle and flocks of fowl, cows and pigs, were evidence of the prosperity of all of us settlers. There was also rye, fruit trees, sunflowers in abundance, apples and cherries, grapes raspberries and gooseberries. Tobacco plantations, sugar beet and mollasses hops and the neighbouring villages benefitted from our hard work.

### Selected excerpts from the memories of Franciszek Źurek.

On the morning of Sunday, September 17, 1939, a frightened Kazimierz Ferens, gave them the news that Soviet tanks and infantry carrying long bayonets on rifles had entered the streets of Krzemieniec. According to Antoni Żurek, on approach to Podzamcze, the Soviet officers told the local population that the forests and land now belonged to the Russian nation. In line with this approach, they began to divide the land and distribute it to the Ukrainian peasants. Only K. Ferens, fled his home in a panic and went into hiding at the home of his brother in law – forester H. Nowak. The rest of the settlers remained at their homes.

A month later, on Sunday 22 October, elections were held for a new Assembly of the People. The Poles who did not participate in the "elections", became the subject of persecution by the Soviet authorities who began a series of arrests. Franciszek Żurek, a 25-acre landholder was arrested (with his family) for trying to organise an election day protest on 23 October 1939. He was then deported to the depths of Soviet territory where he worked hard for two years, felling trees on the Shilka River.

He was finally sent to prison for keeping notes in a diary, and was released in Moscow on December 4, 1941. after the “amnesty” was granted. With great difficulty, he reached the army of General Anders. In his weakened and exhausted state, he fell ill with typhus, and after a few weeks, on 7 April 1942, died in Guzor on Soviet territory. There he was buried in a mass grave by his wife and a few of his closest colleagues, with whom he had shared the fate of deportation and exile.

Surviving Polish families were leaving Guzor in Uzbekistan for Persia. From there they travelled to Iraq, Palestine, Egypt, and by sea around Africa to England, Canada or Mexico. Franciszek Żurek’s family left Guzar two weeks after his death, following this route, arriving in England in mid-September 1942. Four years after the war, in December 1949, Franciszek’s wife, Stanisława and their daughters travelled to distant Australia. She lives in Niddrie Victoria.’

One of the reasons the military settlers survived the rigours of Siberia better than some was their experiences of forestry, gamekeeping, farming and generally hard physical work on the land. It may have prepared and helped them better for the job of felling trees and building shelters.

## Gm. Czaruków – Osada Chrobrów

'The soldiers of the past, of the Polish army who took part in the battles for Poland's independence were given parcels of land taken from the division of larger estate holdings of the gentry.

There two of us children me 10 years and my brother Stanisław 15 years old lived. My Father was from Zyłomierza where at the beginning of WW1 he had finished his schooling at the Russian High School and was fluent in the Russian language. This is why he was able to take a job at the Town Hall in Charuków. We found out much later that he also worked as a civil engineer at the IKOP division and that this part of his work was secret.

Our parcel of land was 14 hectares which was quite large and we had newly constructed farm buildings. Father planted two big fruit orchards and sold the fruit as it became available. Our personal relations with the Ukrainians was fine as Father helped them with a variety of legal matters.

The town Łuck was about 25km from us and Father was often in Równe town and he was there when the Russians invaded Poland on 17th September 1939. The relations with the Ukrainians changed completely.

We lived at that time 'like rabbits hiding in the grass' but we continued living as normally as we could. We went to the Russian school and the Ukrainian children were nice to us although they were shortly to tell us 'soon you will go to the white bear's land.'

We repeated that to our parents and they knew very well what that meant. In secrecy Father prepared a hiding place, a dug out under the wall to the pantry and planned to hide there if the Russians came for him. Without warning in late evening from 9th to 10th February 1940 came 'bojcy' Russian soldiers with bayonets fixed to their rifles. They came with a few Ukrainian neighbours and told us to pack what we could and took us to the station. We could hear the desperate crying of people and the swearing of the soldiers. We were then packed into the train wagons.

We travelled for over two weeks towards the north of Arkangelsk 'oblast' and disembarked at the River Wyczegda. We lived in long single storey barracks in which each family had its own area. We worked cutting and sorting logs.'

These were just a few of the survivors of the deportations to Siberia. From an estimated 1.7ml deportees, it is thought only about 120,000 were able to reach the Polish army in Persia and very few survived even then, many suffering the effects of starvation, dysentery, typhus and malaria.

The Poles are a feisty, brave and strong people, which I can happily testify to, they got through incredible hardship to reach safety and from 9 members of my family having gone through Stalin's purges, 9 members lived to tell their story. One son of Walery and Ziuta, Zbigniew, regrettably did not.

Równe Market

CHAPTER 2

# Invasion by the Warmongers

## The Germans

The Second World War was sparked by an attack on the Polish munitions depot on the Westerplatte in Gdansk, at dawn on September 1st 1939 by the German army.

However, Poland's future had been decided earlier, on August 23rd 1939, when the Hitler-Stalin pact was signed, it contained a secret protocol concerning the renewed partition of Poland along the Ribbentrop-Molotov line. The USSR and Germany spent the first 22 months of the war as allies and their pact was not a cold non-aggressive pact it was a most zealous partnership with the two dictatorships trading all necessary commodities of war. Grain, vital chemicals, arms and ships. Until of course Hitler invaded the USSR and Stalin then switched sides, completely taken aback by Hitler's Operation Barbarosa in 1941.

On 1st September 1939 without any declaration of war, Germany's invincible armies and air force launched a blistering attack on my mother Alicja's homeland, over a million and a half troops stormed into Poland, on three fronts, East Prussia from the north, Germany from the west and Slovakia from the south. This was the Blitzkreig, an attack by Hitler's enormous war machine, with 2,600 tanks and 2,000 aircraft against the Polish 180 and 420. The bombing of Poland was intense, Hitler was wreaking havoc and the Polish army began retreating and regrouping east near Lwów in eastern Galicia attempting to escape relentless German land and air offensives.

My family were living at their apartment in Równe at this time and Hitler's attack changed their lives dramatically, it was the trigger for the second World War in Europe. Germany wasn't the only power that invaded Poland that month, the Soviets were also on their way and were to invade 2 weeks later.

By early September German bombs were falling around their home causing massive explosions and Kazia, Adam and the children ran from the apartment into the courtyard amid the most incredible noise, it was terrifying and their two cats, poor things were running from room to room so frightened and confused looking for shelter. Adam's relatives in the west of Poland had warned him of the German invasion and told him to try and make an escape with his family as Hitler's troops would soon reach the eastern borderlands. Poland's fate was almost sealed.

The family ran out of the courtyard with the aim of getting to their Osada where they thought it would be safer. They were so frightened and Kazia and Adam dragged the children behind them and headed out of Równe. People were scattering, running for cover, screaming, there was confusion and chaos everywhere.

Huge billowing columns of smoke filled the sky, 'such massive clouds of smoke and flames, as red as poppy's'. They could see the German planes coming lower and lower and deliberately strafing the villagers with machine gun fire. Their town was burning and panic was everywhere. Huge craters lined the streets and they had to be very careful where they stepped.

They shouldn't have been out there in the thick of it, it wasn't safe anywhere but they were looking for a quick route out of Rowne and were also curious to see what was happening to their home town. Enormous mounds of rubble lay where buildings used to stand, bodies scattered everywhere, many having been crushed beneath the collapsed buildings. Most residential areas had been bombed and defenceless citizens were gunned down as they ran from burning buildings trying to find safety.

By the beginning of October 1939 'our country was shattered'. A month of fighting had almost destroyed Poland. A country of 34 ml people living on 150,000 square miles had almost ceased to exist. The last operational Polish unit surrendered on 6th October unable to counter the overwhelming German military attack.

The consequences of war were everywhere, every city, town and railway station showed the effects, with skeletons of buildings, ruined homes and depots.

My family had found shelter at the church and from behind its huge door they saw Kazia's brother Walery looking for them, arriving with his wagon and horses he had left his Osada as soon as he'd heard the bombs and had rushed to take them away from Równe into the comparative safety of the countryside. He could see they were in shock, Kazia was white and trembling and Adam was tightly holding onto Janusz, with Alicja and Jasia hiding behind him.

They were so very relieved to see Walery who quickly bundled them into the wagon. They covered the way back to the Osada through the country lanes very quickly, seeing many carts overturned with their dead livestock attached. They were very lucky to avoid any gun fire and they arrived safely. Luck was to play a most important part in the survival of the family. Alicja was in a daze and was wondering what had happened to their cats who they never saw again.

Hitler had authorised his commanders to kill 'without pity or mercy, all men, women and children of Polish descent or language, only this way can we obtain the lebensraum (living space) we need'. Himmler took him at his word, 'it is essential that the great German people should consider it as a major task to destroy all Poles.' Crimes against the Polish population were committed, the Luftwaffe indiscriminately bombing towns and cities, civilians killed by the security police and mayors and town officials hunted down and executed.

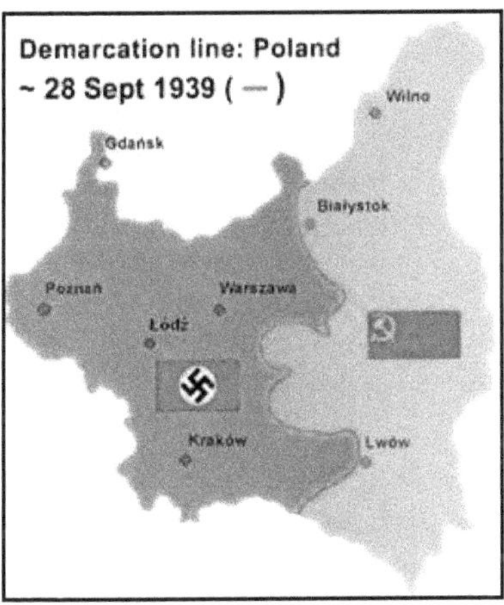


*Map showing the partition of Poland according to the Soviet-German agreement, the Ribbentrop-Molotov pact.*

The Poles were considered by the Germans to be sub human and were to be liquidated. By October 8th 1939 Jews and Poles were stripped of all rights and were made subject to special legislation. Rationing for the barest sustenance and medicine was imposed and young Polish men were forcibly drafted into the German army. The Polish language was forbidden, all schools and colleges were closed, the Polish press was abolished, libraries and bookshops were set ablaze. Polish art and culture across Poland was destroyed or looted, churches were burned and priests arrested and sent to German concentration camps.

Hitler's goal was to identify the Polish middle class and murder them. An estimated 40,000 Poles were killed in mass executions in Pomerania northern Poland alone before the end of 1939. In Poznań about 2,000 Polish intelligentsia were murdered and on 9th November 1939 Professors of the Jagiellonian University were summoned by the secret police, arrested and sent to concentration camps.

Community leaders, mayors, priests, teachers, judges and doctors were executed in public, much of the 'intelligentsia' was sent to German concentration camps spread across Poland. The first mass execution of WW2 took place in Wawer near Warsaw on 27th December 1939 when over a hundred Poles were taken from their homes and shot. There followed street roundups and other executions throughout the war. The goal was complete domination of the Poles, to terrorize them into submission and slavery. Western Poland was now decreed by the Germans as a new territory a 'General Government'.

In the spring of 1940 the Germans began the AB-Aktion (AuBerordentliche Befriedungsaktion) a concerted effort to eliminate what remained of the Polish intelligentsia. As many as 30,000 Polish Academics, intellectuals, teachers and writers were arrested and interrogated by the Gestapo. Most were sent to concentration camps, those considered especially dangerous were charged, a verdict proclaimed and the sentence declared. Those prisoners, around 6,000, were then taken to nearby woods and executed with a shot to the back of the head then buried in mass graves.. Prisoners from Pawiek prison were killed in Palmiry Forest, some near Częstochowa and others near Lublin

Jews were also being systematically murdered in the concentration camps located in German occupied Poland, where most of Europe's Jews were located after the pogroms in Russia during 1881-1884, having found a safer haven in Poland than in other European countries. The camps were Auschwitz, Birkenau, Treblinka, Sobitor, Belzec and Kulmhof. They would wear the Star of David as their sign and the Poles the letter P in a triangle as their sign. They were treated with equal brutality, deprived of all humanity and both Poles and Jews were condemned to death. They lived a little longer in the concentration camps but in the death camps, their murder was immediate, shortly after they stepped off the transports.

The Poles were also the target of extermination and as the population was larger than the Jewish population, the methods employed were different. They were removed from their homes, shot or immediately sent to Germany for labour and worked to death. The German war machine needed people for production and they could not murder the Poles all at once as they were doing with the Jews, Polish factory workers and farmers were needed.

Two days after the Wermacht slammed into Poland, both France and Britain, her closest allies declared war on Germany which was greeted by the Poles with great enthusiasm, people running into the streets waving flags believing their allies had come to their aid. Neither France nor Britain however, intervened nor did other nations of the world. PM Chamberlain dispatched instead the RAF to drop leaflets over German military positions commanding German troops to lay down their weapons and informed them that their declining economy would not withstand a protracted war. A futile and cowardly response.

It did not stop Hitler from carrying out his policy of Lebensraum with ruthless efficiency and establishing over 2,000 German concentration camps throughout Poland, some allotted to Polish Christians, some to Polish Jews as well as camps for women and children. The largest concentration camp was Auschwitz originally intended only for Poles who were its first prisoners in June 1940 in the first transport from Tarnow. There were 728 Poles mostly Catholic and 20 Polish Jews dubbed as Political prisoners and members of the Polish Resistance sent there by the SS. A group of German prisoners were also brought to the camp to act as Kapos.

From Free Radio Warsaw came the report of the bombing of Warsaw on 8th September 1939, 'Warsaw was burning, huge billowing columns of smoke filled the sky with thick clouds as red as blood, railway lines were so heavily bombed they became like twisted pretzels. Huge craters lined every street in Warsaw and other cities. There were enormous hills of rubble where buildings used to stand and protruding from the rubble were scattered bodies of people who had been crushed beneath the collapsed buildings. Military and residential areas were bombed and strafed. Defenceless citizens were gunned down as they ran for shelter from the burning buildings. Peasants were massacred as they worked in the fields and men, women and children were slaughtered. Churches, schools, hospitals, monuments, museums, all were targets for destruction. The Polish people, their culture and the very existence of the Polish nation were targeted by Hitler for annihilation.'

Warsaw, 'the Paris of the east was transformed into a wasteland, an open grave'. The devastation continued in 1941 by Soviet bombing, in 1943 by the Germans at the liquidation of the Warsaw Ghetto and in 1944 during the Warsaw Uprising. The city was 85% destroyed.

## The Soviets

Whilst the German's were exterminating the Polish population on 15th September the Soviets began massing troops along the eastern Polish frontier. On 16th September Commissars went out among the men briefing them that 'this would not be an invasion but a liberation, freeing the workers from the unjust rule of the Polish landowners'. The plans for the 'liberation' contained a large propaganda element, fodder for the minorities of the Kresy, the Ukrainians and Byelorussians, Russia's 'blood brothers' who were 'trapped in territory that had been illegally annexed by Poland'. On the 17th September the Soviets invaded the eastern borderlands on the pretext of helping Poland against the Germans but the Polish population did not accept this, they knew the propaganda methods of their old enemy. Methods used to this day by Putin, glorifying the Soviets by regurgitatng that same old propaganda!

At five in the morning mechanised cavalry crossed the frontier followed by the rest of the army. The Poles were poorly prepared for the Soviet invasion

and the eastern border was badly defended. The threat from the Germans had been clear for many months and most Polish forces had been focused in the west and the fighting had drawn many troops away.

As the massed forces of the Red Army advanced they swept all before them. Defensive positions were quickly overcome and Polish troops were captured or swept aside. During the first day the Soviets advanced up to 60 miles and it wasn't long before eastern Poland was theirs. Poland was now divided in half and the Kresy region was incorporated within the adjoining Russian border and Soviet citizenship was imposed on its Polish inhabitants. Tyranny would replace freedom so long fought for by the Polish people.

As the Soviet troops had broken through into Poland they unexpectedly ran into German troops who in less than two weeks had fought their way through to the east. The Germans fell back when confronted by the Soviets, handing over thousands of Polish prisoners of War to them who were immediately taken into captivity. Up to 250,000 Polish soldiers were taken prisoner, sent to the gulags or killed.

It was impossible for Poland to win against such powerful odds, trapped between two of the most powerful armies in the world. Although they were the first country to oppose the Germans, Poland may have had a different outcome had her allies, France and Britain come to her aid, but they had abandoned Poland to fend for herself but Poland did not surrender, she continued her struggle against both enemies until the end of WW2.

Approximately 20,000 Polish military forces who had escaped Poland, were fighting in France in 1940 and they and the Polish Government operating in exile, were evacuated to England. The Polish troops joined the British army, training in Scotland and its Airforce trained in Blackpool before joining the RAF to fight against the Luftwaffe in the Battle of Britain, where Polish airmen made their mark with the most 'kills' of Luftwaffe planes – a fact not mentioned during WW2 commemorations!

At the sound of the Soviet's 4,700 rumbling tanks, 3,300 aircraft and 620,000 heavy boots, families cautiously emerged from their homes to see what was happening. They had barely survived the German bombing and had lived day to day in a state of great fear. Adam, Kazia and the children had stayed at the Osada with Walery and Ziuta and their children, where they felt safer. When the bombing stopped Alicja rigged up the pony trap and she and Adam went back to their apartment for provisions and clean clothes and to look for food but the shops had very little, mostly taken by the Soviet troops.

What they saw when they came into Równe were Soviet soldiers dressed in shabby uniforms, the rear units trailed out along the roads and tanks, tractors and other vehicles that had run out of fuel, left by the roadsides. Soviet troops had expected to find impoverished peasants but instead had found a country wealthier than their own. The borderlands had been built up successfully by the military settlers after WW1 and also by the many Jews who had settled there and opened up their own businesses, living alongside their Polish, Ukrainian, Lithuanian neighbours.

The Russians began their rule of intimidation immediately, looting shops, occupying houses, flats and offices. They carried lists of names of people to be arrested for deportation, helpfully prepared by their Ukrainian spies, and they checked names off those lists whilst going about their business of harassing the Polish villagers. They had also hung from houses their red flags with portraits of Lenin and Stalin. 'They were a jumble of ragamuffins in their greasy coats and strange hats' one of Babcia's neighbours told her!

When Adam and Alicja arrived at the door to their apartment they found people there who had fled the troubles in Warsaw, who had made themselves at home after finding the apartment doors and windows open. The family had left in such a panic they hadn't had time to think of security, Adam decided to let them stay as they too were in shock and terrified with nowhere to go but they eventually moved out looking for safety elsewhere. Adam and Alicja got clothes and whatever else they could together and left for the Osada in the pony trap, carefully avoiding any Soviet troops on the way who were mostly busy looting and looking for food.

Despite the disruption and the aggression of the Russians, the bombs and the planes overhead, the craters and the horses lying dead in the road, Alicja looked around and tried to concentrate on the country side around her. 'September was glorious, nature just carried on around us, ignoring the turmoil' and she wished that she could ignore the turmoil around her as well but it was impossible.

On the way out of Równe she gazed almost in a trance at the beautiful fields covered in marigolds and wild flowers, the forests where they had picked mushrooms with their Babcia Sofia, the forests that Stalin and the UPA would later raze to the ground. They crossed the river and as they neared the Osada, the fields of white and purple flowers stood out against the clouds of black smoke in the sky. Alicja never forgot that scene, one of very many locked into her memory.

They continued without bumping into any Soviets although they did see a few of them ransacking the homes of villagers. Adam urged the pony on and they saw as they neared the orchards of Walery's Osada, the fruit ripening and acres of sunflowers, Adam's favourite flower which he was later to grow in England. The potato season was approaching and there was much work to be done in the fields but their lives were now on hold, their country was being destroyed and they couldn't do anything about it. Day by day Poland was dying around them and they couldn't see any help coming from their 'allies'. Alicja leant against her Father and cried quietly to herself, the reality was beginning to hit home.

The primary motivation for Stalin was class, he focused on those elements of society who might oppose communist rule and he targeted the people of the eastern borderlands. These lands had been settled by men like my dziadek Adam Góral and Wujek Walery Radomski and many of their military compatriots after the Bolshevik war of 1920. Stalin had not forgotten Russia's defeat and revenge was also his motivation.

One of Stalin's first moves was to deport to Siberia the military families, priests, lawyers, professors, all that he considered the 'elite'. These included the families of the eastern Borderlands where my grandparents Kazia and Adam had settled after marrying in 1923, to develop the land with other military families. Each deportation had a classification according to Soviet law, it defined the location, living conditions and in the end defined the chances of survival.

Like the Germans, the Soviets reigned in terror, a campaign of Sovietization was immediately started, taking over Polish businesses and factories, destroying churches. The Złoty (currency) was removed from circulation and banks were closed. Poland's educated classes were deliberately targeted because both the Germans and Soviets knew it would be easier to oversee the de-Polonization and control of the country if the 'elite' were annihilated.

The Russians then began their carefully planned deportation programme, sending Poles in huge numbers to Siberian labour camps in four phases up to 1941. On 10th February 1940 272,000, in April 320,000, in June 240,000 and in June 1941 between 200,000 and 300,000. Figures are taken from various sources, historians and scholars, the Polish Armed Forces and the NKVD and are open to further research which is continuing. My own research has focused on the Kresy history groups and other historical information which gave the numbers of approximately 1.7 ml.

The deportees of 10th February were designated as 'special settlers' (Spets-pereselentsky-osadniki), also labelled as 'enemies of the state' or 'anti-revolutionary agitators'. From specific Osada's between 100-150 families, the Radomski's and Góral's included, were exiled to the remotest regions of Northern European Russia and Siberia, Arkhangelsk district and the Komi ASSR, Sverdlovsk, Omsk, Tobolsk, Novosibirsk and Krasnoyarsk districts. They were under the direct supervision of the NKVD, the pre curser to the KGB.

Growing up with and experiencing my Babcia Kazia's loving character and sense of humour, which has prevailed amongst many members of the family, I can see how Stalin would have considered her and her compatriots the most 'dangerous of revolutionary agitators' and 'enemies of Russia' and his reason for such brutal action!

Within the 'special settlers' there were large numbers of farmers and forest workers from the Osada's, used to hard labour and together with the other less physically able, they could spread the load of the daunting work ahead of them and this group had a relatively higher rate of survival than many of the other deportees.

The Kresy Poles in particular, were damned in the eyes of the Soviets who hated them, thinking them all aristocrats and officers. They were however mostly enlisted, ex military men, Osadnicy and their families with other minority religious and ethnic communities, Jews and mainly Catholics of which most of Poland was made up of. In the same week that the AB-Aktion was ordered in Berlin in Spring 1940 Moscow gave the order to apply 'the supreme punishment, shooting of Poles' at random.

The April deportees, were POWs and mostly women and children, damned to exile for belonging to the families of men previously arrested by the NKVD, classified as (administrativno-vysslanyc). They were deported to Kazakhstan, Aktyvbinsk, Petropavlovsk, Akmolinsk and Pavlodar. The survival rates were low and very few escaped the USSR following the 'amnesty'. The numbers of survivors for this group are unknown.

The June deportees were classified as (spetspereselentsky-bezhentsy) special settlers. Made up of Polish, Ukrainian and Belorussian and were mostly Jewish. They had fled German occupied Poland for the Soviet zone, others were refugees from eastern Poland who had escaped into Lithuania. They were regarded as 'politically suspect' and sent to Siberia, Sverdlovsk, Chkalov, Yakutsk and Arkhangelsk and lived in NKVD supervised settlements.

Very little is known of their fate as so few left after the amnesty, word hadn't got through to very many labour camps across the USSR and many thousands of Poles were left ignorant of what was happening, completely unaware that they could leave to join Ander's Army to fight against the Germans. The survival rate of those left in the wilderness of the USSR is likely to be low as they had little money, nothing to barter with and would have starved, there are no numbers of any survivors. There are quite likely relatives of deportees  still living across the regions of the USSR.

These deportions were the final part of Stalin's ethnic cleansing programme and were almost on the eve of the German invasion of USSR, Operation Barbarrosa, with the last trains carrying the Polish deportees leaving eastern Poland as the German bombs were falling on the Soviets.

During the following weeks military POWs arrested by the Russians were shipped out of their camps and held by the NKVD whilst their identities were checked. They were then led away arms bound behind their backs and shot in the back of the head, their bodies disposed of in mass graves. This massacre at Katyn in western Russia was discovered in 1943 by the Germans and is synonymous with Soviet brutality. The dead totalled over 21,000 and included one prince, one admiral, 12 generals 81 colonels, 198 lieutenant colonels, 21 professors, 22 priests, 189 prison guards, 5,940 policemen and one woman Janina Lewandowska, an officer and Lieutenant pilot with the 3rd Military Aviation Regiment.

The culture shock faced by the Poles on arrival in the Soviet Union cannot be overstated. They had travelled in the depths of the coldest winter for some considerable time, through deep snow drifts and into deep forests. The only advantage was that they had accommodation in the labour camps built by earlier victims of Stalin's purges and ethnic cleansing of 1933, the Ukrainian Kulaks who had been left there to fend for themselves.

The deportees taken in the February and June 1940 deportations, sent to the north of Russia and Siberia were tasked by Resolution 2122-617ss of the Soviet People's Commissars of 29th December 1939, with 'clearing forests in regions belonging to the People's Commissariat of Forestry of the USSR'.

Work assignments were handed out to everyone aged 16 or over and it involved felling trees, sawing branches and hauling timber, even in winter when the temperature fell to -70.C and there was little daylight. 'If you didn't work you didn't eat' and the meagre rations were allocated only to those who worked, and who met the quotas. They were barely sufficient for the hard labour undertaken and the deportees began to starve and suffer dreadfully. My dziadek Adam and Mother Alicja were tasked with this back breaking physical labour in the most extreme of weather conditions.

Poland had to contend with the Germans and the Russians, their repressions and deportations to labour camps, hard labour within Germany and Russia and then the UPA who took advantage of the desolation of the country to wage their own massacres on the Poles. Murdering an estimated 100,000 mostly women, children and elderly.

## The Ukrainians

The Poles of Wołyn and Eastern Galicia also faced the onslaught of the Ukrainian Insurgent Army which began ethnic cleansing of the area in March 1943. Their aim was to purge the Kresy of non Ukrainians from what was to be the future Ukrainian state and their savagery surpassed even that of the Germans and Russians.

When Soviet tanks had entered Nowy Dwór in Wołyn on 23rd September 1939, the infantry unit commanded by a captain riding a horse stolen from its Polish owner, gathered all the Ukrainians in the main square and said, 'on this day you have been freed by the Red Army from the yoke of Polish capitalism. This whole wealth accumulated by the bourgeoisie now belongs to you. You must exterminate the bourgeoisie! Your rulers will henceforth be peasants and factory workers. I will make arrangements for you to form police units composed of workers'. Soviet propaganda at its best!

With the Soviet invasion and the annexation of the area in 1939-1941 militant Ukrainian nationalist extremists saw an opportunity to cleanse Polish people from the territory they considered historically to be Ukrainian. They were distrustful of Polish territorial ambitions and were intent on exacting retribution for the Polonization which the Polish state had supposedly inflicted upon them. They wanted an independent and ethnically pure Ukraine modelled on Fascist principles, like Nazi Germany and Fascist Italy. They wanted to eliminate all Polish people from southern Kresy to prevent those lands from returning to Poland after WW2.

OUN and UPA nationalism was introduced by Ukrainian agitators in Ukrainian villages in Wołyn and also, in the spring of 1940 the Wołyn Jews showed their gratitude to the Poles by enthusiastically welcoming and supporting the occupying Soviet communists. They collaborated with them and it could be said they sowed the seeds of anti-semitism in Wołyn by their actions. The Poles hated communism with a vengeance and my Dziadek Adam was totally against Soviet state control and the brutality it engaged.

On 22nd June 1941 a terrible chapter began for the inhabitants of Wołyn with the German invasion of the USSR. The barbaric treatment towards the

Stepan Bandera

Polish people began almost immediately. The Germans had promised the Ukrainians a 'free Ukraine' and Stepan Bandera accepted this hollow promise little realising that he was simply a tool of the Germans, used for the mass extermination of the Polish population of Wołyn.

An order from 1942 states, 'liquidate all Polish traces, destroy all walls in the Catholic churches and other Polish prayer houses, destroy orchards and trees in the countryside so that there will be no trace that someone lived there. Pay attention to the fact that when something remains that is Polish then the Poles will have pretensions to our land'.

The Germans encouraged both sides against each other 'we have to do everything possible so a Pole when meeting a Ukrainian will be ready to kill him and conversely a Ukrainian will be ready to kill a Pole' – Erick Koch German Commander. The same as the Soviets with their encouragement to the UPA to 'exterminate the bourgeoisie' Poles.

Their methods were very similar to the German SS which the extreme Bandera faction of OUN-B admired. The group had a monopoly of power within Ukrainian society and had the support necessary for the massacres to take place and the opportunity. They also had the barbaric skills, honed when Ukrainian fighters had joined German SS and Police services where they learned the art of genocide against the Jews before approximately 5,000 deserted to join UPA in 1943 taking weapons and ammunition with them.

The terror campaign assumed a mass scale in the summer of 1943 with massacres in the Sarny, Kostopol, Równe the family home and Zdolbuny regions spread to Dubno and Łuck and eventually into Kowel, Włodzimierz, Wołynski and Horochow regions. On Sunday 11 July 1943 UPA detachments, supported by local Ukrainians surrounded and attacked 99 Polish villages in those counties, as well as in Łuck.

There was no warning for the attacks on defenceless Polish villages, Ukrainian neighbours came to the Poles with axes and murdered whole families. 'Villages were torched, Roman Catholic priests axed and crucified and churches burned with all parishioners inside. Isolated farms were attacked by gangs with pitchforks and knives, throats were cut and pregnant women bayoneted, children cut in two and the menfolk ambushed in the field and led away to be put through other atrocities'.

Ukrainian neighbours who had previously lived peacefully side by side with Poles now took over the empty homes and farms of the Poles they murdered. The initial hostility of the Ukrainians to the Military settlers in the borderlands had improved over the years with relationships becoming friendly with work for them on the Osadas and socially. However, they turned very quickly against them supported by the Germans and the Soviets who stoked resentment between them.

'The perpetrators could not determine the province's future, but at least they could determine that it would be a future without Poles.' – Norman Davies, Europe at War 1939-1945 No simple Victory

The Polish civilians of Lipnicki were ruthlessly slaughtered, their homes destroyed and the villages burned to the ground. Property and life-stock, farm machinery and equipment anything of value was looted and on that day alone it is estimated that there were 8,000 victims, mostly women and children and some elderly. The Ukrainian perpetrators used bullets, axes, knives and pitchforks. Those Poles who took refuge in the churches were not spared and suffered the same fate.

After the first murders the Polish underground began organising self defence units and the commander of the Wołyn District forbade any reprisals against Ukrainian villagers.

'I forbid the use of the methods utilized by the Ukrainian butchers. We will not burn Ukrainian homesteads nor kill Ukrainian women and children in retaliation. The self-defence network must protect itself from the aggressors or attack the aggressors but leave the peaceful population and their possessions alone.' – Col. Kazimierz Babinski, 'Lubon' Commander of the Armia Krajowa, Wolyn district – A most humanitarian attitude in view of the actions of the UPA.

My Babcia Kazia's cousin Tosia and her two young sons were murdered, burnt alive, the only detail we have of their murder. The Ukrainians were ruthless, savage beyond reason in their methods of killing, normally starting with young children. Poles abandoned their homes and fled to the cities seeking escape from their oppressors, the Germans, the Russians and now the Ukrainians!

UPA leaders who committed the genocide in Poland are today national heroes in Ukraine. Their victims number between 40,000 - 60,000 Polish deaths in Wołyn and 30,000 - 40,000 in Eastern Galicia, with the other regions bringing the total to 100,000.

This Genocide of the Polish people by the UPA was never formerly identified as such until 2008 when the massacres committed by the Ukrainian nationalists against ethnic Poles in Wołyn and Galicia were described by Poland's Institute of National Remembrance as bearing the distinct characteristics of a Genocide and on 22nd July 2016 the Parliament of Poland passed a resolution recognising the massacres as a Genocide.

*Polish civilian victims of 26 March 1943 massacre committed by the UPA assisted by Ukrainian peasantry in Lipnicki, Kostopol, my Mother Alicja's birthplace*

I've included some personal testimonies from survivors of the UPA atrocities and I cannot imagine how some of them actually lived through their ordeals. They recount how many of their relatives were horrifically tortured before being murdered. The UPA were Hitler's henchmen, supplied with arms by the Germans they also engaged in guerrilla warfare against the Polish underground.

## Personal testimonies from survivors of the Volhynia (Wołyn) Genocide – *Polandpl/history*

'I saw my murdered friend ... his name was Pronczuk. When banderovtsky were killing his mother he ran to her rescue. The murderers chopped off his arms and legs and put him on a stool, he bled to death.' – *Wladyslaw Tolysz*

'In the first homestead we saw a horrifying picture, a boy aged not more than ten was impaled on a sharp pole at the gate ... Dead bodies of men and two women brutally massacred with an axe were lying at the doorstep.' – *Jerzy Krasowski*

'One of the Banderovtsky saw me and shot me at point blank but missed, he fired another shot but also missed and I managed to escape. My father and brother also fled from the house. My brother was shot, a banderovtsky riding a horse caught up with my father and murdered him. My mother was standing in the entryway holding her baby in her arms, Banderites fired shots through the closed door, one bullet hit the baby in the chest and my mother in her arm. My mother jumped out of the window put the dead child on the ground and crawled into a rosebush near the house. The Banderites broke through the door, plundered the house and set fire to the buildings. The roof fell in, the charred remains of the house fell as far away as the rosebush so that my mother got painfully burned. This is how the tragedy of our family was sealed.' –

'In one of the villages near Detrazny after the pogrom a small child whose intestines had been ripped out was found in a hut. His intestines were splashed against the wall in an irregular shape and on one of the nails a piece of paper was hung which read, 'Poland from sea to sea.' – *Wincenty Romanowski*

'At daybreak I found my father's dead body in the farmyard, he was lying next to a tree trunk used for chopping wood and his throat was slit. I found my mother inside, she had marks on her head from being hit several times with a hammer and a stab wound from a bayonet in her throat. My sister Helena had a deep wound in the head from being hit by an axe so deep that her murderer had left his axe in her head. My youngest brother Edzio aged 2 was lying in a pool of blood with his small head smashed and a knife stuck in his chest. Lying next to him was my 16 year old brother Bronek. It was his voice begging for mercy that I heard for the longest time at night. When I took a closer look I saw something that looked like a lump of battered meat. His arms and legs were broken, it was him the murderer tortured the longest.' – *Michel Wojczyszyn*

'During the singing of 'Gloria' the first shots were fired at Father Bolesław Szawłowski and the congregation. I was in the church with my sister when I heard the murderers walking around the church and saying 'O toj jeszcze zywyj' ('Oh this one is stlll alive') I quickly grabbed a cap soaked in warm sticky blood and rubbed my and my sister's face with it and we pretended to be dead. People were choking from thick smoke so they tried to escape from the church, Ukrainians were shouting 'wychadi chto zywy' (come out if you are alive) and then they would kill people leaving the church at the door. They tried to blow up the church but we only felt a terrible tremor and then there was silence.' – *Jadwiga Krajewska*

'Three of my children, Stanisława, Janek and Leon were murdered by Ukrainians, I took my youngest son and ran out of the barn. I heard a loud noise and heard my son Jozio let out a horrific cry. I fell to the ground holding my baby in my arm, I felt pain in my left arm, blood was trickling from the wound. The dumdum bullet went through the muscle and the bone of my left arm. I wasn't aware if my son Jozio was alive or not. I was very weak from the loss of blood.

I don't recall how long I lay there unconscious, I soon felt thirsty so I began to crawl. I was lucky because I saw my husband's brother Aleksander Soroka miraculously saved, appear. He brought me water so I could quench my thirst. I decided to crawl back to my house so I could die there. I lost everything I had in my life. Those I loved the most passed to eternal life. I wanted to join them there in the other world where God dwells.' – *Marianna Soroka*

Poland's suffering continued at an awful pace by three invading enemies and my family were at this time prisoners in a labour camp under the direction of the NKVD after a journey they barely survived and would never forget.

Had they been left behind in Równe they would almost certainly have fallen victim to the savagery of the UPA.

I had listened as a child to my grandparents chatting away, fascinated by the language being spoken which I was only just getting to grips with. Adam my Dziadek referred to the Soviets as Bolsheviks and wasn't very complimentary about them. I knew enough of the language to learn about their ordeal which later led me to write their story in the prequel to this. What most left an impression later on in life when I was more able to understand the circumstances was that despite the treatment meted out to them by the Soviets, my Dziadek and Walery and many thousands of other Poles who had escaped the USSR labour camps chose to fight with them against Germany!

The Polish people who survived the brutality of a tyrannical force, almost starved in the labour camps and in dire physical condition, journeyed over 3,500 km to join the Allies in their droves to fight against Germany and it is quite incredible that they willingly allied themselves to Stalin!

Their other option however was to remain as slaves of the Soviets in the labour camps and face the demanding physical work and continued starvation. The decision to leave the camp was made easily by Kazia and Adam, with many other hundreds from their camp they went into another desperate situation, a journey of over 3,500km to Persia to join Anders' Army.

### The Allies

Two days after the Wermacht attacked Poland, both France and Britain, Poland's closest allies declared war on Germany. The news of this promised liberation was greeted with some enthusiasm by the Poles who flooded into the streets waving flags and singing. They were hoping their allies had come to their aid in their time of great need. However, neither ally intervened. Their response was cowardly, instead dispatching the RAF to drop leaflets commanding the German troops to lay down their arms! This military farce continued for several months, with British and French troops posted along the Maginot line and conducting pointless raids into No-Mans' land. A farce which was to become known as 'the phoney war.'

They also sat back when Poland was attacked by the Red Army on 17th September, which went on to take control of more than half of Poland. On September 27th, after a siege lasting almost three weeks, Warsaw surrendered to the Germans, and by October 5th all resistance by the Polish Army had ceased. They were totally outnumbered and outgunned, they stood no chance against such overwhelming odds and their Allies had still not responded. – The Poles waited in vain.

On the 29th September Poland was partitioned according to the Soviet-German pact and the two nations each specified their territorial claims, which divided Poland along the Ribbentrop-Molotov Line. The Allies were aware of this and still Poland waited.

Leo Amery MP, lambasted Chamberlain in the House of Commons for leaving the Poles trapped between two of the most powerful armies in the world, 'the Poles have been bombed and massacred and we are still considering within what time limit Hitler should be invited to tell us whether he felt like relinquishing his prey!'

My family meanwhile were in the middle of a wartime hell. Walery had heard from some relatives in western Poland, in Łodz, also under German occupation, that Adam's brother's in law had been arrested and killed when the prison they had been thrown into was set alight. Other relatives barely survived the war. On the Radomski side, Kazia's sister Gienia and her daughter Halina had been taken to the west of Poland by her brother Walery prior to the deportations, to join her husband and they had survived. We have no detail of Kazia's Mother Sofia, whether she survived and on the Góral side, Adam's sisters somehow saw it through to the end.

My mother Alicja's home, Równe was turned into a wasteland. The Germans had used twice the ammunition to bomb Poland than the combined artillery used against France and England, Warsaw was reduced to rubble. People were scattered everywhere, POWs were being sent to either Germany or the Soviet Union, soldiers and airmen who had escaped were making their way into Rumania and Hungary. The huge army of refugees created by the bombing who had abandoned their homes now had to find their way back or make their way to the Soviet zone, find new homes and work.

Their future was very uncertain and the war would go on until 1945 when they then had to contend with communist rule under Stalin and lose their freedoms which they had fought so hard to save. Whilst Germany and Russia were dictating the lives of the Polish people my immediate family were living through complete confusion and terror awaiting the next move of the Soviets. The Poles had been abandoned by the Allies and my family were in despair, their country occupied by two hostile enemies and a very uncertain and dangerous life lay ahead of them.

## Churchill and Roosevelt

'In desperate times the enemy of your enemy becomes your friend.'

During WW2 the US Great Britain and the Soviet Union would never have been 3 way allies had they not shared a common enemy in Adolf Hitler. The only way to defeat Hitler was to put their personal and political differences aside in the name of global security. But, how much was each leader willing to sacrifice to make the uneasy alliance work? It seems that Roosevelt and Churchill sacrificed their common sense, appeased and bribed Stalin, almost grovelled, duped by their advisors Harry Dexter White, later unmasked as a Soviet spy, Sir Stafford Cripps a Marxist and Ambassador to the USSR and pro Soviet Harry Hopkins. Roosevelt and Churchill made a massive error in backing Stalin so fully and letting him get away with so much. They funnelled tons of much needed materials and equipment to the USSR, oil, thousands of planes, tanks and trucks without which Russia would have collapsed. What did they get in return? Stalin had purged his armed forces of many Officers and he was desperately trying to increase production of war materials. Roosevelt and Churchill should have used their aid to force Stalin to make concessions, over Poland for example, or to enter the war with Japan earlier. Instead, Stalin made no concessions and emerged the victor in 1945 with a new empire in Europe and territories in the far east that he turned into Communist states.

*The further a society drifts from the truth the more it will hate those who speak it.*
***George Orwell***

CHAPTER 3

## 'No room for this clique'

'Poland needs to be destroyed as a country' – Hitler. Polish suffering at the hands of the Germans is widely known and has become an established account of WW2 history. Shortly after Hitler launched his invasion of Poland on 1st September 1939 Stalin did the same from the east on the 17th his invasion was in partnership with Hitler to defeat their common enemy, Poland. Which was then divided between them and the devastation of Poland, the horrors of the Holocaust, the persecutions, the executions and deportations, began in earnest. Stalin took about 200,000sq kms and 12 ml inhabitants annexing them directly to the USSR and Hitler took less territory and 20 ml inhabitants. It became the Fourth Partition of Poland.

The Soviet ideology was to completely change the entire framework of Polish life, they had invaded Poland to 'rescue' their fellow Ukrainians and 'help' the Polish people against the Germans but their aim was to impose a Communist revolution which meant the absolute destruction of all political, economic and social elements which would eventually bring Poland down to the level of Russian poverty. Stalin saw the opportunity to spread communism throughout Europe with Poland his main route.

Very quickly, after invasion on the 17th September, Stalin had the annexed lands transferred to the respective Russian republics of the Ukraine and Byelorussia and within a short period there were rumours circulating around the Osadas of deportation orders being levied on the settlers. This would be a huge blow for them but not totally unexpected, they had been waiting for Stalin's next move and somehow it felt a relief. Those lands inhabited by the military settlers, the provinces of Wolhynia, Polesie, Bialystok, Nowogrodek and Wilno were now completely under the control of the USSR. When the Red Army had crossed the Polish borders terror against the population began on an unprecedented scale and Ukrainian and Byelorussian gangs began to attack many of the settlements, looting and killing.

The Poles felt completely abandoned by their allies – 'where were they?' There was nothing they could do against their oldest enemy, the Bolsheviks, for whom they felt only hatred and 'a great despair settled in our hearts.' They and the country were powerless and they had never felt so fearful, vulnerable and alone. Their fears were intensified even further, when very soon the Russians had complete control of their home town of Równe. Poland was now under occupation by two enemies and a very different and dangerous life beckoned. Two dictators were using the family homeland for their own ends.

International reaction at the time was subdued as Britain was facing Germany alone and was hoping to recruit Russia as an ally against Hitler and wanted to avoid any public criticism of Stalin. The Russian deportations have long been ignored by the West and it is prohibited to mention the matter in the Soviet bloc where Stalin is held in the highest regard. The stories of the exiled Poles fully deserve to become part of the wider narrative and they are only now coming to light. from the telling of the story of my own family to the many accounts from children of other surviving Sybiraks and historians of integrity and honesty, rather than the revisionists.

Poland had the misfortune to be crushed between two brutal totalitarian states, both of them hostile towards Polish society. Germany on racial grounds and the Soviets on class. The measures employed against the racial enemy in the west of Poland were strikingly similar to those applied to the class enemy in the east of Poland and almost from the moment the Red Army entered Polish territory, the Osadnicy were singled out in an extensive propaganda campaign as enemies of the Soviet system. The NKVD manipulated the resentment Ukrainian and Byelorussian peasants felt towards the colonizers and the Soviet press in the occupied area labelled the Osadnicy as 'servants of the Polish Government' who 'brutally exploited the peasantry' and exaggerated their numbers greatly to 70,000 when the total did not exceed 8,000!

The NKVD then began to make arrests amongst various Polish groups, the main reason given was the military settlers' involvement in the Polish-Bolshevik war! They knew what their army dossiers revealed and there was also the conviction that all Poles of middle or upper class education living on the eastern borderlands were spies, men who would work powerfully against communism. They were a threat to the Soviets.

A reign of terror was unleashed against the Polish people of the Kresy region, the Soviets dropped leaflets urging the local Ukrainians and Byelorussians to rise up and rob and murder their Polish neighbours and whilst many were happy to be complicit there were those who helped their Polish neighbours in spite of a huge risk to them. Tensions had been inflamed towards the Poles by the NKVD and this resulted in bloody conflicts, criminals were released from prisons and encouraged to attack the Poles and the local militia were engaged to hunt down Polish officers, local government officials and the Osadnicy, the Polish military settlers that Stalin hated. Land and livestock seizures became common, intellectuals, rich people and priests were executed.

In the election of the supreme Ukrainian Assembly and in the Byelorussian Assembly there were many hostile accusations against the military settlers 'as faithful servants of Polish Fascism' and the determination to 'clear them from our land' was intense and they now had the backing of the NKVD to carry out their plans, there was 'no place for them in the Soviet order...' The Germans also stepped in with encouragement, money and training for the Ukrainian UPA. Life was becoming extremely dangerous for the settlers.

All citizens of Równe could see their 'liberators', using their power very quickly to arrest all policemen and Poles of any social standing. Towards the end of September the trains were full of Polish soldiers and officers sent by the Russians deep into the USSR. This was one of the first targets of the Red Army's attack in 1939, a premeditated act of revenge long in the planning and a retaliation for the Battle of the Bolsheviks in 1920 which had been won by Poland.

Large scale arrests were made of local leaders and reservists, government officials, police officers, political activists, landowners, businessmen, administrative elites and the clergy. With incredible speed they accomplished the absolute submission of eastern Poland, setting out new rules to Sovietize the lands The economy was devastated, with land and personal property confiscated and redistributed.

The military settlers and their families were to be banished from their homes and sent to labour camps as they were a particular irritant to Stalin, they were 'enemies of the people' even 'counter revolutionaries,' I had never looked upon my Dziadek as a counter revolutionary although he did tend to get a little heated when the Bolsheviks were spoken of! The military settlers were intelligent and hardworking men with minds of their own who would stand up to Stalin's doctrine, they despised communism and it's why Stalin wanted them removed. My Dziadek Adam was perhaps a little too outspoken about his own feelings towards the persecution and oppression that was communism but knew when to keep his counsel.

Stalin's priority then was the ousting of the military settlers from their properties, told they were safe under the protection of the Soviet authorities, the settlers' belongings such as livestock and farm machinery were already being divided up by the Ukrainian and Byelorussian villagers. the NKVD wasted no time, the Osadnicy were given just a short time to pack possessions they had amassed over 18 years.

My Mother Alicja has spoken of many villagers who did not participate in the campaign of oppression towards them and many good souls at great risk to themselves helped them. Some neighbours had refused outright to be moved and those who had been born in the region were allowed to stay, although they had to rescind ownership of their lands to the Russians and take in many Ukrainian and Russian families to lodge with them and 'help' them on their farms.

One evening the family were together at Walery's Osada, sitting at the supper table with only candles for light they were talking, angry that the Russians had come into their country like thieves, grabbing their land and its people on the pretext of helping them. 'They had come in the dark with their rifles at the ready, to shoot us if we came out of our homes. That's how they were helping us!'

Kazia, Adam and the children returned next morning from the Osada, to their now almost empty apartment, it had been looted as had many other dwellings in the village. Russian soldiers and tanks were everywhere, the schools were closed to the normal curriculum, only Russian teaching and Soviet propaganda were allowed. The days were of sheer terror, spent avoiding the NKVD militia as best they could and having to deal with the patrols checking bags at the edge of the village and the railway station.

There were long queues for everything which meant very long waits each day as the shelves were almost bare, no sugar, salt or soap or bread. Life had changed drastically and women stood in lines to try and get information about the whereabouts of their husbands who had been arrested. Terror and fear was in the atmosphere in eastern Poland. The family made a promise, to try and stay as close to each other as possible, no matter what.

Everyone was very nervous and on edge. It was impossible to cross the border into west Poland or Ukraine as the NKVD was paying well for information from the ethnic residents who were easily bought, old feelings resurfacing against the Poles. Anyone crossing the border would be dealt with harshly, an interrogation would take place with accusations of being a spy, then torture would begin. Wujek Walery was arrested coming back into Równe from west Poland and was sent to the Lubyanka prison and most likely underwent torture with many others.

Life was hard, very sad and gloomy, and the family felt helpless. Dziadek, in fear of being arrested by the NKVD hid in various safe places. He and the other military settlers who had been in the Cavalry during the First World War and in the Uprising against the Bolsheviks were considered as threats to Stalin's aim of spreading Communism throughout Europe

The family and many others had heard from their relatives in the west of Poland that people were being massacred by the Germans as they worked in the fields and men, women and children were routinely slaughtered just going about their daily routines. Hitler was targeting the Polish people, their culture and the very existence of the Polish nation for annihilation, Churches, Schools, hospitals and monuments were targets for destruction and Stalin was doing the same. There was no sleep in Równe, everyone waited, unable to do anything to change the situation and there were no allies to help them. "Where were the English and the French" questions asked by many of the Poles, who grew ever more afraid.

The settlements were gripped by fear and families were not sure what to do. Polish officials were being arrested every day and the Ukrainian Committee elected by the Russians, warned everyone that they would have to move out of their homes and that refusal would cost them their lives. Historical hatred was rife and the lawlessness was spreading ever wider. Walery and Adam's Osada's had not yet been chosen by the Committee but many other settlements had been, the larger ones with machinery and live stock for the Ukrainians who were going to 'look after everything for them.' By October 1939, the NKVD pestered the family each week, checking lists of family members and going over their possessions and the family also had to report to the militia office in Równe once a week.

Adam continued to hide with friends and life went on with much hardship and great fear and the NKVD troopers, mean spirited and aggressive searched their apartment looking for Adam, charging in with guns raised looking for any weapons they thought might be hidden, 'it was terrifying and It was only a matter of time before it was our turn,' and the family waited. Kazia did her best to ease the children's concerns, but it didn't really work. She had seen the effect their few neighbours acting as collaborators were having and their number was growing.

At the Osada Krechowlecka where Walery and his family lived, in Wolhynia, there were as yet no attacks nor was anyone yet arrested but everyone waited in fear. They were accused by the Russians, of being 'the most hostile group for whom there was no place in the Soviet order' and their numbers were hugely exaggerated to over 70,000! which led to further attacks upon the Osada's and started the eviction process in earnest.

The mass deportations that were to follow allowed the Soviets to annex the eastern provinces sanctioned by the secret protocol in the Molotov-Ribbentrop Pact signed with Hitler on 23rd August 1939 in which Stalin would take the Baltic states and Poland. The deportations were decided at the highest level, including Stalin, the head of the NKVD Lavrenti Beria and the People's Commissar of Foreign Affairs, Vyacheslav Molotov. It was personally supervised by Vsevolod Mierkovov, deputy head of the NKVD.

Deportation orders were issued in Moscow on 5th December 1939. The Council of People's Commissars of the USSR, had already undertaken resolution 2001-558 relevant to the deporting of settlers' families and those of the forestry service, from the territory of the western parts of the Ukraine and Byelorussia, which was confirmed by Stalin's instructions of the 19th and 25th December. Instructions for the field NKVD cells were prepared for 'cleaning up' the western parts of the Soviet republics of Ukraine and Belarus and deportations were carried out according to registered censuses compiled by NKVD officers in cooperation with local communists.

Also for exile were officials, forestry workers and employees of the railways, and peasants, those who were considered educated, middle class and those who were overtly religious. The Soviet authorities saw the deportations as a form of extermination of the Polish elite and of using thousands of Poles as cheap labour. The conditions in the Siberian Tiaga at many degrees minus of frost, famine and disease would kill many of the exiles. It was a very well planned crime against the Polish people.

Statistics on the numbers of Poles deported by Stalin are difficult to access. Historians differ in their interpretations and information hasn't been made available by Russia but it is known that the NKVD had information on every member of each family, that the deportation was to follow a routine of arrest, transport to the railway collecting point and then allocation to a particular transport and each transport was to consist of 55 trucks, one coach reserved for the escort and one for first aid.

In each truck to be bolted from the outside, 25 people were to be incarcerated, but the number usually exceeded 50. There was to be one hot meal a day and 800 grams of bread per person every 24 hours. This was not however the case and very many starved on that journey to Siberia. The NKVD regional heads sent progress reports to their superiors who in turn sent information to Lavrenti Beria. The journey of the military families lasted 3 weeks or more. 72% were sent to Arkhangelsk area, 9% to the Urals, 6% to the Vologda region, 6% east Siberia, 2% west Siberia, 2% Komi Republic and 3% to European Russia. They were to work in the forests, felling trees and transporting the timber.

Although a specific reason for the deportations was not given it is well known that the 'guilt' of the military settlers in particular was their military past and their loyalty to the 'bourgeoise' Polish Government. Another reason for the swift removal of the military settlers is that the NKVD were probably aware and apprehensive that these military settlers owned firearms and may have posed a threat to them. The overall supervision of the February deportation was undertaken by Bera's deputy, V.V. Chernyshev and the Osadnicy were given the status of 'special settlers' by the NKVD and they would live under their supervision.

Those deported on the 10th February 1940 were taken to Arkhangelsk, where most of the military families were sent, Krasnojar, Krai, Komi and also to Sverdlov and Irkutsk districts. The conditions on the day were terrible, with the temperature at -40. Sentenced to clearing of the forests and construction of railway lines, the exiles would fight hard each day for survival and apart from the extreme cold, there was hunger and appalling living conditions. Vermin and countless bugs infested the barracks and repression by the Soviet guards was a daily hazard to contend with.

Orders had been given to the settlers to quit their homes in the Osada's Krechowiecka, Hallerowo, Bajonowka, Jazłowiecka, Bolesławice and Woronów. Very little time was given to pack belongings that they had accumulated since arriving at the eastern borderlands. The military settlers, the primary targets, were to be taken during the first deportation on the night of 9th/10th February 1940. Although post war figures state that some 272,000 military settlers were taken in that first deportation the tag of military had been applied to many of the civilian population as well.

The family waited, Kazia knew and was fearful that they would very soon be arrested as Stalin was making his intentions well known. Outside the snow was thick, the winter had been severe and inside the house it was quiet, they were warm in bed and fast asleep. They came on 10th February 1940, a day that is still engraved in my Mother's memory, at 5 o'clock in the morning, with insistent hammering, it was so loud they all jumped up in their beds, terrified '...open the door in the name of the Soviet Union, immediately...' and when they had gained entry the family were subjected to an aggressive barrage of orders in Russian.

'There were 4 Soviets armed with rifles, 2 Ukrainian Police and 2 Jews who were also armed.' Told by the 'leader' waving his gun at them, that they were 'a threat to public order' he read out a decree of deportation... 'Do not run away, your house is surrounded by soldiers, you have an hour to pack...'

'They ransacked the rooms and ordered us to dress quickly, shouting all the time and jabbing their rifle buts at us. They pushed everything over and so many lovely things were broken, papers were torn and photographs were destroyed.' 'Pottery was thrown around and clothes strewn across the floor and the children were sobbing and numb with fright.' – *Unknown deportee.*

They were too scared to move, scared they'd be shot, as this was what had happened to others. The Soviets searched for Adam who was still in hiding with friends, then looked for guns and stole whatever they could. 'Be ready to leave in an hour' the leader said and left.

The remaining Soviets urged them to get dressed quickly, pack their belongings and get outside. The decree of deportation was read out to them again and they were ordered to 'get your possessions.' Any resistance was out of the question. They were terrified and weren't allowed to move freely. The leader asked again where Adam was and Kazia very quickly said he was away helping her brother Walery on his Osada.

'Regardless of the weather conditions or time of day or night the villagers to be deported would be surrounded and forcible entry made into their homes. At gunpoint the family would be given 10 minutes to 2 hours in which to pack their belongings and then driven or made to walk to the nearest railway station.'

'The NKVD fell like wolves with rifles and daggers to our house and began to destroy holy pictures, they broke furniture and challenged us, accusing us of being Polish bourgeoisie. They asked where Daddy was, where the weapon was that Daddy did not have. They tore up the floor boards, threw clothes out of the closets and broke the beds. After an hour of them trying to destroy the house we were ordered to gather together, allowed to take some clothes and only 5kg of flour. We were led onto a sledge and taken to the station, treated as a laughing stock.' – *A teenage boy's recollection, from Dubien in Wolhynia.*

The family did not know where they were to be taken and were afraid to ask. The militia were all heavily armed and were very intimidating and seemed to be enjoying their power. They would not allow the children to move around the house but there was one friendly one amongst the 8 militia who quietly said to Kazia, 'take as much food and clothing as you can' and she went to the larder with Alicja and Jasia and packed salt pork, flour, potatoes and as much else as they could into sacks. Kazia was chilled, she knew immediately where they were being taken, Siberia.

Although the children were almost paralysed with fear Kazia made sure they were busy collecting things to take, despite the guards wanting them in one spot they also wanted them to be quick. She hurried them from one end of the house to the other to focus their minds not to fall into a state of panic. They were young and so very scared but they quickly packed everything they could into a big basket, some pots, a kettle, as many warm clothes as they could wear and carry, it was well below freezing, -40C a dreadfully severe winter, the coldest for very many years. She managed to take money, watches and some jewellery she hoped they would be able to barter. She luckily wasn't seen by the guards who would have put these prime objects into their own pockets.

Kazia's grand father, Walerian Bielawski (1834-1883) who had a big estate in Złoczów on the Romanian and Hungarian border, had been threatened with exile to Siberia after taking part in the January uprising of 1863 and was caught by the Russians. It was yet another of a series of national revolutions against the Russian empire by the Poles. Its failure and the brutal suppression that followed led to the complete Russification of Poland for decades afterwards. He had been involved in the Uprising in Podolia, once under the Polish crown and then annexed into the Russian empire in 1793. He was wanted by Ochrana, the secret police force of the Russian Empire, was arrested and imprisoned at Częstochowa in southern Poland and condemned to death by hanging or exile to Siberia.

He escaped with the help of Cardinal Bielawski a relative, and was forced for safety reasons to change his name to Radomski and was never able to return to his home town, lost his lands and estate. He later worked on the estates of some of the rich gentry he had known in Rozienek. He was married (no detail of wife) and had a son Władyslaw (no record of other children). Now his granddaughter Kazia was to become a victim of the Russians.

Kazia glanced through the window and saw a large horse-drawn sledge waiting outside and she realised she could take more items putting all into a pillow case, they would be invaluable to them on their journey into exile. She took a crucifix and a picture of the Blessed lady of Częstochowa and despite the harrying of the NKVD troopers, had the presence of mind to take the family photograph albums. She must have known they would never see their home again.

Those photo albums travelled with the family for over 20,000 km. They were well guarded, it was the history of the family a treasure and they went everywhere and have given a most important record of the family Radomski/Góral. It's why there are so many photo's in this memoir and which I am forever grateful for such a wonderful gallery of our incredible forebears.

*This poem describes the similar experience of another family who were sent to Siberia at the same time, February 10th 1940.*

In February's snow-filled sleep our world collapsed, Its successor perilous – new-shaped existence. The night-clad Soviet fist directly lunged, Crushing our nest – the family home. Coercive hands – calculated, merciless – Hammer the door, wrench the handle. Understanding dawns... here's Nemesis... Nemesis. A fleeting prayer, 'Lord, by Thy Shielding...' Carted like cattle, in wagons clamped, Through merest window's slit beyond our view Slides our dearest Polish land: sanctum sanctorum, Europe's usual martyr shedding farewell tears. What follows – the grey dolour of Russian fields; Drained, strained comrades on station platforms ranged; Leaded skies – cloud sheeted; Listless eyes; life – lost hands; Vacant steppes, Siberia, the buran' Disembodied wail; Kirghiz' indifference. In gaping Saman shacks the first year groans Long as eternity – mine-shaft black – Amid Life's blood-drained emptiness ...But God stood with us! – *Maria Waridoda*

Kazia had realised that the Soviets had been planning this for some considerable time as in the course of a single day they had collected over 250,000 people. They were ordered out of their home and onto the waiting sledge, one of many in a convoy of sledges loaded with families who like them, had been arrested as 'enemies of the people.' Some neighbours stood outside their houses watching as the sledges went by and waved. Within a short time they were on their way out of the town with the many sledges and horse carts filled with people from the neighbouring villages and saw many others heading straight towards Lubomyrka station. It all seemed very well organised and was over powering. Kazia was in a daze, stunned and incredibly frightened, the children were trembling, they needed Adam desperately but didn't know where he was.

They were on their way to the assembly point in the main square of Równe where many people were already gathered and as they arrived at the Parish offices they were met with very loud crying of children. There were about 20 other military settler families all very scared of what was to happen to them, Kazia and the children waited with the others for further orders, it was incredibly cold, birds had frozen on the branches they slept on. They sat there on the sleigh watching small groups that had begun to gather outside with food for friends and relatives, some came just out of curiosity. The NKVD then began to separate the single men from the women and children.

They were checked off against the NKVD lists which had been meticulously put together and ordered into the Parish offices. A little later a long string of large wagons collected them and moved off down the main road to the outskirts of Równe, towards Lubomyrka station. As they moved along the high street out of the town they noticed how very quiet it was, afraid of possible rescue attempts the Russians had ordered all inhabitants to stay inside. 'Anybody found on the street when transport starts will be shot without warning' the NKVD Kommandant announced through a loud hailer. Slowly the wagons moved forward and when they arrived at Lubomyrka they saw a very long train waiting for them.

There were many hundreds upon hundreds of people standing in heavy snow, wrapped up against the cold and there the train sat, big and imposing spewing out clouds of smoke. When Russia had invaded, Adam and many of his co military friends had gone into hiding fearing that because they had fought the Russians they would be arrested and imprisoned or exiled and they were right. How was Kazia to get word to him?

Some of those gathered were known to the family and aware of where they were going and amongst them were some people who hadn't been given any time to pack belongings and were taken to the station with very little. 'There was the family Mitoszewski from our apartment block in town, standing there with hardly anything but luckily, some of their relatives had heard of the deportations and rushed to the station with food and clothing for them.' The Russians wouldn't let them near so the family started screaming and crying and making such a fuss that in the end they let them through. A young woman with a baby and infant was told to bring only what she could carry, her husband had been arrested and she had come only with the child she carried and the infant holding her hand. The NKVD did not care, they were heartless and the poor woman and her children would probably not have survived.

Adam had escaped all the searches by the Russians and had found out that he would be able to travel with them as married military men were to be allowed to go with their families. Word of the deportations had got through to where he was hiding and he had rushed to the square but missed them. He had then run like the devil desperately trying to find them, checking the apartment and then the Osada and eventually reaching the station seeing them waiting by an enormously long train, he was incredibly lucky and the family were very relieved to see him. Luck would play a major role in the survival of the family on several occasions, luck and prayer.

Adam and Kazia had noticed that only the Polish army settlers and their families were taken away from their town that night and to them it didn't seem a coincidence. What they were to find out later was that Stalin had worked out the detailed deportation plan towards the end of 1939.

That same night all along the eastern borderlands many ex army settlers and their families were arrested and taken from their homes. The Russian dictator was settling old scores, he had been embarrassed at the loss of the Bolshevik War and his own part in it.

The hopes of the Russian leaders of pushing their revolution beyond the borders of Russia were dashed at Warsaw in 1920. Western observers were amazed but relieved at the reversal of fortunes as it seemed that Poland would be overrun by its larger Soviet neighbour, leaving eastern and central Europe vulnerable to Communist Russia and its armies.

The Red command had badly mishandled the final stages of the march on Warsaw and much of the controversy focused on the actions of Stalin. He was serving as a member of the revolutionary military council of the SW front, one of two prongs of the Red Army's invasion of Poland. In early August 1920 the SW Front was attacking Lwów, the Polish stronghold in Galicia, while the other prong of the Red Army's advance, the West Front under the command of Commander Mikhail Tukhachevsky, was aimed directly at Warsaw.

On 11th August Sergei Kamenev the Red Army's Commander in Chief ordered the SW front to send its main fighting force, the elite cavalry unit known as the Konarmia, northwards towards Warsaw to aid Tukhachevsky's weak southern front. Stalin refused to obey this order and the Konarmia continued to fight at Lwów allowing Polish leader Jósef Piłsudski to launch his counter attack into the gap between the West and South West Russian fronts, smashing Tukhachevsky's weak southern front. Stalin's subordination had cost the Red Army a strategic point and the war was won by Piłsudski and his Polish fighters.

It was just two of these Polish fighters Adam Góral and Walery Radomski, whom Marshall Piłsudski had rewarded by granting them parcels of land in the eastern borderlands to secure the border and to show his gratitude to them. This helped to protect the country from it's unfriendly neighbour and more than explained the family predicament. Stalin was out for revenge and those who defeated the Red Army in 1920 were to be 'dealt with.'

The family looked at the imposing train and saw that it stretched a great distance, Stalin had planned this well, in the course of 24 hours the NKVD and their Ukrainian militia arrested people for deportation from most of the eastern borderlands and had filled the train to capacity. 10 trains had already passed through the station filled mainly with professors, teachers, real estate owners and families of military servicemen like them.

They were ordered, at gunpoint, by the Ukrainian militia and NKVD, to move towards the wagon, one of the NKVD was a Jew, the local shopkeeper they knew so well but he wouldn't acknowledge them, so they didn't acknowledge him either just in case it caused any problems. Lists of those to be deported had been drawn up on information provided by collaborators from among the Jews, Ukrainians and local communists and trains had stood waiting for long periods at the railway stations in towns and villages across the region. Columns of trucks, wagons and sleighs requisitioned from the peasants had stood ready for days and Soviet army units, the NKVD and the local militia composed of Jews and Ukrainians, awaited orders.

The train consisted of freight box cars, more suitable for the transport of cattle and the Soviets must have worked hard and long to plan for so many people! Each box car contained primitive beds made of wood planks, like shelves and in the middle stood a metal barrel transformed into a stove. When the stove had fuel it would produce more smoke than heat but it would allow the deportees to cook the food they had brought with them.

At the urging of the militia they stepped into the wagon where the walls were covered in frost, it was incredibly cold. There were windows with small metal grilles set high in the walls which gave out very little light. Everyone would have to make do with a small space on the floor if there was no room on the bunks. In the corner of the boxcar a hole had been cut into the floor and separated by just a blanket which was to serve as a toilet. It isn't difficult to imagine the awful smell that arose from there, not to mention the concerns for social customs.

The friendly trooper who had arrested them was there to help them again. He made sure that the potatoes and pork and rest of the food and bundles of clothing stayed with them as the militia confiscated as much as they could, they were ruthless. Any opportunity to settle old wounds they took with sadistic pleasure. But this particular man felt sorry for them, he had a good heart. He had done his job, with compassion and had taken a risk because if his friendly behaviour had been noticed he would most likely have joined them in Siberia! The family wore as many layers of clothing as they could and it would probably save their lives.

That freezing February day was a day carved into Alicja's memory and is with her to this day at 97 years of age, she can never forget even through her dementia. Adam and Kazia looked back towards Równe with tears in their eyes, bidding farewell to their beloved home, where they had brought up 3 children and lived happily, their life and dreams now shattered. The wagon door was opened wider and more were pushed in to be almost on top of people already sitting on top of cases, bags and mattresses and they had to squeeze through a few people, managing to climb onto an upper bunk. The door was closed and locked and silence and darkness fell all around them. People talked quietly amongst themselves, "how long have you been here" asked Kazia of one of her neighbours, '2 days' they said but some in the other wagons had been locked in for up to 4 days, not allowed to use the toilets in the station. Throughout the night they heard many more horse drawn sledges and lorries arriving and people being thrown into the trains. At the sounds of people being loaded they called out to them hoping for any news but no one had any information.

It was incredibly cold, 'it got through to our bones and our breath froze in the air and no matter where you put your hands or how tightly you arranged your clothing, the cold got through.' It was dark and they waited for hours, the train shunting back and forth. The night of their seizure was one of incredible grief and pain, they were being treated like criminals, dangerous to society, now without a home and country.

As a child, from an early age I was aware of some loss as I listened to my family speak of their beloved homeland, the pain of leaving never left them and I heard those words of loss very many times. I saw sadness in my Babcia's eyes, my Dziadek's quiet, thoughtful manner and I saw my Mother often pacing up and down the lounge trying to clear her memory but I didn't make sense of it all until my teenage years.

Ziuta, Walery's wife, with her children Władek and Marysia, were in another wagon further down the track, but they didn't know this until much later. Her other son, Zbyszek, was with his father Walery, who was taking his sister Genia and her daughter Halina to join her husband Władislaw in western Poland. Zbyszek had been determined to join the Polish resistance and was anxious to do everything he could for Poland. He avoided the deprivations of the Russian labour camps, but what he actually went through must have been equally dreadful. There are very few details of his time during this period. All that is known is that he was killed in controversial circumstances shortly before being able to join his family in England.

Details of the journey into Siberia is credit to Danuta Gradosielska Mączka aged 15 at the time of the exile of the Kresy settlers, who kept a diary of the journey. I have been able to compare her detail with that of my Aunt Janina's and they complement each other extremely well.

They had been ripped away from all that they loved and put onto a journey into a terrifying unknown, a land that would prove to be very hostile to them. Kazia had closed the door of their home and on their life and she never saw her Mother again or her relatives in the west of Poland. Her sister, Eugenia, (who she was to see again), niece Halina and her husband Władislaw, survived the war living under the repressive communist state, where nothing was private and where one family member could be turned against another because only loyalty to the state mattered. What was spoken was spoken in secret because so called friends might report you to the Police.

*Journey to prison camp – adapted from a sketch by an unknown artist*

The train began to lurch backwards and forwards on the tracks and all of a sudden it made one last heave and slowly moved off. They were utterly bewildered, in shock and terrified and they sat there trembling, they had never known such fear. Neither children nor adults realised that something even worse was to come, they looked around, huddled up closer together and waited, it was another moment that Alicja never forgot. It was just after Midnight and they were on a Train to Siberia and imprisonment.

Their journey into exile was beginning. From Lubormyrka station on 12th February where they had spent two days in the wagon it took them through Zdolbunow and on February 13th they changed into Russian trains which were much larger and would suit the tracks, more people had been pushed into the wagon and it was very stuffy. The rhythmic clicking of the train wheels on the tracks did nothing to calm their nerves. They were distraught, weeping and so terribly cold. By 15th February they stopped at Iwanko, and were given bread and water, it was very frosty but sunny and they were still locked into the wagon. Alicja looked through the grill at the top of the wagon hoping to see something, anything of Poland. The train travelled slowly, at a snail's pace, stopping frequently, but when it stopped at any station they weren't allowed out of the wagon.

Most of the prisoners had candles so they could see inside the wagon, but these would soon run out as did the fuel for the stove until the guards eventually brought some on one of the many stops and they were able to cook the provisions they and others had brought and share amongst them. After a couple of days they realised it was just best to accept the situation, they didn't know how long they were to be in the wagon and there was absolutely nothing they could do to change the situation.

'The journey was simply indescribable, during our sleep we froze to the walls, our hair, clothes and bedding. The train rocked so badly that people were falling onto the burning stove and onto the ground from the bunks. After 3 days we were given some water and when we could we caught snow through the window but when the guard noticed he beat the butt of his rifle onto the dish and broke it. At the end of March we came to Irkutsk region in Tajshta. In the barracks where we were placed we were told to forget about the rotten bourgeouise Poland forever as here we are to end our lives and work.'

*– Resident of Grodno, wife of non-commissioned officer of Polish army recalls.*

The journey would follow a pattern, it seemed the train would move as slowly as it could through sleeping towns at night to avoid notice and halt on a branch line out in the country during the day to refuel. Signal delays and long stretches of inhabited country meant over running the schedule until well into daylight the next day. On these occasions there was near panic from the Soviets and train staff. Alicja often wondered from her perch on the top bunk, what civilian Russians standing on station platforms made of the very slow, long lines of trains crawling past them.

Ethnic Poles, were a minority in eastern Poland but were the majority of those deported and no social group was spared, this included workers, artisans, peasants, foresters, soldiers, judges, the clergy, professors, scientists, attorneys, engineers and teachers. where many hundreds of thousands suffered awful misery and many perished in circumstances defying description. Anyone listed as an 'anti Soviet element' was deported and this was the most unfortunate ordeal that had befallen my family.

The land, as far as the eye could see was flat and there were a few dilapidated buildings a few scattered settlements and mud huts with thatched roofs and small windows, which looked dirty and run down. It was very gloomy and when the train stopped Alicja saw other deportees who seemed in worse condition than they were. Babies were hungry and were crying and mothers were in despair. Day after day, night after night they heard only the constant moan of the wheels on the tracks picking up speed, taking them further and further away from their country.

Passing daily through villages, fields and forests, all covered in snow. It was bitterly cold and the wagon walls were frozen and their skin froze on contact. In the mornings when they awoke they had to prise their clothes away from the walls. They were dejected, wondering what was going to happen to them. They talked amongst themselves, held each other and waited for the next move and prayed and sang patriotic songs and hymns. Their faith was all that was holding them together as they travelled into Soviet territory.

There were stops at intervals to fill up with water and coal and at these times they were given buckets of hot water and cabbage soup (łapsza) but they could only drink the water, as the cabbage leaves were inedible. They were sometimes given soup with fish heads floating in which despite their hunger they left and just drank the thin soup with the black, sour bread which was handed out at intervals of two or three days, it was hard and they dipped it into the putrid water, it's disgusting but it's all they have. A sense of powerlessness has settled on the wagon and they feel very vulnerable.

Passing into Soviet territory at Szepetowka on February 16th, it was much colder and everyone had noticed the big drop in temperature and put on any extra clothing they had. They were given coal and water and were able to cook a meal on the stove. They were hungry and tired but glad they had brought so much with them. They pass through Orzenin, Korosten and Owrucz, where they again are given coal, water and some potatoes but are still kept locked in the wagons. They see a bleak landscape, flat and endless snow covered fields, forests and towns, and villages through the open door before it was slammed shut.

The train passes over the river Prypet (scene of the Chernobyl disaster in 1986) on 17th February, and travels alongside fields and pastures that looked like ice rinks and they go through small villages and Alicja sees orchards and forests of pine, oak and birches planted in rows all along the railway tracks and there are rows of firs that protect against drifting snow. It's dark in the truck and the air is hot and reeks of human waste. Those sitting on the floor are shoulder to shoulder and rocking back and forth with the movement of the train.

She continued to look out of the small shutters hoping to still see Poland, just a small sign of her homeland but they are now in deepest Russia and she sees kolkhozes, (collective farms) and small houses. The train stops and they get a whole bucket of much needed water and some coal for the stove. At the next stop there is a small hut at the station with outside taps and running water and they are allowed out of the wagon and fill as many buckets as they can for the many thirsty people. Some villagers approach them carrying bread and bottles of water but are sent on their way by the guards.

On 18th Feb the train travels slowly over the Dneper bridge with yet more flooded fields, mostly frozen and forests of pine, oak and birches. There are again rows of firs along the tracks which would continue for most of the journey. Alicja sat on the bunk looking out of the small shutters, she was very cold and very sad. Janusz was by her side trying to keep warm and they cuddle up and together gaze through the shutters. They had stopped at Gomel an industrial town where two of the men in the wagon were allowed out to get some broth and returned with two buckets which were divided up amongst the starving occupants. When the train stopped to refuel and was ready to continue the journey, it didn't wait for those who had got off to find food or water or just to stretch their legs, it would move off regardless leaving those unfortunates to find their own way and many never saw their families again, they would freeze to death.

*Adapted from a sketch by anunknown artist*

On 19th February Alicja's 16th birthday, one which she would never forget, they pass through Bryansk and Orzel and on the 20th Feb they cross the river Don and the train starts to veer further north. Late at night they stop at Karaczew where they are given soup. They are allowed to leave the train and despite the awful cold several get out to stretch aching limbs to see where they are. Alicja and Jasia take the opportunity to look around and get away for a moment from the cries of the hungry babies and crying mothers who cannot feed them as they have no milk. The guards ignore their pleas for milk just sneering at them. Other mothers begged for water only to be ignored. Many of the deaths on the journey were of babies and children, thrown from the train into the snow by the guards. The mortality rate was high, the guards incredibly cruel and uncaring and would continue to be throughout the journey.

The condition of the human freight in the box cars defied description. There were now only about 30 as some had already died, squashed into the wagon some slept on the wooden bunks while others were on the floor. Beria's instructions had been for only 30 per wagon but the NKVD just packed them in regardless. In some wagons there were up to 80, which must have been unbearable and tiring with people only being able to stand. Deprived of food, warmth and the most basic sanitary requirements, thousands perished during the journey, which was of course Stalin's intention. Their bodies were left by the side of the track and it was heart breaking, no burial was to be given to the deceased who were mostly children and the elderly. Worst was seeing young mothers losing their babies or infants, unable to survive the cold and lack of milk, holding the lifeless child in their arms, silent with grief and if a guard noticed he would grab the child, throw it out of the train and would do the same to the dead mother only days later.

In the late afternoon of 21st Feb they reach Aleksandrowka and 22nd February sees them at Rybna station and they take on coal and water and carry on towards Holworsk and Woskriesensk where they notice many destroyed churches, Catholic and Orthodox. God doesn't exist for the Soviets, only Stalin. Next stop is Oriechowo where they collect snow in buckets and after it thaws, which seems to take for ever, they wash off the dust and grime. They are covered in lice and scratch constantly. Many are suffering, children and the elderly the most, children dying from hunger in the arms of their parents and being left in the snow, it was hard to witness.

The monotony of the landscape come to an end when Alicja saw a range of hills, and dry river banks, sandstone cliffs and bundles of peat piled up. She saw a large barn and a stable with sheep, stacks of straw and small huts. They are now all desperate to be free of the box car, packed in so tightly, under guard in locked wagons, sleeping in such crowded spaces. The slates on the roof are rattling adding to their frustration, they haven't eaten for two days and at 4pm they are given dumplings made of white flour and some cabbage soup. It's watery and sour but they eat it. The Soviets had only made meagre provision for their 'passengers' leaving them to suffer from hunger and thirst. At best they got one bucket of water for the whole wagon a day.

On 23rd February in the early morning the train heads towards Pokrowa passing through nice countryside and again they are surrounded by endless stretches of flat land covered by sand blown around by the wind. It is sometimes boring for Alicja watching from the grille but it is something to take her mind off the lice eating away at her, it is also bitterly cold. They pass through Pietruszki which is a big station, with many tracks and they are given soup with noodles but not any water, they can't wash and the conditions in the boxcar are awful. The lice spread from one person to another and everyone is infested. 'There is much unhappiness, a few days ago a woman gave birth and the child didn't survive, there was nothing for the new mother to feed her child and she was desperate and how she cried for her little one.' The guards did nothing at all to alleviate her agony.

The endless plains stretch before them, the train rumbles on and they stop at Untow and get off to talk to people they meet on the platform and hear of very many other Poles being deported. In the evening they arrive in Wlademir and rush to get out of the boxcar, to use a toilet and get water but there is no water and no toilets so they head to the bushes and trees. They are given thick barley and wheat soup which they eat very quickly, they ask for water but no one is listening. People faint, there is so little food and the effects are beginning to tell on very many. Alicja constantly looks out of the tiny shutters to see where they are, and mostly sees other steam locomotives loaded with people like them.

On 24th Feb they cross the frozen river Volga and the situation in the wagon is desperate. Alicja and Jasia are now taking it in turns to look out of the grill and see very many destroyed churches, Christianity was not compatible with Communism and the Soviets destroyed many. They are given coal, water and cabbage soup and the NKVD tell them if there are no delays they should reach their destination very soon which will be Gorki near the Volga river. Someone begins to sing, over and over Boze coś Polskie (God save Poland) and others join in, they are bitterly cold but haven't given up.

They arrive late afternoon and they leave the train and walk to an Orthodox church where they will stay the night. There is no fire and it is bitterly cold and they spend the night on the floor. Kazia and Adam look at each other and wonder how they and the children will survive the hardships to come.

On the morning of Sunday 25th Feb they leave the church with the Sieradzkis, the Zajdels and others from the Osada Krechowiecka for a smaller train and are told they will be going further north and given more coal and bread. They see on most days many planes flying over and anti aircraft guns and other military equipment as well as trains loaded with tanks. They notice that the main train they've left is going further north east, and they wave the others off hoping that they survive, their friends and neighbours the Mączka's from their Osada amongst them. Meanwhile they are heading towards Sharya and Kotlas.

Kotlas was a deportation facility, a transit prison location where deportees were held whilst awaiting transport to their ultimate destinations further north and east. The camp system was spread out along the railroad line, with camps, camp offices and camp stations every 5 to 10 km along the rails and there were also farm camps. No statistics exist but it is believed that a few ml people have passed through its portals, with the numbers peaking during WW2. It had operated from the late 1920's and very many others, Estonians, Lithuanians and Latvians passed through in 1939, also victims of Stalin's deportations. In 1940 very many of the Poles from the eastern borderlands were transferred through Kotlas to the forestry work camps in the Taiga where most perished in the forests. – *Irina Dubrovina – Sovest.*

They had travelled for over two weeks and many hundreds of km and they began to be gripped by fear and panic, not sure sometimes if they were shaking from fear or the cold. Their food supplies were very low and they didn't know how much longer they were to travel, there was little interaction between them and the guards. Many were sick from the cold and the lack of proper food, but worst of all was the lack of water. Some had scraped snow off the roof of the wagon as they had been so thirsty.

They had left many bodies at the side of the track having no time or strength to bury them. No one had any energy and all they saw around them was deep snow and very high snow drifts. Many babies and infants had died and some of the elderly and they were left in the deep snow most likely to be found by the wolves. The grief of their relatives was unrelenting and people were full of sadness.

They board the smaller train towards Sharya and the journey continues very slowly and at just after midnight on 27th February they stop at the end of the track and have reached Gorki where they have to wait until the following morning to disembark with several other families. Their next journey will be onto Sharya a journey of 690 km and from there the NKVD tell them they will head to the labour camp which is about 15 km away from Sharya and is called Poldniewica, The later camps they are moved to are Darowatka and then Duraszowa during the course of two years which are only a short distance from the main camp Poldniewica.

On 28th February 1940 they brace themselves for yet another journey after a gruelling one so far of over 2,000 km from Poland. They board another train, tired and frightened and the inhabitants of the wagon are exhausted, dirty with lice and starving. Some are trying to catch snow through the grille to quench their thirst and they are desperate. Kazia and Adam do their best to reassure the children who are wide eyed and very frightened. The next day on 29th February, after arriving at Sharya the door of their wagon is thrown open and the guards are pointing guns at them and shouting for them to get off the train, a wilderness of snow stretched before them. So much snow!

There were endless wastes of snow, forests and nothing else. It was almost blinding and they were exhausted and very hungry. They saw horse drawn sledges and more guards waiting and they're told to quickly collect their belongings as it started to snow, these are then put onto the sledges and they are instructed to follow the lead sledge. The snow is very deep and small children like Janusz who was only 10 struggle although his sisters Alicja and Jasia also have difficulty as it's up to their waists but the exercise keeps them warm and eases the load on the horses. They looked at each other for reassurance and slowly set off resigned to their fate. The elderly and those barely surviving, are at least able to travel in the sleighs including Kazia.

Sharya is in deepest Russia, a town in Kostroma Oblast on the left bank of the Vetluga river and dates back to the days of the Russian Empire of 1849. It gradually increased in size under the Soviet era and now has greater devolved power after the dissolution of the Soviet Union.

The bedraggled group were forced to march at gunpoint, although there was little point of the guns, there was nowhere to escape to! They walked through the very deep and heavy snow heading to the labour camp. The lead sledge headed off slowly towards the forests, deeper and deeper into the white cloud of snow and it was very quiet and still and after what seemed like hours, wet, very hungry and exhausted they reached the labour camp. The snow storm had by now became a blizzard and they were desperate for shelter. They were in the furthest labour camp, Posiolek Poldniewica. Szarynskij region, Gorkowskaja Oblast.

There had been considerable distress in the wagons, pregnant women had lost their babies and infants had died, not able to survive the inhumane and cramped spaces and having to relieve themselves in a bucket or through the floor had made the situation considerably worse, it was hellish. They went for days without food or water having to catch rain and scrape snow off the roof to quench their thirst.

The guards did little to help them ensuring a high mortality rate. There were suicides as powerlessness had overtaken many, they were completely under the control of the Soviets. Many men quietly raged at the Bolsheviks, my Dziadek amongst them. He struggled to keep his rage to himself even when Poland became an ally of the 'Bolsheviks'.

Less than half the people crammed into the boxcars, survived the long journey to Sharya. Many had starved and those who had left the train to look for food in the forests, would have frozen after becoming lost. Parents buried their children, digging graves with sticks into the deep frozen earth hoping that roaming wolves wouldn't unearth their bodies. Families were decimated, children orphaned and survivors were already suffering the effects of malnutrition.

At one of the stops on their journey they had seen other trains taking Russian 'dissidents' even further into Siberia and those who had died or fallen were just left piled up on the platforms or by the side of the tracks, their families unable even to cover them to give them some dignity. The thought of leaving loved ones behind in such circumstances must have been unbearable. They were pushed beyond anger and tears, beyond protest and grief, until without any energy some would just sink into acceptance, hoping somehow to survive. Only their faith, confidence and love for each other and their determination to survive, kept the family going.

That they had all been together on this journey was a stroke of luck as the assignment of people to boxcars had been random. They had been forcibly ripped away from all that they had known and worked for and put into the terrifying unknown, to a land that would be difficult to work and live in. The stove in the middle of the car had mostly spewed out more smoke than heat and they had been frozen for most of that unbearable journey but had physically kept close together. The train went very slowly, the Russians ignored them and when they stopped anywhere, few approached them to help, it was as if the Russians had been forbidden to speak to the 'capitalist bourgeoise' from Poland.

When they had first boarded the train they had made a point of getting to know their fellow passengers. They were all Poles, Catholics and Jews and like them had similar stories to tell. Some had been arrested for refusing Soviet citizenship, some for a made up crime they had no way of proving they didn't commit and so very many of them on this train alone perished on the journey towards Siberia.

'That freezing and gloomy day 10th February 1940 when we left our family home and with tears in our eyes, bade farewell to our beloved town, is engraved in my memory.' – *Maria Kielan*

Stalin thought the extreme conditions of the labour camps would ensure the liquidation of the 'enemies of the people' but he did not reckon on the resilience or the faith of the Polish people, especially those of the eastern Borderlands, those 'simple people', my family, the Polish Military class, representative of the multi-ethnic Polish State.

What the Bolsheviks had failed to do in 1920, they succeeded in part in 1939 through the signing of the Ribbentrop-Molotov pact. The Red Army took the eastern borderlands as the Bolsheviks had intended and then went on to deal with their slayers of 1920, the Osadnicy.

Whilst the Poles of the eastern borderlands were being deported to the USSR, those left behind fell victim to the Ukrainian Nationalists and the Ukrainian Galiizen Division who were planning the massacre of Polish citizens with the support of the Germans, ethnicly cleansing the Poles in eastern Poland, soon to be Ukraine under the USSR. The massacre of Poles in Wołyn and Eastern Galicia were carried out by the Urkainian Insurgent Army (UPA) North Command which included the cleansing of Równe, home to the family.

My family without any doubt would have fallen victim to the UPA's savage methods, having lived and worked amongst many Ukrainians who were very quickly turned against the Polish population. It is estimated that there were between 76,000 and 106,000 victims, mostly women and children at the hands of the UPA in the Wołyn area alone. Of the Jewish population at the hands of the Germans from this area, approximately 26.000 died which made up about half of the population of Równe. So very many deaths from just a small area of Poland.

Their lives were filled with loss, hardship and displacement, they would have a desperate life ahead of them and it would be their resolve, faith, spirit and sense of humour that sustained them through the deprivations of the Russian labour camps.

*'To choose one's victims, to prepare one's plans minutely, to slake an implacable vengeance and then to go to bed..... there is nothing sweeter in the world'*
*– J.V. Stalin*

CHAPTER 4

# Surviving Siberia

The exile of Polish citizens by the Soviets between 1939 and 1941 is still not familiar to many people, what Stalin was doing to the Poles barely reached the West and when he became an ally of the two main WW2 powers, any discussion of this episode was discouraged.

The true story is only now emerging having begun very slowly in the post war years, over shadowed by the better known German occupation of Poland and the rest of Europe. Stalin's actions were no less brutal and yet despite the evidence of survivors and written testimonies, the West seems to think his crimes were not as evil!

Their walk at gunpoint from Sharya had taken many hours and they were exhausted. They arrived at a school in a small village where they were to spend the night in freezing conditions. The NKVD told them they would be marched to the labour camp, Posiolek Poldniewica, in the morning. They were all very frightened, the group looked at each other got their children together and made a circle in the middle of the floor. There was no food, water or heating and they resigned themselves for another long walk in the morning to the labour camp and a very undecided future.

Arkhangelsk is a region in north European Russia on the river Dvina near the White Sea. It was the seaport of medieval and early modern Russia until 1703. It has significant wood resources with forests mainly of pine, birch, aspen and fir which cover 86,000 square miles and it was to this area of north European Russia that many Polish military families were exiled by Stalin.

Forced labour was used extensively in the USSR as a means of controlling people, as manpower for government projects and reconstruction in a Police run system of colonies and special settlements, ultimately working people to death. Conditions were harsh and deadly and it was a way for the Soviets to imprison anyone for any reason.

It was deemed a necessary tool by the Bolsheviks to rid the country of internal enemies while using their labour to achieve stronger socialist unions and it was no different during wartime. In July 1937 with war imminent Stalin ordered the removal of Germans from Soviet soil on the grounds that they were working for the enemy. A month later the liquidation of Poles was also approved by the Politburo and in 1938 many others, Latvians, Estonians, Romanians, Greeks, Afghans and Persians were swept up in similar operations. They were arrested, shot or placed in the forced labour system.

In order to de Polonize all newly acquired territories, the Soviet secret

Police, the NKVD, rounded up and deported the Polish nationals to Arkhangelsk, the Urals, Kazakhstan and Siberia, in an atmosphere of absolute terror. There were four waves of deportations of entire families from 1940 to 1941.

There were several categories of labour camp:-

Corrective labour camps – the principal type of punitive institution in the Soviet Union, with 5 classes, exile colony, ordinary regime camp, intensified regime camp, strict regime camp and special regime camp.

The 3 main labour camp inmates were 'Kulaks,' 'Osadniks' (my family) 'Ukazniks', then the dedicated criminals, 'thieves in law,' and people sentenced for various political and religious reasons.

***Exile colonies*** were for prisoners who were deemed to be 'solidly on the path to reform.'

***Ordinary regime camps*** held prisoners serving sentences of less than 3 years for less serious crimes or, serving the initial portion of longer sentences for major offences.

***Intensified regime camps*** were for men sentenced for more than 3 years for serious offences.

***Strict regime camps*** housed those convicted of serious state crimes, political dissent, political crime and especially those considered 'especially dangerous recividists'.

The ***special regime camps*** were for those with commuted death sentences and 'especially dangerous recividists'.

Prison officials had the power to change a prisoner's category depending on their behaviour, moving them from a camp to a prison where conditions would be even harsher. Apart from the lack of freedom the semi starvation diet was the most punitive aspect of the labour camp. The quality of food was extremely poor, there were no fresh vegetables and the fish, which was the main protein was rotten. Food was often infested with maggots and cockroaches, the poor diet and the hard work resulted in illness and many deaths. Hunger was used as a weapon, it was a tool of war for the Soviets.

The labour was strenuous, fatiguing and quite often dangerous, with broken old tools and primitive machinery. Failure to meet the high production quotas was punished with lower rations and withdrawal of correspondence or parcels from home. Living quarters were not well heated or ventilated and clothing for the prisoners was wholly inadequate for outdoor work especially in temperatures that could fall to -30 in winter. There was over crowding, poor hygiene, toileting and washing facilities. Medical treatment if any was poor.

The size of the inmates' ration depended on the percentage of work quota they delivered and whilst this compelled many to work harder, depending on the size and needs of their family, it only accelerated their exhaustion sometimes causing death.

After the German attack on the Soviet Union in June 1941 the conditions in the camps worsened drastically.

*Map of Labour camps in the former USSR and Arkhangelsk*

The camp routine was made up of a long list of orders given after the early wake up call, the instructions shouted out by the guards each morning to the inmates assembled in the dark, freezing cold outside their barracks. Then came the line up and marching in line into the forest to their forced labour. They had to gather all their strength to cope with the daily routine and then later in the day waiting in line for the meagre rations, a piece of black bread and maybe a bowl of watery vegetable soup, it was simply not enough for people working at incredibly hard labour.

Siberia is one of the most sparsely populated places on earth. During the winter average temperatures range from -23C to -45C, almost impossible for the body to function and if the intense cold didn't kill the arctic storms would do Stalin's work. They came with very little warning and would quickly cover the working parties in freezing white fog. It was to this vast wilderness that up to 1.7ml Poles were to be used as forced labour in lumber camps, excavating canals, laying railway lines, mining, working in factories and on collective farms.

Those transported to the isolated regions of north eastern Russia to the Siberian Steppe or the deserts of Kazakhstan had a low survival rate, succumbing to major ailments such as tuberculosis. Those deported to the western Siberian Russian-speaking communities often fared a little better. There might have been a medical student or a nurse in the community and some basic medicines available.

The deportees were housed in posiolki, settlements of wooden barracks or huts surrounded by high fences. Many ex military Osadnicy deported in February 1940, amongst them my family the Góral-Radomski's, ended up in isolated lumber camps in Arkhangelsk in north western Russia, where the accommodation was basic and over crowded. The barracks would be heated by wood burning stoves which kept the inhabitants from freezing but there was no running water. Some were housed in Russian villages and the freezing temperatures, hard labour and lack of food and medicines contributed to a very high death toll.

To the Soviets these families, 'enemies of the state,' were a resource to be exploited, a disposable workforce. Men would be separated from their families on the day of deportation and sent to other camps. Sometimes the men and boys lived in the family camp but were sent to work very deep into the forests for weeks or months on end. This would leave many women with children alone to support them with very little chance of survival.

Men and women over the age of 15, my Dziadek Adam and my Mother Alicja, carried out heavy and dangerous manual labour for 10 hours a day six days a week and they would receive a daily ration of a few hundred grams of bread and a bowl of watery soup, but only if the quota was fulfilled. 'If you do not work you do not eat', was the Soviet mantra and they were either paid in vouchers or cash. Many of the Polish families had brought items to barter and they were able to with their Russian neighbours. Some families received parcels from Poland including seeds and could grow vegetables in the short summers. Babcia Sofia, Kazia's Mother sent parcels for as long as she could. The Osadnicy with their farming backgrounds fared better than the townspeople and knew what to collect in the forests.

In some camps the children were sent to Russian schools to learn about communism and this fate fell to Janina, Marysia and Janusz.

Women and children were sent to collective farms in Kazakhstan and Uzbekistan, placed in local communities and usually treated with hostility. The living conditions were dire, filthy and infested with vermin. Life was tough and food sometimes non existent. The death rate was extremely high due to the extreme changes in temperature and exhaustion, malnutrition and disease. Mothers were in despair for their ill and starving children. The authorities were heartless and made no effort to help them, the basic conditions of the posiolek depended very much on the Kommandant.

The brutality of the gulag system is well known. Instigated by Lenin and perfected by Stalin, to remove counter revolutionaries and undesirables from society by placing them in camps in the most savage of environments and starving and working them to death. In 1942 alone, Soviet statistics tell that 352,560 people died in the gulags and in 1943, 267,826 died from illness, exposure and over work. Many were shot, the Soviets were ruthless.

Stalin had developed the system which was wound down in the late 1950's and finally abandoned in 1960 but they continued in all but name until the collapse of the Soviet Union in 1991, but I would be very surprised if there were not still some in the Russian wilderness. There were many hundreds of them and deportations continued up to the late 1950's. In 1956, the Supreme Soviet Presidium decided to rehabilitate the majority of the punished peoples authorising them to return to their region of origin. However, this did not include the Crimean Tatars, the Russian-Germans or the Meskhetian Turks. These three groups were neither rehabilitated nor allowed to return to their regions of origin but condemned to remain in exile deprived of all rights.

After leaving the train at Sharya, the group my family were with had finally reached some wooden barracks at a logging camp. They had walked for hours, had frostbite and were covered in lice after the long journey from Poland. Many had died on that gruelling journey. The barracks had previously been a prison camp for Latvians and it had a huge gate at the entrance which Alicja thought looked quite intimidating.

It was very quiet and still, no birdsong or sounds from any animals, it was so quiet. The camp was surrounded by a very tall wooden stockade with guard towers at the corners, and it looked exactly what it was, a prison. There was a wooden fence around the camp and there was nowhere to run to. The gates were locked only at night but the guards manned the towers 24 hours a day. The barracks were surrounded by forests which extended for hundreds of kilometres. There was nowhere to go to so any attempt to escape was futile and they were watched constantly, those who did escape froze or starved to death in those forests.

There were 18 barracks poorly made of rough wooden logs, and these would house about 2,500 prisoners, with 12 rooms in each barracks and a stove to be shared between two rooms. Each barrack would house 14 families and the barracks for the guards and the Kommandant were set further away in a clearing in the forest. The gaps between the logs were stuffed with moss and clay and were full of bugs of all sorts. There were clouds of bugs and insects that came out to feed on their blood at night, piercing their skin and also tiny flies and mosquitoes which bit and stung them incessantly. Multitudes of lice were also a huge irritant but as time went on they would gradually become used to them. The floor crawled with cockroaches and the fight to eliminate all these irritants would never be won.

*Adapted from a drawing by Sobierajski*

The family stood looking around their living quarters, and could see they would have many problems keeping warm as there were many large cracks in the walls through which the cold would creep, and at times the temperature would fall to minus -30 degrees, sometimes colder. They were all checked off yet another list by the NKVD, and some families were packed off into the unknown, being marshalled off out of the gates. Those left which included my family, were allocated a tiny space to live, one family on higher bunks, one on lower bunks. There was just enough room to lie down, and they would have to sleep tightly together, holding each other for warmth and comfort. They looked around them and resigned to their fate with the several other families they were billeted with helped each other to settle in and found themselves somewhere to store their belongings.

Chief of the NKVD, Beria had informed Stalin that 'in all the Posioleks the barracks are not prepared for the winter, there is a lack of stoves and unglazed windows, as yet normal conditions do not exist for the deportees, families live in cramped barracks, poorly supplied with food and medical care for them is sparse, which leads to epidemic illnesses.' Conditions would not improve.

The NKVD was all powerful in Siberia, were the overseers of the labour camps and they were always ready to punish any Poles for any offences which could be severe. One man was sentenced to 10 years hard labour for criticising Stalin and others were imprisoned for singing religious songs. The more frightening contact with the NKVD was at night when officers would come into the huts in the early hours, usually about 2am to question and check up on them.

The questions were usually aggressive, centred on any missing male member of the family. Ziuta, Walery's wife was constantly asked where her husband was and all she did know was that he had left to take his sister Gienia and her daughter Halina to the west of Poland to be with her husband. What she didn't know was that he had been arrested and charged as a spy on his way back to collect his family and imprisoned in the infamous prison in Moscow, the Lubyanka.

After arranging their belongings they were called together, made to stand outside the camp gates awaiting instructions when the Kommandant arrived with his dog and several guards. He looked quite imposing and had a huge bushy moustache, he began pacing up and down with his hands behind his back, in front of his 'audience' glaring at them wlth contempt. It was bitterly cold and they were stamping their feet to keep warm. He welcomed them by telling them to "Settle down and work because you'll never get out of here. Hairs will grow on my palms before you leave this place. Forget about Poland, it doesn't exist and never will.'

On hearing his views many were outraged. They looked around at each other and a voice from the back said, "That's what you think." It was Ziuta who stood up to him then and several other times. She was so small in stature, but she could be very assertive and she took outrage at this 'oppressor' who dared to doubt her passion for her homeland. This man, the highest authority in the camp, had insulted everyone and she couldn't hold back her feelings, the arduous journey had taken it out of them all! There did come a time when she was able to remind him of those words.

Life in the camp depended on the Kommandant, his powers were wide and the settlers could not question his decisions. All transgressions were liable to a fine or a few days in custody in the lock up. Being late for work was punishable by 3 months hard labour and a reduction in any payment they received. Settlers were arrested for simply having evening devotions and expressions of anti Soviet views had the same fate. Ziuta had been instinctive in her comments and it seemed the Kommandant had let it go, for now.

The very next morning they heard the heavy tread of boots outside the barracks, it was still dark and they hadn't slept well, they were cold to the bone and so frightened. A guard opened the door and 3 of them stepped in with their 'daily assignments.' They were to be sent to work in the forest to fell the trees and were issued with axes and saws. They were given half an hour to get dressed and eat but before breakfast each person was called into the Kommandant's office and given a form to complete which specified the reason for their 'resettlement.' The authorities would only accept one reason, 'enemies of the state' and there was no alternative but to sign. This condemned them to a sentence of 25 years hard labour in Siberia. They walked out of his office stunned, the thought of 25 years in this hell was too much for some of them, they hadn't committed any crime!

There were mornings at roll-call when the Kommandant would say to them all, shouting at them, 'you Polish Lords will die here, Poland never existed and never will. Here, he said, pointing at the forests, here you will die, Polish dogs.' Then turning on his heel he would leave the prisoners with angry looks on their faces as they went off to work in the forest.

They had only time for a breakfast of balanda, hot water mixed with flour, and a piece of very hard black bread. Not very nourishing, but it had to do. This would now be their daily diet, along with 400 grams of slightly less decayed bread. Compared with what they were to live through later, these conditions didn't seem impossible? They still had their strength and warm clothes from home, but it would be difficult to come to terms with their life as exiles! They already missed their home badly.

The Guards came back and ordered them out of the hut and they were all lined up, shivering in the cold. They had put as many clothes on as they could and they waited, there were about 50 of them with axes and saws, including my Dziadek Adam and Mum Alicja. They were urged on walking past the high wooden fence and towards the gate, the guards shouting 'come on come on, form lines' they were being continually checked by the guards, from the front and back. Two guards came out of the watch tower and the gates were swung wide open. There were 4 watch towers Alicja remembers, and she looked up to see sentries perched in the others, watching their every move.

They moved out of the camp and towards the forest keeping their heads down against the icy wind and intense chill, which cut them to the bone. The snow crunched under their boots and with the guards' urging they hurried on. Beyond the boundary of the camp the biting cold and the head wind stung their faces and their hands were already stiff with cold. Adam and Alicja rubbed them together and pulled their collars and scarves tightly and silently thanked Kazia for bringing their fur hats and scarves which they would have to guard carefully. They would later be given fufaika, a thigh length buttoned to the throat kapok-padded jacket and a pair of padded winter trousers and rubberised canvas boots which came to just above the ankles. On top of their own clothes, this did help towards keeping some of the extreme cold out.

'Attention, attention from the leading guard, keep to your lines, no talking, watch where you're going.' The column slowly moved forward, Adam looked at Alicja to try and reassure her and they walked on with as much confidence as they could muster. It hadn't snowed for a few days and the lane was quite worn from previous columns marching this way yesterday. Everyone hunched their shoulders, looked ahead of them and moved slowly onwards, they were all very despondent. The sun was rising over the forests and on any other day it would have been a beautiful sight.

They passed the wood processing building and moved out onto the plain right into the wind and the snow which stretched all around them and in the short distance were the forests where they would be working. By this time, they had marched for about half an hour and the frost had caught Alicja's scarf where she had breathed on it and formed an icy crust, her feet were almost numb as were her hands and all around her people were clapping their hands and stamping their feet trying desperately to get warm but being urged on by the guards.

They went to work in that Arctic weather with their saws and axes, trudging deep into the forest to fell trees in deep snow every day. Alicja's job was to strip the bark from the birch logs, load them onto a cart to be fed into the saw mill. Life from now on would be very difficult for them, they lived in complete isolation, there was no radio, no newspapers; they were not even able to talk freely. They did master some Russian in order to get by, it was very similar to Polish, and it helped them to trade what they had brought with them for food with the local Russians.

Meanwhile back at the barracks Kazia and other women who had been excused hard labour due to health problems and age, were faced with the most dreadful sight. They had been very cold during the night despite all cuddling up together under the blankets and rugs she had packed. She had noticed thick ice on the window panes and white cobwebs of ice all along where the wall met the roof, conditions were simply awful. The bunk beds and mattresses were infiltrated with bed bugs so she and a few of the other women organised themselves to clean bedding, they removed it and beat it with branches to rid it of as many of the different kinds of bugs there were. In the summer the bunks would be dragged outside and boiling water poured over them to kill the bugs.

It barely made a difference and exacted a toll on everyone. The bugs attacked them at night and sucked their blood out of their under nourished bodies. In the mornings they would see the creatures scurrying away full of blood and they could easily be squashed but there would be an army waiting to replace them. On top of this there were the lice that crawled into their scalps and clothes and played havoc with their skin. It had all very quickly become a part of their existence and Kazia wore herself out trying to give the family a clean bed at night.

The one range stove in the barrack used for heating and cooking burned continuously, there being a plentiful supply of wood from the forests. They also used the stove for drying their clothes, which were always wet from walking through snow up to their waists and they were still damp in the morning, there was never enough time to dry them thoroughly.

The stove was also a magnet for cockroaches crawling up the chimney and other bugs, which absolutely covered it. 'It is amazing what you learn to live with, what you accept as normal when you get up in the morning in this strange place.' Nothing was done to get rid of these vermin and a typhus epidemic broke out with many deaths in the camp. The Kommandant ignored pleas to help with this situation and the lack of hygiene due to overcrowding, lack of soap and very primitive toilets (outhouses or slop buckets) was far worse in the summer months. Contaminated water later caused a typhoid epidemic and many died without any strength to fight.

After cleaning the bedding Kazia, Jasia and Janusz would walk to one of the different villages they had found on their wanderings and exchange some of the belongings Kazia had packed, many small items to barter for food, sugar or potatoes. The winter was severe and had brought incredible hardship and people would collect as many stores as they could, any food that came into the camp was very quickly snapped up.

We Poles, said Słowacki (a Polish Poet 1831) "must learn to breath underwater," and this stubborn mentality helped them through every wretchedness the Russians threw at them.

Those under age which included Jasia, Janusz and Marysia, had to attend school to be indoctrinated into the Soviet ways which didn't quite penetrate their stubborn Polish minds and when they could they would escape the classroom and walk along the railway tracks to look for any of the settlements and people who might have some food. They were aware that there might be wolves or bears in the forest but luckily never saw any, their hunger overcame any fears they might have had.

The courage of the women in particular stood out, those faced without husbands, fathers or brothers had the impossible task of feeding and protecting their children and the physical skills needed to carry out the work, they somehow managed to survive and then were able to take on the arduous journeys ahead of them. Like my family, their faith and strength got them through each day. Mothers with babies found it hard, they would lose milk due to malnutrition and had to improvise with watered down honey and flour but it wasn't enough to save their children.

Everyone scratched, day and night, the lice were everywhere and many suffered from malaria, shivering so hard. Alicja remembers one of Kazia's new friends, Genia, with unbelievably swollen legs who was shaking with a very high temperature, whatever she ate she couldn't keep down and she became terribly thin. She began to lose her strength and her family cried as there was no medical help and within a few days she died. Those who died had to be buried twice as the ground was too hard in the winter to dig through so they were preserved in deep snow until the spring which must have been doubly heart breaking.

Relations with the guards were varied. The highest authority was the Kommandant and at times he was hard and at other times forgiving. Some guards pushed them mercilessly to work, but there were those amongst them who were considerate. Some of them suggested ways of preserving their strength, discreetly and the family were quietly grateful for their kindness although it was noticed that these few guards did not stay long at the camp!

One of them had initially frightened Alicja, he had looked very scary and was quite brusque but when she got to know him better he turned out to be a good natured guard who didn't put many into lock up or haul them off to the Kommandant on the flimsiest of excuses. He was very kind compared to the many who weren't.

Guards would come to their hut in the night and question Adam, asking him what political news he was receiving in their letters from Poland, despite them being heavily censored. They would threaten him saying that 'political activity' could be punished and he would be sent to another gulag many km away. Adam explained that he was not receiving anything political, he wasn't interested in politics. The troopers did not have any hard proof and stopped questioning him.

They would then call out Kazia and shouted at her to frighten her, asking her the same questions to which she answered in the same way as Adam had. They told her she was lying, would never see her children again if she didn't tell the truth. Kazia then became angry and shouted back at them that she was working hard, wasn't lying and they eventually backed off. The guards took sadistic pleasure in taunting their prisoners for any minor reason. Adam and Kazia were so very lucky as they could have been arrested. They stood up to the NKVD and how proud am I of my Babcia and Dziadek, and my Polish heritage.

In Siberia winter came early in September, and spring came late, in May. Work in the forests was in teams and Adam and Alicja became a very close team. Everybody above 15, or those considered big enough and strong enough – this included Włodek, had to work in order to eat. Here in Russia this was the rule – if you didn't work you didn't eat. The under-16s, including Jasia, Janusz and Marysia, went to the camp school to learn Russian.

Those who couldn't bear the incredibly harsh conditions, mostly the elderly, numb with cold, arms and legs swollen and hungry and ridden with lice so close to death, very soon gave way despite trying their hardest not to. So many of them, forced to trek daily across frozen wastes, so weakened they collapsed were left in the forest, stripped of their clothes and left to die, becoming food for the wolvers. Loss of life meant nothing to the Soviets, to them the imprisoned were just work horses and there would always be others to replace them.

Day after day at six o'clock in the morning Alicja and Adam and all the other workers had to get up in the dark, roused by the guards and hurried along to get ready. Marched off in columns out of the camp through the plains then into the forests, guards front and behind them constantly being checked. They would have to wade into deep snow up to their knees and in some places their waists, to fell the trees. The men would cut the trees down while the younger people removed the branches and stacked them into big piles ready for the horses to drag them away on wagons to the processing depot.

There was a sawmill with electrical saws and generators and the men worked in groups cutting railway sleepers or props and pit stops. The younger men and women cut wood into slices with electric saws and fed them into a machine which cut them into cubes, which were then used for fuel in the substation. There were many accidents as it was difficult to use those tools with frozen hands and there wasn't medical or nursing help at the camp and people died from infections to their wounds.

Alicja and Adam took the wood they cut to the drying house and as it dried the wood sent out a gas that was highly noxious, it would sometimes send heads spinning and made Alicja dizzy but she couldn't refuse to work and continued through the dizziness and nausea, no work meant no bread ration and no pay which hurt all the family. If she had refused she would have been sent to the 'coop' or detention cell, a small freezing cold shed in the woods.

Circumstances suddenly changed, they were not paid for many weeks and the rations barely sustained them. Finally, the Russians began to pay them for their toil but the wages were very low, just a few roubles, but it helped them to buy some goods from the nearby villagers. They were forbidden to have any contact with the local people, but hunger forced them to break the rules. The Kommandant mostly overlooked this in the beginning, as he realised he needed them to be strong enough to work and meet the deadlines imposed on him from headquarters.

Their work was back breaking, some worked in the collective farms or mines, while others slaved in the quarries. Most worked in the forests felling trees regardless of their fitness and health, braving the most inhumane climatic conditions so that the Russians could continue the railway track that had ended at Sharya, where they had left the train. The Soviets intended to build deeper into Siberia to give easier access to other labour camps and the 'special camps' and gulags. How my Mother at only 16 survived the physical toil I will never know.

Some of the more able and experienced men were given the responsibility of building new barracks. They worked very hard for slightly better wages and larger rations of bread. These projects were usually completed in good time as accommodation was needed for newer intakes of prisoners as there were many more 'undesirables' coming into the camp.

Although the prisoners did not present any danger the NKVD spied on them constantly. They had their informers and it was necessary for everyone to be constantly on their guard. They had to watch what they said because 'the walls had ears'. If someone was suspected of 'political activity,' a 'denunciation' would be made against them by a person who would then be rewarded by the authorities for their help, by assigning them lighter work, or extra rations of bread. To a hungry person, as they all were, but who was of a weaker character, the acquisition of an extra piece of bread was possibly life saving!

*Arrival at camp – adapted from a drawing by an unknown artist*

All transgressions were punished, sometimes a fine, sometimes a few days in custody. The powers of the Kommandant were absolute, with the settlers having no possibility of questioning his decisions, which made some of his future actions regarding my Dziadek very interesting. One could be arrested for devotions to the Blessed Virgin but the Osadniks did not capitulate.

Despite the dreadful conditions imposed on the Polish deportees, they maintained as best as they could their cultural and religious activities and made every effort to keep their identity. There are drawings and illustrations of camp life, illustrated in (Stalin's Ethnic Cleansing) and some wrote on scraps of paper keeping diaries, one was a friend of the family 15 year old Danuta Mączka from the same Osada as my family who kept a most incredible diary. The families conducted prayer meetings despite pressure from the guards telling them there is no God, only Stalin!

The days were long and if they were lucky Kazia, Jasia and Janusz were able to give the workers hot water with maybe raspberry twigs that they'd foraged for during the day on top of the daily sour, black bread which didn't have much taste, but took the edge off the hunger pangs. Kazia also sometimes managed to find mushrooms. There was very little else to eat. They had received some seeds from Babcia Sofia but these were not yet ready for planting. Everyone was desperately hungry and sad, they were aware of having to be careful and the stress was beginning to tell. Of all the memories that my Mother remembered, the one in sharpest detail concerned food, it would come back to her clearly and unbidden. There was never enough of it and the thought of it always nagged them. 'Some would have given a handful of diamonds for an extra piece of bread in those circumstances, because only food had value, it was beyond price'.

Sometime that month a northern snow storm hit the camp, it blew in without warning and it covered the workers with a white fog. For 3 days the cold was so intense and the winds so icy cold that not even the well fed and clothed guards ventured out and the workers resorted to using ropes to find their way around the camp. They had even less food over those 3 days and on the 4th day work was resumed regardless of the weather. On this day Adam saw a horse frozen, the poor over worked thing abandoned by the guard. He and a few men tried to cut some meat off with their axes but they just bounced off they were too blunt, but they did get some meat off and took it back to the cabin cooked and shared it. It didn't last very long and Adam went back the next day after sharpening his axe only to find that there was very little left of the horse. Others had got there before him.

One day Janusz had seen the Uzbek guards brutally beating a man to death, he had allegedly killed their dog cooked it and shared it with his family. Janusz saw his hands up in prayer, begging for his life, screaming that his family was starving and Janusz ran, afraid at such brutality, it didn't happen very often but left a mark on those who witnessed it.

There was a small village about three kilometres from the camp and the villagers, mostly Russian 'dissidents', were very kind to them. They held markets on occasion and the prisoners were able to buy or barter for much-needed food. At the last moment before boarding the sledge to leave Równe, Kazia had grabbed as many scarves, and other small items and trinkets as she could and filled her pockets and sacks knowing they would probably exchange well. People from the collective farms around the camp would sometimes come to the fence to exchange food for clothing with the prisoners which would later be a life safer for them.

The Russian villagers on the collective farms and villages, had been exiled from their homeland after the Russian revolution of 1917 and like them had been given little notice. They had been arrested and physically removed from their homes, loaded onto transport and brought to this wasteland to work on collective farms. They had not been able to take many possessions with them and had arrived with little but the clothes they stood up in. They were then expected to build their own homes and work for their Russian masters, sending a great proportion of their farm goods to the major towns, probably via Kotlas, surviving on very little themselves. 'Yet they were able to help us, they were so kind especially the older ones who could empathise with what we newer prisoners were experiencing, we were so very grateful to them.'

There were many good Russians, but the Soviets soon filtered these out and sent them either to the Gulags or collective farms across the vast wilderness of Russia. These older Russians couldn't even be open with their own children, who would without hesitation report them to the authorities for any outspoken comments. Their children had been indoctrinated from early school age into the ideals of communism so they knew no other way. A similar country today would be North Korea, the inhabitants under constant surveillance and control.

One old Russian, Constantin, had become friendly with Adam and they chatted to each other whenever it was safe. They were both very much against communism and spoke out about it but as the NKVD jumped on the slightest anti communist remark as being almost treasonable, they were extremely careful. The village markets soon stopped, because prisoners and villagers were getting too friendly, which was not tolerated by the Russians. Everyone had to be careful of what they said and did from then on. Maybe they had been careless and had been overheard saying something completely innocuous but considered anti-communist and were now punished for it!

There were two occasions in the labour camps when the family experienced absolute terror. The first took place in Duraszewo camp, where they lived with three families, two Polish families and a family from the Ukraine, who weren't very fond of the Poles and more often than not worked with the Russians to gain special favours. The atmosphere at times was tense and Adam wondered if they had been put amongst the family to spy on them. Extreme hunger affects the mind in a very negative way as do old adversities.

During their incarceration they tried very hard to keep their spirits up. Sometimes singing and dancing, and they were singing one evening when all of a sudden the door opened and the Kommandant stood there with his rifle and dog and told Adam to go with him. It wasn't the usual evening head count, when guards would come with their dogs. The family froze, knowing that so many men had been taken by the Kommandant for interrogation and were never seen again. They didn't know why he was there and were terrified thinking about what might happen. All of a sudden the Kommandant seemed to change his mind, he spun on his heel and walked out without saying a word leaving them confused.

The Kommadant never mentioned the incident again and they later learned that the father of the Ukrainian family had sent his son to the Kommandant to tell him that Adam had been making fun of the Russians, which was completely untrue and malicious. From then on they were even more alert and the Ukrainian father was even more hostile, as his spiteful effort to gain any indulgence from the guards had failed.

The family were still receiving packages from home, which were thoroughly examined at the regional office before they were able to collect them. Sofia, Kazia's mother, had been able to send parcels and they had exchanged letters with her for a little while, heavily censored of course, it was such a comfort to keep in touch, and to know that she had so far survived, as she was now quite elderly.

The regional Post Office was a long walk from the camp and they had to collect the mail and packages, walking through muddy country roads and fields and in winter very deep snow, which made it very difficult. It took most of a day there and back and Jasia and Janusz used to go together, with Marysia tagging along sometimes. They often didn't get back to camp until after dark, absolutely exhausted but so happy with their post, although sometimes they were empty-handed and despondent.

These letters and packages seemed to cause the authorities great discomfort and they began to show a lot of interest in them. The prisoners shared all their news from home with each other and this raised their spirits hugely. Some of the letters contained news that the NKVD regarded as 'political' and it was easy for them to eavesdrop in the barracks, by just standing in the corridor by a door listening in to what the prisoners were sharing.

Senior NKVD officers would arrive at the camp unexpectantly to investigate, questioning people about their political views, 'where did all the news come from, who was writing these letters' and then they would threaten them saying that this 'political activity' would be punished in a gulag. Had they had irrefutable proof of any 'political activity' they would have most certainly arrested and imprisoned anyone and the unfortunates would never be heard of again! All gatherings were then banned and very suddenly, there were no letters, no contact from home and no parcels of desperately needed food and seeds. They had been confiscated by the NKVD, which wasn't a surprise.

One evening after work Adam in desperation made the decision to take Kazia's wedding ring, (his had already been bartered) and despite his emaciated state, go to one of the villages to look for food and he set off for one of the nearest which was about 2km away. His family was slowly starving, it was a struggle to maintain the work commitments, and "if you don't work you don't eat" was the Russian principle. The situation could not go on much longer, the family had to survive, they needed food desperately.

Kazia, Jasia and Janusz had been able to collect sorrel and chives from the meadows on warmer days and had also spent time fishing not far from the collective farms and as well as the mushrooms and cabbages it had kept them going although the situation was now desperate. They had seen bodies being collected by the Uzbeks and loaded onto arbas, skeletal corpses, Poles from various collective farms and prison camps, dumped into ditches that would become their graves. It was becoming an everyday occurrence.

It had not snowed heavily and was still light as he left the barracks and he looked around for any guards, the searchlights hadn't yet come on and it seemed clear, he was very nervous but he set off in determined mood running towards the path to the village and after a short time safely reached it. He knocked on the door of his friend Constantin who helped him to exchange the ring for potatoes and flour from some of the other villagers. He was exhausted as the trek to the village had taken a lot out of him, the snow was deep and he was feeling the effects of malnutrition, but he had to get back. He had a hot cup of tea with Constantin and his family before he set out on the return journey.

He had only been going for a short time when it started to snow quite heavily, the storm had come down very quickly and he lost his way completely. The cold hit him hard and his face was numb, it was way below zero, everything looked the same and all he could see was a wall of white swirling snow, the big white flakes falling on him, he was very cold and he noticed the light was slipping away as he struggled through the drifts. The sky had become darker and he hoped he wouldn't have to survive the night in this wilderness.

He was desperate, this time the Kommandant wouldn't be so lenient he thought. He couldn't go any further, he couldn't see a thing, no path, nothing but a blanket of snow. He stopped, gathered his thoughts and collected some kindling from under the trees and bushes which was still fairly dry and he was able to light a fire, with his battered old army lighter, although it took some time as his fingers were almost frozen.

He then squatted down by the flames in total despair, clinging onto his sack of food, wondering if he'd see his family again or if the wolves would get him. Which way should he go? He had no idea. He was so tired, so cold and so hungry, and he was becoming disorientated. He thought it was hopeless. How would he get back? What should he do? Oh how he needed Kazia, his rock. He cried until he shook, he just wanted to sleep and felt at a complete loss, how had he got into this nightmare? And how could he get out of it? He was distraught, it had all come to a head and he was in a complete panic, all his army training was to no avail.

With the snow falling heavily around him still not seeing any landmarks, let alone a path, he prayed as he'd never prayed for a miracle, a way back to his family. The Poles were deeply attached to their religion and praying was a means of helping them through many problems. Praying had given Adam what he needed, an incentive. All of a sudden, with what little strength he had left, he got up, his mind absolutely set, he had decided on a direction. He put aside his hunger and weariness and started walking, his life and that of his family depended on action, one foot in front of the other, that's all he had to do. His body was beyond exhaustion. He was soaked by the snow which had got through to his bones and he was achingly cold. His hands could barely keep hold of his precious goods, but he was determined about one thing – to get back to the camp. His family was waiting for him. It was a major effort and every muscle cried out for rest.

The snow flakes seemed to be easing, a light wind was starting to gather pace and the night sky was clearing, he could see the moon and the stars so very bright and around him a frozen, white emptiness, he was even able to notice how beautiful it was. His nose and cheeks were frozen numb and his eyes were watering as he pulled his jacket up around him trying to shield his face, his lips were cracked and so cold. He recognised a clearing ahead of him and realised he wasn't very far from the camp. He stepped on huge sheets of ice cracking and crunching under his weight and the wind suddenly stronger pulled him along, sliding along those sheets of ice. It helped him a little as he was exhausted with very little energy left and he couldn't feel his body.

After what seemed like hours, he arrived at the outskirts of the camp and at the gates stood two figures, one tall, the Kommandant with his rifle and the other his dog, by a large fire. The fire was like a magnet, drawing Adam ever closer to someone he really didn't want to face. Should he go round the other side of the camp? Try getting in another way? But it was surrounded by wide open spaces and the forests were so far away. So many escapees had never made it, they just disappeared. And he was so tired. He felt resigned to his fate. His legs shook and were about to give way as he made his way to the gates, but his fear suddenly left him he was ready to face the Kommandant.

"Góral, where have you been?" said the Kommandant, and Adam answered, so close to anger, the adrenalin taking over, "I had to go for food for my family, they are starving, I had no choice, you left me no choice," he screamed. The Kommandant was taken aback, not expecting this from one of his prisoners. "We'll talk about it in the morning" was his response and he went through the gates back into the camp, leaving Adam just standing there, exhausted almost to the point of collapse, confused and not sure what to do next.

Kazia had been watching out for his return and ran up to him, grabbed him and pulled him back through the gates and into their barracks. The children were still awake, curled up on the bunk together waiting for his return. They couldn't sleep, how could anyone sleep? They'd kept as quiet as they could so as not to alarm the guards, and after keeping their feelings in for so long they just burst into tears. They were so relieved to see him. Every day was torture for them, wondering whether they would survive it, avoid the guards and their aggressive behaviour, have any food to eat? It was beginning to tell on all of them.

Adam still held the potatoes and flour, he had never let go of the sack and Kazia had to prize it away from his frozen hands before throwing a blanket over him and dragging him to the burning range, his ears burned and his nose and chin felt like pins and needles, he would have to thaw out slowly and it would be painful. The dread the family had felt that night was never forgotten. There were many occasions over the first few years of her new life in England when Alicja would very suddenly be reminded of these times. 'They just crept into my thoughts without warning and would leave me in such a state of panic for some time. I still think of them occasionally, but without some of the awful panic,' over the many years since then those thoughts haven't left her, she remembers Siberia when her father went into the forest to get them food and how frightened they had been although these thoughts are fading over time and dementia.

Adam had risked his life to keep the family alive, he had seen their physical state, they had lost a great deal of weight, and were wasting away in front of him. Their muscles ached so much it was painful to move. Alicja and Jasia couldn't lift the heavy saws to cut the trees and were anaemic, lethargic, dehydrated. Their skin was becoming cracked, they were so fatigued, how could they work? It was far worse for Kazia, this was having a dire effect on her heart and she was struggling to get through each day despite her determination.

In spite of everything, the Kommandant seemed to have a conscience. He had been kind to the family on two occasions. After the signing of the Amnesty in 1941, he simply vanished into the night with his wife and dog. Where could they have gone to find safety? Or had he been sent to fight the Germans?

I remember my grand parents telling that story so many times when we all got together. Each time something would spark the memory and they would all chip in with their thoughts and each time they found a reason to laugh, to look back with humour and then it would go quiet but not for long and chatter would continue around what prompted the memory.

Ciocia Ziuta also risked her life, although in a different way. She was quite outspoken, the words she aimed at the Russians and Ukranian guards could have had enormous impact but she seemed to escape any significant punishment. She was a very small woman with a massive heart and personality. How could an NKVD guard possibly take delight in responding harshly to the insults of such a little person, a 'non-person' at that? What bravado could he have gained in the barracks in front of his fellow guards? The sheer strength of human spirit and unbreakable bond between the family got them through unimaginable privations.

The prisoners were finding the winter months extremely severe, temperatures falling to -40, and the snow and frost were intense. All prisoners had been given padded trousers and anoraks filled with wool and wore shoes made from wicker, and around their legs they wrapped strips of woollen pieces from their shoes to their knees. They were very light and warm if wrapped around properly and with some added clothing they had brought with them Alicja and Adam were able to cope a little better out in the forests.

Life was very sad and very hard, and could be demoralising, but the youngsters amused themselves after work even on an empty stomach by singing hopeful songs and praying when they could. Praying in groups wasn't allowed but day after day they hoped and prayed that some time soon, somebody would rescue them from this inhuman land. Children and the elderly were dying in their hundreds and there had been many burials in the hard icy snow. Some of the deportees could afford to have relatives buried in the cemetery at Monastyrek in Kotlas but many of the dead were buried in the ice ground of Siberia.

The year progressed and after the snow melted they had to dig deep into the ground cutting trees whilst others worked to lay the railway tracks. Standing in deep snow digging all day and coming back to the barracks cold and wet and tired for something to eat, and of course there was very little and they usually went to bed hungry. They had by then finished the food Adam had risked his life for sharing it out as carefully as they could. They lay close together for warmth and comfort, holding tight. At times there was no bread because no food was delivered. When they received a parcel from Babcia Sofia it cheered them up and they smiled.

People were dying every day of dysentery and typhus, malaria and starvation, the privations of life in the camp were hitting hard, the family were living on roots and the herbs that grew on the bank of the river, the very barest necessities of life! There was grain in the fields around the forests and wild fruits which some of the smaller children gathered when the guards were distracted, they filled their pockets and returned the next day to do the same. The guards knew what was going on but turned a blind eye, some of them seemed sympathetic to them.

There had been many deaths in the workforce, younger girls and boys as young as 13 were now being sent deep into the forests and forced to do very heavy labour. Hardly able to carry the heavy axes they were marched into the forest in the same columns, with the axes on their shoulders and worked tirelessly cutting down trees and trimming the branches. Alicja was lucky as she worked with Adam who insisted on being with her despite threats from the guards. Other fathers started to follow his lead to work alongside their children  to protect them. Once the Kommandant saw the benefits of families working together he raised little objection and now Jasia was also working in the forests.

The Kommandant's orders had been to keep his prisoners going for as long as possible as their labour was important to the cause! One of the  awful aspects of this ordeal was the contempt and hostility of the guards towards them and if  people didn't die from the cruelty, the frost, the deep snow and extreme temperatures would see them off. In this climate their lips would chap and ears would freeze and it was very difficult at times to breath.

The day was from dawn to dusk and at the end on leaving the forest they would be gripped by the fear of the wolves out on the open plains watching their every move. They would wait and watch them, it wasn't a very long walk but a fearful one before they eventually reached the safety of the camp seeing the clear strip with the guards and barbed wire of the camp they would relax knowing they would soon be with Kazia.

They still had some clothing and trinkets to exchange for food, and would have gone to the Kolkhozy to get some potatoes or flour so that Kazia could cook something for the family but the Kommandant had put a stop to the visits. They had very little to eat now during the day, usually just a piece of bread and a drink of tea made of raspberry twigs. They had no coffee, so they experimented with a brew made of acorns and called it coffee which wasn't very tasty. In June some were lucky enough to get seeds from relatives and grew potatoes, cucumbers, beans and onions and it was warm enough to bathe in the river and get clean. In the summer months they picked mushrooms and cranberries in the forests and they could sustain themselves as they were plentiful, Kazia and Janusz spent most of their time searching for anything to eat.

Did anybody know they were there? Perhaps no one knew they had been forcibly deported? Exiled from their homeland. They felt they had been deserted, forgotten. What was happening back home in Poland, how was Sofia coping, life was very difficult to bear and the guards were very cruel which put a great strain on them all.

The guards would come around each night for roll call with their dogs, at a different time each night to try and catch them out and to keep everyone constantly on alert. Some were very rough with them and abused everyone verbally. If a girl happened to be pretty she would be singled out for attention, but mothers and fathers kept a keen eye on their daughters.

The youngsters had accepted the situation more easily than their parents who were very depressed, only waiting for the day when they would be free again. To think of escape was impossible as there were always guards and dogs around. The camp was surrounded by wide open spaces and then the forests which very few escapees made it to or through. Accidents, starvation and sickness took its toll on the prisoners, but the most distressing cause of death was psychological. Anyone who lost faith in their survival did not last more than a few days. It was quite unnerving.

Kazia and Adam, although quite subdued, never, ever gave up hope, somehow they knew they would be free, that they would survive. They never doubted it, their resolve served them well.

After a few months in the camp at Poldniewica, the family were moved to a smaller camp, Duraszewo, in August 1940 which was about four kilometres away. They were sent with four other families in carts with their few belongings and hoped they would be housed in better conditions. The routine was the same, they had to work as hard as they had done before, on even poorer rations and conditions. At the new camp they met the Krawiec Family, Bruno and Maryan, their sisters Krysia and Irena and their parents which was to lead to a very close friendship over many years.

Bruno and his brother Maryan fought at Monte Cassino once they had escaped the camp. He later met and married Halina who had lost both her parents in the Russian labour camps where they had succumbed to the privations. As orphans, she and her two sisters were eventually sent to India after reaching safety in Persia from the USSR. Of all the groups of Polish orphans escaping the USSR into Persia in 1942 the largest group was sent to Africa. The Commonwealth countries were very hospitable to the many refugees fleeing the labour camps and accepted many of them willingly unlike the US and UK.

Wigilia 1941 had been and gone and with it the memories of their homeland that had been brought to their minds. Christmas decorations and barszcz, uszka, śledzie, fruit and cakes and everything else that came with the memory of Wigilia. The snow kept falling and it was dark and Kazia prayed that they would return from the forest safely for the potatoes and soup and dark Russian bread that she had prepared. They were together which was the most important thing and another day had gone by safely as she saw them appear at the edge of the forest.

Winter was well established when they were told they were going to be moved again, they were being sent to a smaller camp, Deralwelka with 6 other families. Moved by sledge, on another very bitterly cold day, it was February 1941, very frosty and the snow very deep and food was becoming even scarcer. It was a year since they had been taken from their homeland, hundreds had died through starvation, exposure to the climate and injury. Kazia had some spare clothing and trinkets left and exchanged some of them for potatoes which was all they could get from the market. The Kommandant had relented and allowed several families to visit the villages again for food, but by then they also had very little to barter for, the villagers were stockpiling for another hard winter and couldn't let them have very much. The new camp was a slightly better one and they had a family area to themselves, it was surrounded by forests and the narrow gauge railway came by the camp which made them feel less isolated.

The guards took them through the usual routines of how much they were expected to do each day, when they were to get up, when to assemble outside the barracks and their days followed a routine, the physically demanding work continued with great difficulty, felling trees and building the railway line further into Siberia, their health was suffering and was becoming a matter for great concern to Adam and Kazia. Signs of acute hunger were beginning to show in the children with gnawing pains in their stomachs, hunger pangs and Alicja was slowing down with very little energy and low moods, it was a constant battle not to give up.

One of Jasia's jobs was to collect water from the well at the outskirts of the barracks. It was a long walk and it was her dreaded chore as the snow was always very deep and it made it difficult to walk. A thick layer of ice covered the opening of the well and she found it difficult to get the bucket into the opening. She always carried an axe in this weather and she carefully made the hole bigger and got the bucket down. The walk back was exhausting with the heavy bucket and Adam usually met her half way if he wasn't in the forest. She was also beginning to show signs of exhaustion, finding each day getting more difficult to get through.

The snow was heavy and was to cause many problems. The temperature was low and the wind freezing, many did not have proper boots or clothing, what they had been issued with had worn out. There were several accidents with people slipping on scaffolding carrying heavy boards, people went down with colds and pneumonia and every morning they put on the same wet and cold clothes they hadn't been able to dry on the range. Everyone went back to the hut each day frozen, soaked, sometimes trees would fall injuring people and they would be brought into the barracks in great pain. The equipment was primitive and caused accidents and they didn't have any medical help and so few of the injured would recover.

There was one young girl of about 14, Ewa, who was exhausted beyond endurance working for her siblings having lost her parents. She left the hut at dawn each day and returned in the evening and then had to prepare a meal, clean the hut and wash and repair clothes with some help from her younger brother, her younger sisters were too young to help. She was exhausted and had to face the most strenuous demands to cope with the extreme cold and hard labour with a malnourished body. She had the responsibility for her younger siblings and they did what they could to help her. If she had asked the Soviets for help they would separate them and she would never see them again. It isn't known if she and her young siblings survived the camp or were shipped out to a Russian Orphanage.

Spring was late in 1941 and they were recovering from another extreme winter. They were still receiving letters from home which were very heavily censored so they didn't really know what was happening outside the camp. There was no news of the War but the Soviets were still so full of their alliance with the Germans. People in desperation tried to escape and two young men did but were recaptured, badly beaten and imprisoned. No one tried to escape after that.

The Poles took great comfort from praying, it gave them strength to get through each day although the Soviets were determined to stamp this out, telling them there is no God, there is only Father Stalin! It was relentless. If a parent tried to stop his child from attending the school he would be punished with prison or heavier work. Despite the threats they prayed when they could, it was their faith that got them through this terrible ordeal. Adam and most of the prisoners hated communism, seeing it as oppressive and would not bow to Stalin's indoctrination methods. Communism had genuinely transformed society but in a very destructive way. The regimes' policies caused famines that killed millions and never before had any government terrorised so many of its own people.

One day whilst Alicja was cutting branches off a tree and putting them onto a bonfire she noticed a young man sitting on a fallen tree with the foreman, watching her. When she finished work and she and Adam were walking to the barracks, the young man walked along with them. They talked, and when Alicja got to the barracks he told her he was a member of a young communist party (Comsomolts) and that he would come and see her again. Adam very watchful, called her into the barrack then, as it could have been a very difficult situation.

They didn't want to antagonise the guards but also didn't want to encourage any friendships either, especially those of a romantic nature, as this might have led to an even worse situation. The young man did come again several times to their barracks and each time he brought a balalaika and played for her, and 'I didn't even remember his name', said Alicja. Adam wasn't happy that he was seeing her and did his best to quietly discourage him. The last time he came he very solemnly told Alicja he loved her but that he had to go to war. She never saw him again. This young Russian was the very first man who expressed romantic love for her and she didn't remember his name! Soon after that the guards began leaving them to their own devices. There was hardly any bread and anything else was rotten, completely inedible.

By late Spring 1941 they had been forbidden to visit the kolkhoz to barter for food but rules had been broken because they were starving and people would break out of the camp at night despite the search lights and try to get back in without being noticed although the guards watched them constantly. Those who were caught were imprisoned in the cellar in the admin block where there wasn't any heating and they froze.

There were times when the villagers from the Kolkhoz, knowing the dire conditions in the camp would hide in the bushes on the verge of the forest bringing them some food to barter. The Camp stores sometimes had food and clothes but of very poor quality and line ups would start very early and they often went away empty handed. There might be salt, cookies and shoes and people would crowd in but there was never enough for them all. Those kolkhozniks hiding in the bushes would catch their attention and Adam would take a risk and go up to them to see if they had anything. They were very kind people and shared their spare rations whenever they could.

Everything, especially food was now being sent to the front for the Russian soldiers who were now fighting the Germans on Russian soil. The guards seemed restless and the prisoners sensed something was happening. One day, June 22nd 1941, they found that the guards with their dogs had left the camps. They had just disappeared overnight, then news filtered through from some of the villagers who had been watching from the outskirts of the camp that Germany had declared war on Russia. Maybe Russia would become an ally of America and Britain? Everyone began to hope that things might change.

The absurdity of the situation was that the prisoners were saved by Poland's first aggressor, Hitler, with his attack on Russia. Churchill had persuaded Stalin to release all Polish prisoners on Soviet soil to allow them to fight against the Germans, becoming allies with the USSR who now had German troops deep in her territories and Stalin desperately needed allies and re-established diplomatic relations with the Polish Government in exile in London. He agreed to grant an 'amnesty' to all Polish citizens who had been forcibly deprived of their freedom and exiled to Russia in 1940-41 and when this news came through to the camp, everyone cheered, they were elated.

Amnesty, a period during which a law is suspended to allow offenders to admit their crime without fear of prosecution, a general pardon especially for offences against a government. The Poles had been arrested without having committed any crimes!

The amnesty referred only to a one time immunity in the USSR, for those deprived of their freedom following the Soviet invasion of Poland in September 1939. The signing of the amnesty by the Presidium of the

Supreme Soviet on 12th August 1941 resulted in the temporary stop of persecutions of Polish citizens under Soviet occupation. General Sikorsky, on behalf of the Polish Government, signed the first diplomatic agreement on 30th July 1941.

The agreement also included a special statement concerning Polish prisoners of war and Polish civilian deportees in the USSR. Stalin promised to release Polish prisoners of war and the huge number of the deportees who had been exiled to Siberia. The Soviet Ambassador to Britain, Maisky, then announced that the Soviet-German treaty of August 1939 relating to the territorial division of Poland along the Ribbentrop-Molotov Line 'was no longer valid.'

*Picture of one of the many burials endured by parents of a child who could not survive the utter deprivation of life in Siberia*

Stalin had put the Poles in those camps to work them to death, and if it hadn't been for the 'amnesty', he would have succeeded. Poland's history shows Russia's greed for her land, to expand the Russian Empire even further and seek revenge for past uprisings. It was also Stalin's intention to spread Communism throughout Europe via Poland. The Russians' hostile feelings towards the Poles were returned in full.

Although emaciated by disease and exhausted from the harshness of the life they had led, the survivors were ready to make their way in their hundreds of thousands from the most remote corners of Russia, out of the camps and towards freedom and their Army. They were to leave behind so many of their number, buried in crude graves and those too exhausted, aged and worn down by starvation to be able to make a journey of any distance, even if it meant freedom.

Very many of these poor people were skeletal, wearing only rags, their feet covered in paper. They were so very thin, as the family and everyone else was but these people looked old and wrinkled. They were bloated and their skin was yellow, their eyes sunken. They were so weak some of them couldn't stand up, mentally they hadn't given up but physically they were incapable. There were not enough of the prisoners who were strong enough to help them and they had to be left behind. It was heart-breaking for Alicja and the family to watch and it would be another image of very many that stayed with her, she would never forget those they left behind.

Many of the prisoners had not been told about the formation of the Polish military units on Soviet soil, the news was kept from them, they were not told about their rights and obligations to join those Polish units until a young Polish soldier had walked into the camp shortly after the' amnesty' and surprised them all. He confirmed to them what had happened and said it would be best for them to head towards Persia, a journey of over 3,500 km where the Polish army was forming under British command.

The NKVD did everything in their power to limit the number of Poles leaving as they needed their slave labour. After the German attack on Russia the conditions in the camp worsened drastically, quotas were increased and rations cut which led to a sharp rise in mortality which made the prisoners more determined to take action during the short period they had to leave. They had to make haste as the window would not be open for long and after listening to the young soldier they were now even more determined to join the Polish army. They did not trust Stalin with very good reason, they had to leave as soon as they could.

General Anders, their Polish military leader, had been freed from the Lubyanka prison in Moscow and news then reached the camp confirming that the Polish army was reforming under his command in the Middle East, with some units being formed within the Soviet Union. Everyone was excited and wanted to join the Polish army. They knew what they had to do, but not how to do it. Leaving was not as simple as it might seem, 'amnesty' documents and transport had to be arranged, and there was much to do and think about. Only in flight from Russia could safety and freedom lie and they had to move fast, the journey to Kotlas would be their first aim.

Not many weeks after the amnesty had been declared, Uncle Walery had walked into the camp, he was unrecognisable, he was very badly bruised, very thin and gaunt, with long hair and dirty clothes and a beard down to his chest. Despite his malnourished condition he had found the strength to look for them. Walery had been coming back to collect his own family when he had been caught by the NKVD had been arrested accused of being a spy and transported to the Lubyanka prison. He had avoided the deportations but was then sent to a prison at Swierdlowsk then onto a camp in the salt mines of the Urals, many hundreds of km from their camp. He had been lucky as there was a lot of movement along the Soviet lands with many people leaving camps heading towards the Polish army.

There were transports and centres set up for the deportees to register at and he had managed to get onto some of those transports but had also walked many km to reach them. He also met with other Poles who were wandering the plains looking for their relatives.

Ziuta had earlier found out where he was and written to him to make sure he knew where they were and contact had been maintained between them. Despite such isolation, no papers, no radio, contact was always somehow made. Word was always able to get through, although it did take some time.

It was so very difficult for them at this time and they longed for freedom, anxious to leave but there was now a typhoid epidemic throughout the camp and the death toll was unbelievable leaving very many orphans to fend for themselves wiping out whole families. It lasted for 2 months and the population of the camp halved. They had lost so very many friends and had to learn to keep their emotions on hold, it was the only way to function. The camp authorities let them trade with the villagers again and they had food to build their strength for the arduous journey they were soon to face. They still had to work in the forests and were driven very hard and mentally found it extremely difficult.

They felt downtrodden and it brought many to despair but to lose courage now, to let the Soviets destroy their spirit would be disastrous. The days seemed endless, life was monotonous and they were very sad. They were physically and emotionally exhausted and always hungry but they prayed and kept their faith. So many more tragic deaths through accident, death through illness of friends was difficult to cope with. Climatic conditions and cruel treatment by the guards and near starvation was taking its toll by the day.

Alicja had another friend in the camp, Elzunia, who was 14 orphaned with a sister of 7 and a brother of 12, she was the head of the family and worked in the forests as a lumberjack with grown men. If she didn't work her family would starve as there would be no rations. The Soviets made sure she worked as hard as the men did and produce as much as them. They were heartless, 'the more of you that die the happier we will feel'. There were 10,000 orphans from the labour camps who arrived in Persia after the amnesty, they had somehow managed to travel from the USSR towards the Polish army in the most malnourished of conditions.

In August 1941 an NKVD officer had arrived at the camp to confirm to people that General Sikorski, Commander in Chief of the Polish army and Premier of the Polish Government in exile in London, had signed a pact with Stalin. The family and those around them were overjoyed. They were told they would receive documents quite soon stating that they were free to leave.

The first discharge papers were issued on 5th September 1941 for some of the surrounding camps and very soon groups departed to travel towards the Polish army, so very eager to fight. By October other groups were getting their discharge papers and travel documents. The family hadn't yet received theirs but waited with patience. It was getting much colder and the wait for papers was getting longer and it looked like they would be caught in the beginning of the harsh Siberian winter, a very difficult time to travel the distances ahead of them.

The Kommandant explained that there were very many people waiting at the station in Kotlas and not enough wagons for them all. He asked them to be patient but they were keen to get out of this prison. Without the travel documents though they couldn't leave as they wouldn't qualify for food stamps for soup and bread at the station canteens. Some of the older boys so very keen to fight ignored him and left.

In November 1941 Antoni Maj, the camps' representative and the Kommandant were notified that it was time to transport some of those who wanted to leave and horse drawn sledges were sent from the collective farms in the area. Over 700 Poles left the camp and were taken to the nearest railway line in the middle of a forest. There was no station and they had to wait for 3 days and nights in the open in deep snow for the train.

There was plenty of wood available and camp fires burned continually to keep them from freezing. When word reached them that the train was on the way they gathered as much wood to load onto the train as they could for the long and cold journey to Kotlas which was over 450km away. A few hundred Poles from camp Dorovatka near the railway line joined them making a very large grouping and they hoped there would be room for them all.

The train arrived and they loaded on and when it left there were many tears and high emotion, people were excited but afraid. The journey ahead was again unknown to them, it was over 3,500 km to their destination, meanwhile, Adam and Kazia and several others still waited for their official papers to leave.

It was now a war situation, the captive Poles left in the camp awaiting their papers had now become Soviet allies and it was a very strange feeling for them! They weren't getting paid and were still expected to work but at least they were getting 800 grams of bread and watery soup a day. Their main concern was their documentation and there were just a few of them left in the camp in this situation. Soviet soldiers needed shelter and the prisoners were moved to a very small hut. Adam was angry thinking that the Kommandant had other motives in keeping them there and was ready to 'escape'. Kazia was more measured and argued that they settle down and wait.

From the Russian wastelands there were almost 200,000 POWs who were released from the gulags to form the Polish army on Russia soil. Stalin would cut off their supplies however and the NKVD would sabotage them at many stages of their journey so General Anders in 1942 ensured they were evacuated to the Middle East making their way by whatever means they could to Persia, Iraq, Syria and Palestine under the main command of the British army, but under his command whilst ensuring them safe passage out of Russia. This exodus included many thousands of women and children and very many orphans.

At about this same time relations between Stalin and the Polish Government deteriorated over disagreements over the borderlands between the eastern provinces of Poland, Stalin insisting they should be absorbed into the Soviet Union after the war. Vyacheslav Molotov, Soviet Foreign Secretary, was in London to press the case for the territories of Poland and the Baltic states, formerly carved up by Hitler and Stalin.

Stalin was keen to have the Allies endorse this same deal. The British Government thought this utterly immoral and Churchill refused, only granting a general treaty of alliance and no promise of any territory but this was overturned at the Tehran meeting and later at Yalta with Roosevelt's support. Stalin would have his territories and the Iron Curtain would later close down on Eastern Europe.

Although Germany was beaten and the Allies had won the war, The Poles were the real losers. Over half a million fighting men and women and six million civilians died. About 50% of these were Polish Christian and 50% Polish Jews. Approximately 5,384,000 of the Polish war losses were the victims of prisons, death camps, executions, annihilation in ghettos, epidemics, starvation, excessive work and ill treatment. So many

Poles were sent to concentration and labour camps that virtually every family had someone close to it who had been tortured, interred or murdered there.

There were one million war orphans and over half a million invalids. The country lost 38% of its national assets (Britain lost 0.8%, France 1.5%) and the country was swallowed up by the Soviet Union, including the two great cultural centres of Lwów and Wilno. So many had died in the camps, of disease, bad water, mosquitoes, ill treatment and starvation. They had been worked to death and told they would never leave.

Families' buried their dead in the mud, under little mounds of earth, singing their patriotic songs, some of the coffins lay on the high water table unable to be buried. Yet so many did survive, mostly by simply believing they would, with their determination and resilience and their faith, it saw them through. They had indeed 'learned to breathe under water.'

Deportation had been a way of eliminating economically strong and intellectually enterprising elements of Polish society, a plot designed to weaken the Polish population of the newly Russian occupied eastern borderlands, it also strengthened the Russian speaking population.

Those frail and starving people had incredible, psychological strength and refused to abandon their beliefs. They had shown a heroism and resourcefulness in sustaining their physical lives under terrible conditions and also their humanity and friendships and their concern for others which helped them to survive. They worked together as best they could for each other and would need every resource to survive their journeys towards Tashkent.

Kazia, Adam, their children and her brother Walery and his family had no alternative than to wait for the documents that would guarantee them food and water at the various stations along the route to Tashkent. Without them they would starve as so very many did in their impatience to leave the camps to fight.

They were still one strong unit and had survived this far because of that, the strengths I had seen growing up in such a close and loving family almost devastated by war.

*Two of the labour camps in the Gorkowski Oblast where the Polish military families from the Kresy were exiled to in 1940*

*'If you are afraid of wolves, keep out of the woods' – J.V. Stalin 1936*

CHAPTER 5

# Liberated

In Operation Barbarossa in June 1941, the Germans invaded the Soviet republics, Ukraine, Byelorussia and Russia. Stalin now needed allies and as a condition of joining forces with the USA and GB against the Germans, he grudgingly agreed to the repatriation of all Poles on Soviet soil. This was the price he paid for the Soviet-Polish pact of 31st July 1941 which re-established already tenuous diplomatic ties with the Polish Government and began the creation of a Polish Army to be assembled on Russian land.

Although Stalin ordered the release of Polish POWs from the gulags and labour camps, he allowed only a small proportion of them to leave, about 114,000, over 1ml were still detained and the NKVD were to obstruct the passage of those fleeing refugees towards reaching any checkpoints. Due also to the endless sabotages from the Soviets the Polish Army was quickly evacuated to Iraq, Persia, Syria and Palestine coming under British command with General Anders ensuring as many as possible left the USSR safely.

At the camp, local men and the guards were quickly mobilised into the Soviet army, food, coal and kerosene were diverted to meet the army's needs and all others left in the camp were faced with starvation but they at least had an escape to plan and freedom to look forward to. Their remote settlement had been shocked by the news on the camp's radio of these events, which always followed a familiar pattern, announcements with a build-up about Soviet bravery and large German casualties and then admission about a Russian retreat, Soviet casualties were concealed while German forces were in full retreat on all fronts!

Leaving the camp was not as easy as it seemed and preparations had to be made for a long and arduous journey of over 3,500km. The food situation in the camp was dire, the prisoners were at the end of their strength and most had exhausted any items they had to barter. The Kommandant tried to stall their departure but unable to block them from leaving he made no effort whatsoever to help them.

In general the Soviet authorities made it almost impossible for the Poles to leave the gulags and camps as had been provided for in the agreement with the Polish Government. The re-classification of the prisoners as 'free citizens' guaranteed nothing, as the Soviets did not recognise their right to join the Polish free army nor their right to leave the USSR. The prisoners had to achieve this on their own, and it was hardest on the single women with children who had lost their husbands.

A few days after the radio announcement a telegram arrived at the camp from the Polish Embassy in Kuybishev. It stated 'that all officers, the soldiers of the military settlers and those who were able to serve were to report to the nearest HQ of the Soviet Army, from where they would be directed to the new Polish Army. All Soviet authorities had this information and those who reported to them would receive the necessary travel documents and food stamps.' Many of the Soviet 'authorities' ignored this information and diverted the Polish transports leaving the USSR towards collective farms along their route out of the USSR.

Camps Poldniewica, Derawalka and Duraszewo, elected a representative who would go to the army posts set up by the Polish Embassy scattered throughout the region, who would have information about what the deportees would need to do with their newly gained freedom and how to move on to the next stage of their journey from the USSR. They would need to know how to progress now that they were able to travel freely regardless of the cynical tactics of the NKVD.

Antoni Maj was the representative of the remaining prisoners. He was from a village in eastern Poland, Jadwipol and one of four children of Ludwik and Stanisłowa Maj. His father had a small farm and was a forest ranger working for Prince Janusz Radziwil. Antoni had just returned for a short visit to his parents in the Kresy with his new wife and happened to be on the deportation list held by the NKVD. Many years later when he visited his Aunt in Poland she told him that shortly after the family had been driven away by the NKVD, their Ukrainian neighbours descended on their property like vultures!

Antoni would need to visit the Polish embassy in Kuybyshev, (named after the Bolshevik leader Valerian Kuybyshev who took the city in the October revolution of 1917) which was the administrative centre of Samara and about 800km away. He had to argue very strongly to get transport to the railway station in Sharya about 90km away, which the Kommandant very reluctantly agreed to. The journey was long and the deportees would have to get used to the vast distances to be travelled across the USSR in their journey towards Persia.

Kuybyshev is a major river port situated at the junction of the Volga and Samara rivers in close view of the Zhiguli mountains and in 1941 the prospect of Moscow falling to the invading Germans seemed so likely that it was chosen to be the new capital of Russia. The Communist party and governmental organisations, diplomats and leading cultural establishments were evacuated there. After the Russians defeated the Germans most of the area's 1.5 ml German inhabitants were dispersed into exile or into hard labour camps. In 1991 the city was given back its historical name of Samara.

Antoni returned a week later with the necessary paperwork which gave him authority to act, a certificate from the Embassy officially nominating him as a spokesman for the refugees. Alicja remembers when Antoni got back and told them they were free and able to go where they wanted, there was such joy and tears of relief!

The Polish Ambassador to the USSR, Stanisław Kot, and his small team had the enormous task of organising relief for the hundreds of thousands of Poles dispersed throughout the vastness of the Soviet Union. The first task was to find them, as they were spread over such a huge area. The aim of his delegates was to set up orphanages, feeding centres, hospitals and schools throughout Russia for all who had been released from the labour camps and to somehow get them all to where the Polish Army was being formed. Embassy delegates were sent all over Russia to arrange this massive programme of relief.

It took time to organise the necessary individual papers (the amnesty document which would serve as the family identification and passport and as a one-way travel permit to the destination of choice) and transport from Kotlas, and Antoni, with several able assistants, was working hard to organise everything, he had a huge job on his hands. Transport was to be arranged for the entire community to go south east, as the Polish army was being formed in Buzuluk, in the southern Ural Mountains. General Władislaw Anders, commander of the Polish Army, had set up his headquarters there. Without the amnesty papers everyone would be faced with hunger, as the papers entitled them to soup and bread at various station canteens. It also helped prevent any arrest by the Soviets.

However, Adam's papers were withheld and the family couldn't leave and were in absolute despair. There were several other families denied permission to leave who were also considered 'social undesirables' for their part in the Uprising of 1920, the Russian-Polish war, when all around were busily getting ready to leave, the 'social undesirables' were being held back. The records of the men in question, their military history and political views were known to the authorities, it was why they had been arrested in February 1940 and the NKVD had made objections to them leaving because of their military history! 'I cannot describe our feelings of hopelessness. We were absolutely desperate and how we wept.'

The Soviets went out of their way to postpone as many departures as they could, determined to keep their slave labourers as long as possible and they refused to allocate places on a train for them. However, a few days later Antoni successfully acquired the necessary amnesty papers for all the camp residents remaining including the 'social undesirables' and tickets would be allocated for them despite the Kommandant's efforts to prevent them leaving.

Those in the most remote labour camps of the Kotlas region didn't hear of the amnesty for months and as soon as they could they moved south desperately seeking recruitment into the army or at least their protection. Many from this remote region would need to make rafts to drift down the rivers to reach the nearest railway station and at Yarensk every family who wanted to leave had to build rafts, which then meant cutting down trees, gathering vines and boiling them to bind them to the logs before setting sail. It was long and tiring work. Those who decided to travel in later winter had to make sledges and cope with the snow up to their armpits in places which made their escape very difficult. They trudged this way for over a week covering incredible distances of up to 60km a day they were so determined.

From the moment they heard of the 'amnesty' tens of thousands of Poles travelled south from their labour camps towards General Anders and his army. Some hitched rides on carts, some walked, some sailed part of the journey on basic boats, some boarded cargo trains again, keeping alive by eating raw potatoes or weeds and grass. Many thousands died of mainly typhus en route, Uzkek villagers would open train doors and skeletal bodies would fall out.

The family were at last free to go leaving the labour camps behind them and Antoni had got them all together before leaving and told them to guard these identity papers very carefully as without them they would be arrested and sent back to the camp or worse and they wouldn't ever see freedom.

Although they were free to go there was considerable hardship to endure before they were truly free of the restrictions of the Soviets. Some of the families in the camp stayed behind by choice, they were mostly White Russians or Ukrainians with communist sympathies and they didn't see any reason to travel into more conflict and danger. Although how they would survive in that inhospitable land, in one of the most extreme geographical and climatic regions in the country? They would have to survive a harsh and sometimes deadly climate, hard labour and meagre food rations!

On 28th December 1941, after a very unhappy Wigilia, with little to eat or celebrate, with their papers in their grasp they started to pack everything together, they had a horse and sledge borrowed from Constantin, Adam's

Russian friend, to take them to Kotlas. They were frightened that it would all go wrong, but also excited, it was desperately cold and there was a lot of very deep snow and they had heard from the Soviets that the German forces had now reached Moscow and Leningrad. How would this affect their journey? The camp was now almost empty but for the graves of over 270 of their fellow countrymen, women and children, driven to their deaths by the extreme cold, overwork and starvation. Only about 10% of prisoners in some camps survived to escape.

Kazia, Adam and the children looked back on almost two years of abject misery and hardship and took a very deep breath realising they were on the way to freedom although with a mountain to climb. They had their few scraps together including their most precious photo albums, hugged each other, and with 3 other families, looked ahead to the journey towards Kotlas 450km away, with lighter hearts and great determination. They travelled many miles on foot, with Kazia on the sledge and were able to stay overnight with local Russians they had met previously at one of the markets. They had probably saved their lives as it was bitterly cold.

They started early the next morning on the long journey to Kotlas which would take a few days but they were focused, they thanked their Russian hosts and set off. Everyone was happy because they were moving away from the dreaded labour camps, going south towards the Polish army in Bukhara and away from Stalin's grip. Their hearts were lighter and their shoulders already dropping. As they were about to leave army trucks appeared at the farm with Russian soldiers on their way to the railway line in Kotlas and asked them if they wanted a lift. They couldn't believe their luck, Russian soldiers – and so friendly! They left the horse and sledge for their Russian friends and got into the trucks.

There was a lot of movement of Russian soldiers at that time across the plains of Russia after Hitler's attack and the soldiers were very helpful. The trucks passed over the river Dwina, which was frozen, it was -20 degrees and extremely cold, the wind was very strong and they shivered from cold and excitement. There were three other families with them on the truck and they would support each other throughout the harsh demands of what would be an arduous journey.

They reached Kotlas late afternoon on 30th December and saw a very crowded station, people were begging for food, so thin, eyes so dark and they couldn't ignore them as they made their way to the station forecourt. It was full of Polish families, all hungry huddling in rags because of the cold and like them eager to board any train out of Russia. They waited in line for 400 grams of bread and a bowl of soup and this was marked on their permit of travel. They had paid for their place on the train as Kazia had saved what she could and bartered for the rest, it cost her 80 roubles per person. There were about 7 families from their camp and they waited at the station for 3 days, waiting as train after train packed with Poles passed through the station without stopping. They had been reassured that there were Polish officers there to help them along the journey but they didn't see any.

Kotlas was the first town they had seen as newly freed people and they noticed when coming in that most buildings were of wood, the only brick building was the NKVD headquarters and a smaller building for the district communist party. There were wooden walkways each side of the streets and the roads were just dirt. Most of the inhabitants were ex Zeks (Prisoners) who had been allocated to live in Kotlas after their release from the labour camps. Some had worked on the Kotlas-Vorkuta railway and many others in the mines in Vorkuta district, the canals and dams.

Kotlas is a city at the tip of the Arkhangelsk Region and lies at the junction of two wide rivers, the Northern Dvina and the Vychegda. It has a river port, a shipyard and rail junction as well as a timber processing combine. It was probably inhabited from ancient times and was only granted official town status by Russia in 1917. During the 1930's Kotlas became the place to where Kulaks were deported and made to work as slave labour in the forests, they were affluent and independent farmers in the Russian empire who emerged from peasantry and became wealthy by their own hard efforts and had resisted Stalin's collectivising of the peasantry and refused to hand over their grain to detachments from Moscow.

During 1929 and 1933 peasants with a couple of cows or 5 or 6 acres more than their neighbours were labelled as 'kulaks' and 'class enemies' of the poorer peasants! Lenin described the kulaks as 'bloodsuckers, vampires, plunderers of the people and profiteers, who fatten on famine' and according to his political theory and his Marxist revolution, he intended to liberate the poor peasants and labourers. In practice however, government officials seized, with violent force, kulak farms killing resisters and deporting others to labour camps, which existed in the area until 1953. It was Stalin however, through one of his 5 year plans who caused the worst famine in history, the Holodomor, which killed millions.

2nd Jan and the train arrives late. It's made up of lots of boxcars and they join the long line, lucky to get on as so many were fighting for a space. They have tickets and were allocated seats amongst the Poles from the gulags and POW camps. The family were to witness a sight that would be a constant at each stop on the journey to Persia, the burying of people who had died on their long trek to freedom. They had already seen lightly covered mounds on the outskirts of the station which were the graves of Poles from the earlier arrivals.

The sliding door of the train is left open and the only sign of guards were the uniformed men driving the train, no NKVD guards to shout orders at them. At every station these men had to negotiate hard with the NKVD to have the train moved onto the next station and they also arranged food for the Poles at the communal feeding places. They didn't bother them and the family began to feel a little freer. There were however still the many watch towers manned by guards near every settlement on route.

There were men designated at the stations to bring them food, soup, bread and boiled water and being classified as military transport enabled the newly freed Poles to receive small rations for which they had to show their identification papers. At other stations and city's there were Polish Consular officials to help them on their way.

The train moved towards Kirow and they began to relax a little. After arriving at Kirow station, a journey of 520km they were faced with many hundreds more people waiting on the platform. Some were able to board, but others were left to wait for the next transport. People sometimes waited many days for a train, vulnerable to the weather and thieves. They were very often shunted onto a side rail to wait, as other transports carrying military equipment were given priority and they sometimes heard Russian soldiers singing. They also had to be very careful if they got off the train as they would set off without any warning.

The journey from Kirow to their main destination Bukhara, was over 3,000km, and they braced themselves for a very long and gruelling journey. Everyone sat huddled together and chased hunger away with the little food left, ground oats and potato pancakes. As they moved on from Kirov through forested countryside with small villages at intervals the watch towers were less frequent as they moved onwards on the Trans-Siberian route. They were able to get out and stretch their legs, very aware that the train could leave the station without any warning. Many people were caught out by this and were separated from their families, never to see them again, as had happened on their way from Poland to Russia.

They were heading towards the Ural Mountains and had to change trains several times, there were hundreds upon hundreds of weary travellers heading towards the Polish army and the trains were very crowded and also very unreliable as everyone was to find out. Some of the routes were guarded by a network of spies and the NKVD who only worsened the evacuation process by relocating thousands of Soviet citizens at the same time. This was a deliberate ploy to cause as much difficulty as possible and an attempt by the NKVD to resettle as many deportees in the poorest part of Turkestan as they could. They thrived on creating problems for others but in this they failed as so many determined Poles got through to other south eastern republics of Russia. The Polish spirit was unbreakable, they would not let the Soviets get the better of them, they still had the spirit that had won them the Bolshevik War.

The Ural Mountains extend for about 2,500km and run from north to south through western Russia from the Arctic Ocean to the Ural River and north western Kazakhstan. It is probably the richest range of mountains with salt, silver and gold mined there since the 1500's. Famous for its gems and semi precious stones, it forms the boundary between Europe and Asia and during the German invasion of Russia the mountains became a key element in German planning for the territories they expected to conquer. Faced with this threat the Soviets evacuated a large part of these territories especially the industrial units and three giant tank factories were established in Sverdlovsk and Chelyabinsk out of the reach of the German bombers and troops.

Everyone was tired and hungry as they pass through Zuyovka but their spirits are good and the children chat to their companions and stay very close to their parents. They spend their time watching the countryside go by and sometimes see elk and the odd brown bear which excites them and they see many wolves. They pass stations the names of which they couldn't remember. If the train stopped for any length of time it was for the disposal of the dead, both young and old died but most frequently death hit the former gulag prisoners, so badly malnourished.

The bodies were not buried, as no one had the strength to dig graves, emaciated children died in their mother's arms and it was heart wrenching to look at the mothers abandoning the bodies of their children to be devoured by wolves in the forests or the jackals in the deserts. Sometimes the train wouldn't stop for many hours and the decomposing bodies would have to be thrown from the moving train. How many thousands of Poles were left by the railroad tracks in Russia during that trip to freedom will never be known.

They stop at Molotov for 2 days to allow Russian troops to go through ahead of them, troops heading to fight the Germans who have invaded their country. Would the fleeing Poles have any contact with the Germans? It was a thought that crossed Adam's mind constantly. They shared their thoughts with others, but sometimes were just lost in their own, thinking of home and wondering if they would ever see it again. At times they just huddled together to give each other warmth and the reassurance to go on, Kazia always had a word of comfort or humour to keep them going. She truly was the glue that held the family together, they had always been a close and happy family but were even closer and reliant on each other now.

'We journey on and it's been many days of exhausting travel. We never know when there will be a hold up and we make the best of the delays to hunt for food'. The journey continues over the river Kama, to Shalya, Kuzma, and Hropik going through a more industrialised countryside. 'We get off at Hropik and stretch our legs and as usual we look for food. We find the queue for the bakery which is so very long, many people as dusty as we are in threadbare clothing and so very thin and we probably looked the same. When the bakery started selling bread the queue moved slowly forward but after about ½ an hour it stopped as a convoy of NKVD lorries had arrived and they took the whole batch of bread, we were very hungry and very angry.'

They travelled through the most beautiful landscapes of forests, valleys, rivers and mountain ridges, and arrived at Swierdlowsk on 19th Jan a major station in the Ural Mountains. This time they were able to get out and speak to friends from other wagons and see the happy faces of people who didn't seem to have a care in the world for the first time in two years. Alicja and Adam go out to look for food, they had their papers and were able to get soup and bread. Their train was classified as a military transport but it didn't make any difference to the speed at which they travelled, it was very slow as they were shunted onto side rails to let the troop transports through which sometimes left them waiting for hours at a time.

Swierdlowsk was formally known as Yekaterinburg, founded in 1723 and named after Peter the Great's wife, Yekaterina. It was the mining capital of the Russian Empire and a strategic connection between Europe and Asia. She gave the city the status of a district town in Perm province and built the main road of the Empire, the Siberian route through the city when it became a key city to Siberia. It is on the eastern side of the Ural Mountains and is surrounded by wooded hills, several lakes and rivers being located on a natural watershed.

Yekaterinburg was also the place of imprisonment and execution of Tsar Nicholas II, his wife and 5 children together with their loyal servants who had chosen to accompany them. They were shot, bayoneted and clubbed to death on 16-17th July 1918. Killed by Bolshevik troops led by Yakov Yurovsky under the orders of Lenin and the Ural Regional Soviet, Yakov Sverdlov and Felix Dzerzhinsky. Their bodies were then taken to the Koptyaki forest where they were stripped and mutilated. Initially thrown down a mine shaft called Ganina Yama, the bodies were later disposed of in unmarked graves in a field, Porosenkov Log. Russian President Boris Yeltzin described the killings as one of the most shameful pages in Russian history.

The Soviet leadership claimed in September 1919 that the family was murdered by left wing revolutionaries and then denied outright in April 1922 that they were dead. The Soviet cover up of the murders continued until 1926 when they acknowledged them after a publication of an investigation by a White émigré. The burial site was discovered in 1979 by an amateur sleuth but the existence of the remains was not made public until 1989 during the Glasnost period. The remains were confirmed by DNA and forensic investigation and they were reburied in the Peter and Paul Cathedral in Saint Petersburg in 1998, 80 years after they were killed. Key members of the Russian Orthodox Church did not attend the funeral disputing the authenticity of the remains.

They had been travelling for many long and very uncomfortable days, always hungry and it was very hot and dusty and there would be much hardship to follow. At some stations they saw huge piles of salt and wheat, the salt being sold on the black market by the matchbox at a very high price. At other stops there were quite unpleasant scenes with men driving horse-drawn carts collecting the corpses of those who had died, eventually giving in to illness and starvation.

Jasia, Janusz and Alicja took the opportunity to explore Swierdlowsk, as they had been assured that the train had to refuel and take on provisions and would not be leaving until the next morning. There were many buildings and beautiful monuments along the streets, one of Catherine the Great, but in the end they were too malnourished and weary to really look at the sights so headed back to the station.

As they approached the sidings they saw a very long train filled with people who were probably being transported to the camps the Poles had come from. Their cries for food and water were desperate, there were many such transports of human misery heading into Russia, many Germans from Kuybyshev which had a large German population. As Hitler had invaded Russia the Soviets were rounding up all Germans from across the regions and sending them to prison and labour camps in Siberia, Uzbekistan and other Russian areas. The children quickly ran for their wagon and climbed on. This had frightened them as it immediately brought back memories of their own journey into Russia from their homeland. Adam had been told by one of the 'officials' at the station that the Polish recruiting office had moved to Kuybishov which he shared with his companions.

From Swierdlowsk on 21st Jan they continue through the Ural mountains towards Chelybinsk 250km away. They disembark to search for rations which are now becoming very scarce and they manage to get some hot soup. The next stop is Orenburg where Polish Officers are there to help them on their journey. There were Polish army units camped along the route from Siberia to Tehran. The train then heads to Kartal and Aktyubinsk after taking on more fuel and some time for rest, it's an even longer journey of 1,670km and the train stopped in a siding by open fields. The landscape is very different here with houses of brick or mud.

They had passed a village a short way back and they were very hungry, they always were and Jasia and Janusz decided to try their luck and search for food but they had only gone a short distance when a loud whistle was blown announcing the train's departure and they raced back. They wouldn't eat that day. Trains had been changed there for Oktiabirsk a shorter journey of only 102km and they get out again to look around for food and there are many people waiting who tell them they've been there for days and that there isn't any food.

These had been very long, arduous journeys, so far over 3,000 kilometres, it was hot and everyone was filthy and exhausted and had lost track of time. The shortage of food and the unwashed bodies and clothes were irritants, but they were together and safe, that was important.

The train rumbled on to Shalkar and the Aral Sea, now on the Trans-Aral railway, and finally, after a journey of about six weeks and a total of over 3,500km, they arrived in Tashkent, the capital of Uzbekistan. It was a drab and very old station, still marked with the Turkish moon and star. Everyone was exhausted, hungry and filthy, they disembarked and sat on the platform, talked to friends, looked for food and waited. This had been a most fatiguing journey and very many didn't make it despite their determination. Worn down by starvation, typhus, dysentery and malaria with no energy left to go on, they just dropped. The girls would be chatting to their friends one day and the next morning their friends didn't wake up.

The surrounding fields and platforms were filled with Polish escapees from the Russian work camps. Representatives of the Polish authorities milled around doing as much as they could to provide food and basic shelter. More trains of Polish refugees were arriving every hour which made matters even worse. The assistants from the Polish Consulate started to explain to them how to reach the local Polish Army unit. 'Once you join up' he said, 'you'll be safe, the Russians won't be able to touch you, you must get into a uniform.'

After several hours they board another train which stops first at Samarkand, a journey of 300km. They get off and will have to wait on the platforms for 2 nights, some of the passengers were to wait for barges to take them to Nukus on the Aral Sea and Russian military trains were let through. They were exhausted, they hadn't slept well on the platform and were very hungry, they board another train and after 200km they reached Bukhara, where some of them were told to leave the train. They said their goodbyes to their friends, including the Krawiec family, Bruno, Maryjan and their sisters Krysia and Irena and their parents, as the family and others were going further east. They had become very close to the Krawiec family and would meet them again.

Many years later my Mother Alicja became friendly with Halina a Polish woman, while taking my younger brother Chris to junior school in Birmingham in 1962 and she was taking her daughter Elizabeth. She invited her to her home once and "I noticed her wedding photograph and I said I recognise that woman" and Halina said but how can you, she's my mother-in-law? 'Just then a tall dark man walked into the lounge and we recognised each other immediately. He was Bruno from the Krawiec family to whom we had said goodbye in 1942 in Bukhara.' There were many hugs and tears, 'how can you hold back tears when such vivid memories suddenly overwhelm you' Alicja remains friends with Halina to this day, Bruno died some years go.

During the journey south they had suffered many hardships, typhoid, red and common dysentry raged, food had been scarce and the death rate had risen higher than ever but everyone had held on to the hope that the Polish army would be there to protect them at the end.

They were now in Uzbekistan, the site of one of the world's oldest civilised regions. An ancient Persian province, it was conquered by Alexander the Great and the Nomads, Arabs and Turks over the centuries. From the 4th century BC to the 16th century AD Bukhara and Tashkent, situated as they were on the major trade routes to China, India, Persia and Europe, were centres of prosperity, culture and wonderful luxury. The Uzbeks invaded in the 16th century and extended the domain over parts of Persia and Chinese Turkistan. The empire then began to break up into separate principalities, one being Bukhara. Sorely weakened by warfare, these regions were conquered by Russian forces who took Tashkent in 1865 and Bukhara in 1868. These areas then became vassal states of Russia and after prosperity, peace and luxury came communism, domination and poverty.

It seemed the end of the line and there were very many hundreds of people gathered, cold and dirty, hungry and waiting for someone to tell them where to go, some were on the platform and some had stayed in the boxcar. The train would go no further, it had made a very short stop, and no one moved, they didn't want to get off as they thought they would never leave the USSR. They had a very unsettled and fearful night in a field across from the station.

Next morning the Polish civilian authorities came and assured them that they would remain there only temporarily and that the boxcars were needed for military purposes. They were persuaded that resistance was useless and reluctantly they left the train.

Bukhara was very busy with Uzbeks with very colourful straps around their caps and midriffs and Turkmen in black khalats, long robes with huge caracul hats lined with long haired fur band around the outside. The roads were full of people riding camels and donkeys loaded with bundles of dry twigs and bales of cotton. Lists were being drawn up by the 'authorities' dividing the occupants of the train into smaller groups and the thought of further forced labour crossed the minds of the waiting Poles.

They waited for another night in the field and were terrified of their prospects. Morning came and they were given their instructions by the Uzbek authorities, they were being sent to a Kolkhozy. Their fears about working in forced labour are realised! They had wondered what their fate was going to be, knowing that the Soviets were keen to retain their labour and prevent them from leaving, they were not surprised at this turn of events. They were still slave workers for the Russian collectives! Adam, Władek and Walery had left for the recruiting office in Bukhara which had re-opened and said they would be back as soon as they could thinking it was safe to leave them.

They had been assured by the Polish authorities that this was only temporary, until the problems of feeding and accommodating the large numbers of Polish Army volunteers had been overcome. Kazia and other mothers were most anxious, the Russians had been taken by surprise at the numbers volunteering for the Polish Army and had made attempts to limit the terms of the amnesty made with the Polish Government.

The numbers attempting to reach Buzuluk and Kuybyshev where the Polish Army was being formed in camps at Totskaya and Tatishchev, were an embarrassment to the very inefficient Russian rail system already under strain from the wartime demands of Soviet soldiers. To this end, without consulting the Polish authorities transports were secretly ordered to bypass Buzuluk and travel towards Kazakhstan and the fleeing Poles were affected hugely by this, left fending for themselves in desert and collective farms almost cut off from civilisation.

The many numbers of Poles involved had completely over run the Uzbek, Tadzhik and Turkmen Republics. They were now at the vast Steppes of Northern Uzbekistan and access to the collective farm was possible only along a dusty clay road. In the long severe Siberian winters, this route was snowed over and in spring, when the snow melted the road vanished under a raging torrent of ice cold water.

Some hours later, several arbas, with mules driven by quite wild-looking men wearing black fur hats got off their carts and through gestures told the weaker ones to get on board the arbas. Kazia was allowed to ride and those like her who were too weak or ill to walk. This time their walk to enslavement just outside Vobkent was about 30km or so and the stronger ones set off walking. Alicja, Jasia and Janusz follow the arbas confused and frightened. They were captives again, were in shock and very frightened. Kazia was almost in despair but she knew that Walery or Adam once in uniform would find them.

By lunchtime they still hadn't eaten and had just reached the Kolkhozy, which was in very barren countryside, with clouds of dust everywhere. It filled eyes, mouths and noses and made everyone cough and almost choke. The Uzbek took them to a big clay hut with an open fire in the middle full of smoke with a group of people with strange faces looking curiously at them. 'We had never seen an Uzbek before, and the Uzbeks had never seen a European before.'

They were strong sturdy people, with broad yellow faces, flat noses, very prominent cheek bones and cool dark eyes. 'We just watched each other, it was a strange meeting, but despite the differences, especially in appearance, they were friendly towards us.' They would need these new recruits to work for them! Early evening came and they were so hungry, they were given some uruk, dried fruit to eat, for which they were very grateful. The diet from then was frozen turnips and linseed cakes and cattle feed, which was tasteless and indigestible. After eating each family was allocated a kibitka, where they were to sleep.

They had no lights, no beds or furnishings. The huts were fashioned from home-made clay and bricks mixed with straw, and the roofs were either thatched or tiled with a hole in the middle. The village foreman managed to get some boards and straw, so they had something to make beds with although they didn't have any bedding.

*A kibitka of the nomad Uzbek tribes, also known as a yurta*

They were free to mingle with the local population of many mixed ethnic origins, the native Uzbeks of Mongolian race and European Russians who like the Poles had been deported there. There was no escape from this isolated and inaccessible settlement. The land around was flat and had a small tree covered area where the Kommissar lived. On the northern side of the Kolkhoz was a forest plantation and a small lake with a supply of fresh water, there was a store and a post office and the offices of the NKVD headquarters.

The NKVD told the Poles that anyone wishing to travel beyond Tashkent needed to obtain special permission from them and that the Polish deportees especially were not allowed this privilege, 'they had been misinformed that they could travel freely.' However the family knew that if they had a relative in the Polish army they were allowed to leave Uzbekistan, which is why Adam, Walery and Władek had left to reach the army HQ to get into uniform but the Soviets did not share this information wishing to keep them on Soviet soil.

Their first priority was a long soak in the lake after weeks in the trains it felt so good to be able to wash their hair and clothes. They were filthy, covered in lice and scratching.

Work was organised by the village master, who came to their kibitka in the morning with a horse drawn wooden cart and asked them to follow him into the fields, where he explained what had to be done. They were made to clear the cotton fields of the stems of the previous seasons' plants and various other dried weeds which the Uzbeks used for fuel. They later had harder work assigned to them, which involved digging irrigation canals and carrying soil from one place to another to level the ground for the cotton fields. It was work far beyond their strength, but if they didn't work they wouldn't receive the dhzugara, similar to wheat, – their 'payment.'

The Mothers left to fend for themselves looked around them and shrugged, they had no choice. Kazia would not be able to handle the strenuous work with her heart condition and would look to the children to help out, even Janusz.

The younger people picked cotton in the fields and the norm was for everyone to produce three large bags of cotton a day, which was very difficult for the Poles being malnourished and in such poor health. The Uzbek women did manage to achieve the norm but with difficulty, they bent into the work stooping, using both hands with very few breaks throughout the day. Even infants were taken by their mothers to earn their 'payment'. Some of the men working at harvesting the crops, shoe making and repairing wagons had come from the Osada's in Poland and were skilled in farm work and proved to be very useful despite their poor condition.

Other groups were sent to weed the planted wheat and barley crops which stretched for many kilometres across the Steppes. They laboured for seven days a week from dawn to dusk with meagre nourishment, perhaps a little water, cold tea and bread. The work was very hard, women were bent double moving along the rows of wheat in heat of 50C pulling out the rough wormwood and everyone returned to their kibitka's exhausted. The sun was extremely hot and the wind which often brought with it sandstorms, burnt them and dehydrated them quite badly.

As well as terrible hunger people succumbed to typhoid, fevers and dysentery, they were all terribly ill. They ate anything they could find, hog weed, nettles and sometimes when they were brave enough, stole melons and apricots. They even hunted for hedgehogs, lizards and crows. People were haggard and swollen with hunger and they died and those with enough energy dragged their bodies to ditches and covered them with branches. No one had energy to dig graves, they had to drag themselves through each day.

The Kolkhoz administrator told them what was to come later in the year, that at harvest time the whole of the Kolkhoz would move onto the steppe to gather and cut the hay working into the night and how important it was that the harvest was good for the survival of the population as the state would take a fixed amount of wheat and if more than this was not grown the population would starve in the winter months. They listened with other ideas on their minds as they had between them been planning an escape. They would not survive more strenuous labour, they were almost physically spent.

All the children gathered what they could, mushrooms and wild berries in the forest plantation and everyone queued up daily for their food provisions from the store. They gathered firewood for cooking an evening meal and Kazia tried to have something ready for her exhausted workers, Jasia and Alicja. Their standard fare was a soup called zutyerka, salted boiling water with pieces of dough and potato.

On a good day Kazia added an onion and cabbage and if they were very lucky Janusz caught a fish from the lake. Kazia was the source of their survival, her sacrifices and heroism, and all-embracing devotion got her family through this most awful ordeal. The family owe her everything, especially her resourcefulness after Adam had left, her superhuman efforts and for offering them the last spoonful of soup from nettles, a crumb of bread or a potato, leaving herself with very little.

In September the potato harvest would also begin and this again involved back breaking work, and by this time the weather would be colder and it would be the rainy season. The Administrator showed them how the potatoes had to be collected and put into large casks made from wood with large heavy iron handles and that the best of the potatoes of course would go to the state. He was planning for what he thought would be their future, his to decide.

The deportees however, had no intention of seeing the potato harvest, already making plans to leave. They were all suffering from various illnesses and wanted to use their remaining energy for the trek towards Tehran which was another lengthy journey of many km. They took in the detail on their rounds with the Administrator giving nothing away to him of their plans.

There were also dairy farms at the Kolkhoz and in the summer the workers would be sent far out into the steppe to guard and milk the cattle. There was no accommodation and they would have to build their own shelters. Again the women had to meet a quota of cheese and butter and would be fined if they produced less than expected. They were given very little milk for themselves or their babies or any other dairy products as generally the entire produce of the farm was sent to the authorities. This was Stalin's collectivisation.

There was no meat or fruit or vegetables and their bodies were badly undernourished, they were always hungry and were growing thinner and weaker. It was relentless, and it was now critical they made their escape as soon as they could. Most of the workers, were women and children who were extremely weak and malnourished.

After the amnesty, when they had received their evacuation papers, on 27th December 1941, with most of the men heading to join the Polish army most women had been left to cope on their own and were not expecting further forced labour, which was not the intention of the Russian-Polish pact of 31st July 1941. Also, unless the women were related to one of these men who had joined the army, they wouldn't be able to leave the kolkhozy and the fate of many of these women and children, left under Soviet control, is unknown.

The Soviet methods of working surprised the women, despite Stalin's movement for industrialisation and collectivisation in agriculture the tools the women were expected to use were ineffective and quite primitive and the work was not organised well and it looked like the appearance of work was more important rather than the actual output as the overseers never seemed to be there overseeing which was an advantage for these emaciated workers!

This land, had once been known for its riches, but through communism and collective farming it had suffered poverty and severe hunger. Before the October Revolution of 1917 it had been regarded as a paradise.

There wasn't much help from the Polish authorities at that time as they were so far stretched organising the evacuation of so very many thousands of fleeing Poles from such a vast area. They did at times meet some delegates from the Polish Embassy on the roads, recruiting personnel from amongst the deportees to help with the organisation. The Russians went out of their way to disrupt everything they possibly could. They were determined not to let their labour go free. Stalin's grip was tight.

The solidarity of their Polish group remained strong in spite of being scattered over such a large area and daily contact was continued whilst at work in the fields with their Polish friends and many new ones amongst the locals. Although they hadn't been able to see Ziuta as often as they had liked, they were too exhausted for the walk to the other Kolkhozy.

The trains, trucks and food were now being diverted to serve the needs of the Russian army while all the exiled Poles were left to their own ends for their daily bread again. The amount of food they received was dependent on the weight of cotton they picked or the number of heaps of soil they had moved, 70 being the required quota. They were given maize flour and sometimes dried fruit, again only so much per working person. It wasn't much and they didn't always get it. Everyone was hungry and at times there wasn't any flour, so Kazia picked some weeds and boiled them so that there was something to make a meal from. Survival was the order of the day, Jasia and Alicja were the workers and Kazia and Janusz searched for herbs, sorrel, anything edible.

Things were getting desperate, would they ever eat a proper meal, would their hunger pains ever go away? Janusz was still gathering what he could from the plantation, but had to be careful not to be poisoned as had almost happened when he mistook something that looked like a beetroot. The most prized item would be a dog or cat but this was almost impossible, there were some creatures like frogs and lizards but for the moment he left those alone.

By this time they had heard a Polish army unit was in Kermine about 400km from their kolkhozy. Word had reached them confirming that families who had a member in the army had a better chance of getting out of these inhumane conditions and children could join the cadets and this would allow them to go to the Middle East, where the main Polish army HQ was.

Their 'amnesty' papers had by now become useless, deliberately invalidated by the Soviets! Thinking their families would have been safe, Adam, Wujek Walery, Włodek and other men had left to go and enlist in Kermine Adam was immediately posted to Iraq and others were sent to the Middle East and the remaining families were forgotten, left to their own devices.

They weren't aware but at the time Wujek Walery had been left behind in Bukhara in an Army camp and he was able to come back for them, another stroke of luck for the family and the main reason that they were to survive. He was able to get them out of incredible difficulty. Food was so scarce, everyone was very thin and working so hard and were so very miserable, and Kazia was desperate to feed her family. Their love for each other and faith had got them through incredible hardship but they knew they also had a great deal of luck on their side.

Sometimes children would catch a dog but they weren't brave or strong enough to kill it quickly with a hard blow to the head so instead they pushed it into a sack and suffocated it, so desperate had they become. This land had once been so abundant with pheasant, quail, wild goats and game, all now extinct, victims to Stalin's collectivisation programme.

The Uzbeks were generally quite friendly, they spoke in their own language but addressed them in Russian and as Kazia spoke Russian and most of the deportees had picked it up in the labour camps, they were able to get along quite well. Soon after this Kazia was taken ill with typhus and had to go to the medical station and Alicja helped her there as Jasia was having to work, 'one of us had to work'. The foreman had obtained an arba for them, pulled by mules, and they got Kazia to the hospital in Vobkent. Alicja had to leave her there and walk the five kilometres back to the collective farm.

The children were now alone and they prayed that Kazia would soon recover and be back with them. A couple of days later they were lucky enough to get some maize flour from one of the Uzbek women in exchange for an embroidered handerchief so Jasia and Alicja baked some buns. The next time they visited Kazia in the medical centre they took her some of those buns. They were only able to see her from the window as she was on an isolation ward, but though she was still very ill she recognised them. The children walked back to camp with lighter hearts, knowing she was still alive.

They met one of their neighbours on the way back, Ivan, a Russian, and former sailor in the Tsarist navy and for his service he had been deported to Siberia. He had been very kind to them. His wife and daughter had remained in Russia, free citizens and once a year they travelled the long distance by train to see him. The family came across many older Russians, some devout members of the Russian Orthodox church, who after the Communist revolution had been exiled to Siberian gulags. Believers had to be secretive about their faith to avoid persecution by the NKVD who were especially vigilant in all USSR communities. Children were taught to spy on their parents and religion was never discussed.

So many people were ill, they bartered and begged for food for their survival and many hadn't the strength to get up, many had blackouts from the hunger. They were exhausted and desperate but never ever defeated, they were determined to join the army but hopes of getting out of the USSR alive were fading. There was no more flour, no food to share and the situation was desperate. There was a great shortage of drugs for treatment of anything, certainly no antibiotics, children were going down with measles and diphtheria, pneumonia and pleurisy and many did not survive.

Traditional herbal remedies were relied upon which sadly did not work.

The next time Alicja went to the hospital to visit her Mother the Sister on the ward told her she would soon be discharged and Alicja was so happy when she left the hospital she ran across that bridge with such relief. They all three went to visit Kazia together a few days later with a donkey to collect her from the hospital. She was still very weak and wobbled on the donkey but somehow managed to stay on and they got her safely back to the kibitka. The children were so happy to have her back, although she would need nursing and some nourishing food, and as usual there wasn't any food to be had. The fact that she was with them somehow gave them all the strength they needed to carry on.

Soon after Uncle Walery arrived at the collective farm from Bukhara in uniform, he had come to take his family further south so that they could be closer to the Polish army and have a better chance of surviving and then hopefully he could follow Adam to the army in Iraq. Ziuta and Marysia were in a collective farm further away, which was a very long walk, and they hadn't been able to see each other very often but had managed to keep in touch and to be together sometimes despite objections from the overseer of the kolkhozy.

Only uncle Walery's immediate family could be registered and allowed the necessary papers for food and travel and because Adam was already posted to Iraq, Kazia and her children were left with nothing, no food or money and no papers had arrived for them to travel. She was still recovering from her illness and was far too ill to work and the children were in despair. With only Alicja and Jasia working how could they all be fed?

Kazia had made a decision, despite being forbidden to approach them by the Soviets she and Walery contacted one of the liaison officers at the Polish Consulate Trustee and 'encouraged' him to let her enrol Jasia and Alicja into the young cadets school in Guzar so that they would be looked after. Janusz was too young, so Kazia and Janusz would stay behind at the Kolkhozy for now waiting for their papers from Adam.

Włodek, Walery's son, had already left to enlist and Uncle Walery then persuaded Kazia to go closer to where he was stationed so that she and Janusz would have a better chance of survival and it would be easier to get him into the cadets. Unless you had a family member in the army or were in the cadets, basically in a uniform, you wouldn't be allowed to leave the collective farm. So many of the deportees were left at the collective farms and their survival is unknown.

The Kolkhoz authorities would not allow them to move but with intense opposition from Walery and Kazia, she and Janusz did move to Bukhara nearer to Walery. Kazia would later persevere despite further opposition from the Soviets and the overseer of the Kolkhozy, to get Janusz into the cadets and then permission to later travel south. It would take time and argument but in the meantime Alicja and Jasia would shortly be on their way to Guzar to join the cadets and to receive medical attention, food and at last, freedom.

Many thousands died travelling on foot from the labour camps through the Russian Steppes, they had no food or water and their clothing wasn't fit for the sub-zero temperatures. Even when they reached safety, already sick and emaciated, Stalin would not allow them food and the NKVD made it very difficult for the American Red Cross to provide the refugees with food, medicine or clothing. Stalin's plan was to kill as many as he could either from starvation or on the battlefield. His intention was to send the fledging Polish Army straight into battle against the Germans. General Anders the Polish Commander of the 2nd Army Corps refused, his aim was to get as many of his countrymen out of Russian imprisonment and fit to fight.

Later in March 1942 he negotiated with the allies for an immediate evacuation, which was one of the largest in modern history but his attempts to get the release of the remaining Polish prisoners and deportees in the USSR failed. Stalin refused to give them up insisting they were now Russian citizens and part of his labour force, he had reneged on his pact with the Polish Government, the man was evil.

Alicja and Jasia left Kazia and Janusz in Vobkent, to join the cadets leaving Wujek Walery and the rest of the family in Bukhara, knowing that their uncle would help Kazia and Janusz, they were in safe hands. They were quietly confident that they would all meet up soon. For now Adam and Włodek were in Iraq with the Polish army and the sisters set off for their journey via the station in Bukhara, to Guzar the Polish enlistment centre and Cadet School in Uzbekistan.

The Polish and British governments were now aware of the deportations from Poland but were completely unaware of the conditions of those exiled Poles. Everything had changed on 22nd June 1941 when Germany invaded the Soviet Union in Operation Barbarossa. This proved to be the salvation of the Polish exiles from regions of the USSR and saved many lives in the 'amnesty' of 1941 granted to the deportees in the Polish-Russian pact.

A world at war had forgotten the many hundreds of thousands of starving Poles in captivity in Stalin's forced labour camps. After being told by the camp Kommandant that 'hair would grow on my palms before you leave here' the Soviets now needed these Poles but still disrespected and enslaved them! Stalin suddenly found his country was in danger from the Germans and the destiny of my family was changed that day in June 1941 when Hitler had attacked Russia.

Stalin had agreed to Churchill's plea to release all the Poles held in captivity, he was in need of allies to fight the Germans and he had agreed to the creation of the Polish army from these released prisoners from the gulags and prison and labour camps. This army was comanded by General Władislaw Anders who rather than mobilise the new army against the Germans as quickly as Stalin had wanted, held back to allow the Poles to recover their health after 2 years of captivity and to also allow as many as possible to flee the camps.

This did not please Stalin who then put a stop on any further release of Poles in August 1942 leaving many hundreds of thousands on Soviet soil, they were now citizens of the USSR and their future was cast. He withheld food from women and children travelling with the men, who mostly starved and his NKVD did all in their power to disrupt the travel of those heading towards the Polish Army, yet these people were travelling to fight with the Russians against the Germans!

*I've included a series of notes on recollections of some Sybiraks fleeing the labour camps in Siberia,*

'From Kharitonovo where people worked as foresters and loggers, we left 14th October 1941 on a small steamer over the river Vychega to Kotlas. The place was awash with Polish families, all hungry and huddling in rags because of the cold and like us anxious to board any goods train travelling south. Reached Tashkent and the collective farm end of October. Christmas 1941 was a cruelly cold winter, very little fuel in the collective farm, Engels, in Kagan. Searched the fields for frozen carrots, turnips and potatoes. Typhoid epidemic and many died. Conditions were terrible in the half ruinous Uzbek huts in which we were housed.

By Easter, April 1942 news filtered through of the Polish army being formed in Vrevskoye and Cadets, girls and boys being enlisted into the cadets. Many left for Tashkent and then by train to Vrevskoye. Many girl cadets were sent onto Guzar. We left Guzar on 11th August and by then many cadets had died from dysentery and hepatitus and on 14th August arrived in Krasnovodsk and on 16th August aboard ships for the 2 day journey to Pahlevi in Persia. It was like a fairy tale, the shops were full of goods and we spent our time sunbathing and swimming and we had plentiful food and fruit. This lasted until October 1942 when we left for Tehran.

The journey on army trucks took us through the most beautiful scenery, sparkling with flowers, greenery, vineyards and rice fields and the tree covered slopes of the mountain of Elburs on the horizon. After an hour or two the scenery changed as we wound our way through high mountains and deep ravines and a wilderness of bare rock to an almost uninhabited sandy plateau through Kazvin to Tehran. Underwent quarantine. Left cadet school end October and joined family in Camp 3. Left Tehran in August 1943 for transit camp in India. Left India in November 1947 for England.'

'Xmas 1941, people receive certificates, documents of release, representing freedom, where to go, people knew that in Kotlas there was an agency dealing with Poles so when we were supplied with sledges in early Jan 1942 we ignored the hard frost and headed there. There were very many of our compatriots from many different Posioleks, like us intent on moving south. They were all haggard, wrapped in rags, but full of hope and determination. A herd of human bodies clambered onto the train and fell onto the bunk beds. We passed through forests, mountains and steppes. The train would stop whenever and wherever and we passed through Kirov, Svierdlovsk, Czelyabinsk and Tashkent. Every station looked the same, drab and miserable and covered with multitudes of people. At these stations the dead were taken off the wagons and taken for mass burial.

Went onto Turknenia where Polish units were encamped March 1942. Were worked on collective farms. Many fell victim to typhoid and dysentry. In Hospital recovering. Lived in a mud hut surrounded by an apricot grove. End of March 1942 heading to Krasnovodsk to join cadets. Soviets on the station preventing the sick from going on board the ships. In Pahlevi Persian men selling pancakes and hard-boiled eggs and cigarettes. Underwent quarantine. End of August next stage towards Africa and sit out the war. In 1948 join family in England.'

'August 1941 Liberated Poles left their places of exile, posiolek Lednya on the river Vychegda. Working in forests and housed in little villages built by previous deportees. They headed south towards Kermine, clad in rags and tatters and not all of them reached Kermine. A lack of water and unbearable sun caused outbreaks of typhoid and dysentery from which thousands died. On arrival in Kermine we saw an Uzbek leading his arba loaded high with corpses and skeletons. They were Poles from the collective farms and he stopped by a ditch and offloaded them and this became their grave. This was an everyday occurrence. We stowed away on trains as there was no official transport for us to leave Siberia. End up in England at end of war after India.'

'Nov 1941 from Posiolek Komartikha on news for the formation of the Polish army, deportees were heading for Kotlas and on arrival we camped in Kotlas railway station in fearful conditions with vermin infesting the concrete floor. The cold was intense and we had to endure this for two weeks before once again finding ourselves in cattle wagons but the atmosphere was entirely different. We had no planned route but knew we were heading south to the Middle East. There were very many stops as the green lights worked in favour of the Russian army transports.

At each stop the corpses of dead children were taken off. The entire route was strewn with the bodies of children. By Jan 1942 the transport came to a halt at an oasis in Uzbekistan. Not far from Sari-Assiya there was an assembly point for Poles. All healthy men joined the army and all those too ill were taken by ambulance to the hospital in Denau. Many had chronic inflamation of the lungs, dysentry and anaemia. Hundreds spend several months in hospital recovering then onto collective farms housed in Kibitki, June 1942.'

'September 1941 Many men left the camps, Yeluga, as soon as news of the amnesty had been announced. Telling their families that they would let them know when and where to join them. Unfortunately in many cases no news ever came and the families were left to sort themselves out with relevant documents'. 'November 1941 rest of the family set off for Kotlas on foot walking several km a day and at night stop at ancient villages, luckily finding places that took us in and often gave us food. Reaching Kotlas in Dec there were thousands of people arriving from all points of the compass, all waiting for trains to take them south.

There was a Polish Mission there but it could offer no help at all only advising us to make our own arrangements. Friends we met there warned us to be very careful of our belongings. There were Russian escapees from the gulags and some Poles who had been there for some time with nothing. We got a train, throughout the journey the carriages would be uncoupled and attached to other trains. Supplies ran out, there was very little food available. People were getting lice, it was filthy. The route was difficult to judge, but we did go through Kotlas, Kirov, Perm, Sverdlovsk, Chelyabinsk, Karaganda and Tashkent. Onto collective farms, cotton growing.'

'When we reached Kotlas the sight that met us made our hearts drop, we were faced with thousands of ill looking starved people camping under open skies whose number stretched down both sides of the railway tracks and well into the forest clearing. Many at the end of their strength died from hunger, whenever the train stopped the corpses were taken and placed on the platforms. Trains stood at sidings for hours as army transports took priority. Typhoid, dysentry and other infections decimated many people'.

Of the Polish prisoners deported by Stalin 415,800 died and were buried in registered graves, 434,300 were either lost or disappeared and 681,400 were never allowed to leave the USSR. My family made it out of the Arkhangelsk region, and were on their way towards Uzbekistan and safety but they experienced sabotage by the NKVD throughout the journey to Tashkent.

From the 20,000 Poles sent to the Kolyma mines only 170 made it to the Army camp on the Volga. Prisoners released from the Navaya Zemlya gulag walked more than 3,000 km to reach the camp and the only survivor died on the day he arrived. The 3,000 sent to work in the lead mines of North Kamchatka all died of lead poisoning.

After Germany attacked Russia on 22nd June 1941, General Anders had been freed from prison and he then sought to form an army from the men imprisoned in Russia. He was initially told a blatant lie by Stalin that only 20,000 men had been captured by the Russians but he ignored this lie and began the formation of an army corps and had within weeks established a HQ's southeast of the Ural mountains. Troops and deportees started to gather in the area of Buzuluk after fleeing their respective labour camps and gulags. The first parade of the army corps from the words of General Anders were as follows:-

'There for the first time I saw 17,000 soldiers paraded for my arrival. I shall not forget the sight as long as I live, not the mingled pity and pride with which I reviewed them. Most were in tattered relics of Polish uniforms. There was not a man who was not an emaciated skeleton and most were covered with ulcers from semi-starvation. To the great amazement of the Russians including General Zhukov, who accompanied me, they showed a fine soldiery bearing. Old soldiers cried like children during Mass, the first they had attended for many months. For the first time I took the salute of a march past of soldiers without boots. They had insisted upon it. They wanted to show the Bolsheviks that even in their bare feet they could bear themselves like soldiers and march towards Poland.'

This parade of skeletons was on the 14th September 1941 and was the beginning of an army that was only allowed to begin to leave Russia a full year later and it would be over a year later before the soldiers were ready and fit enough to be transported to Italy to be trucked up towards a shell-pocked mountain that was the strategic key to the Valley of the Liri River and Monte Cassino. The 12th Podolski Lancers would win the battle to raise their Polish flag at the top of that hill and these were the men who had marched past General Anders in their bare feet such a short time ago, proving their point to the Bolsheviks.

To someone who does not know the Russians as intimately as my family did, it would seem that all of Russia's cruel hostility against Poland would cease when she became Poland's ally against Germany, especially when, with the treaty of July 1941, the Polish army was formed to increase forces against a common enemy, Germany. Stalin had no intention of giving up the eastern territories seized at the beginning of the war. His aim was to dominate all of Poland and turn her into a communist state, and it was clear from the later Yalta conference that the Allies would not oppose Stalin's plans, that Roosevelt would again give in to 'Uncle Joe'. Without Polish representation or that of any other occupied country, the existing annexation of the eastern half of Poland had been decided. The Poles, their ally, had been betrayed and abandoned.

*The forming of the Anders Army in Buzuluk*

***General Anders had the deepest loyalty to these men.***

The Yalta agreement had consigned Poland to the "Soviet sphere of influence" and for many Poles to return to their homeland meant death or another deportation to a Gulag in Siberia. Many settled in the UK, US, Canada, France, South America and several other countries. Unless you were a communist, there was no future in Poland. Adam and Kazia, Walery and Ziuta and their families did not return to their homeland to live and the younger members only visited on holiday. Marek Skocyzlas son of Marysia and grandson of Walery and Ziuta, moved to Poland after College and still lives there with his family.

The sisters were looking forward to joining the cadets although were reluctant to leave Kazia and Janusz but hoped that it wouldn't be too long before they were able to be together. They were heading towards Guzar which was a reception depot and health inspectors at that time were rounding up the very sick for isolation in hospital. During their stay here many civilians and soldiers would die like flies from typhus, malaria and dysentery, suffering from the deprivations of the labour camps and gulags.

The trek to freedom was being made at huge physical cost to the Osadniks and there would be many stops along the route for anyone who needed medical treatment. The journeys had been exhausting on top of their treatment in the labour camps and most of them were almost spent of energy, physically and mentally but they resolved to carry on towards the Cadet School.

# CHAPTER 6

# Flight to Freedom

The relocation of the Polish army took place in January and February 1942 and was spread over a massive area with the journeys between the camps taking many days through Kazakhstan, Kirghizstan and Uzbekistan. The HQ moved to Yabgiyul, south west of Tashkent, the 5th Infantry Division was in Dzhalyal Abad almost on the Chinese border, the 6th Infantry Division was in Shachrizyabs near Samarkand in south Uzbekistan, the 7th Infantry Division was in Kermine in central Uzbekistan and the 8th Infantry Division in Czok-Pak in Kirghizstan. The set up had taken time and further organisation would prove to be very difficult.

The 9th Infantry Division was near to Ferghana in Uzbekistan, the 10th Infantry Division in Lugivoy in south Kazakhstan, the Artillery at Karasu in Tadzhikistan, the Engineers in Vrevskoye in east Uzbekistan, the Armoured forces in Otar in west Kirghizstan and the army depot in Guzar in south Uzbekistan not far from where the family were in the Kolkozy. Communications were poor as the telephone only worked for an hour a day and the camps were primitive, thousands of tents pitched on a wide and muddy plain. It was a massive undertaking.

From 7th August 1941 an Embassy of the Polish republic existed in the USSR and opened 19 delegation centres and provided a network of social workers for the protection of Polish citizens, 10 such centres being in Kazakhstan and Soviet southern Asia. At the time of the breakdown of Polish-Russian relations in April 1943, 271,325 Polish citizens came under the remit of the Embassy and the Embassy's welfare activities faced constant hindrance from the Soviet authorities including the arrest of its social workers. Russia was treating its ally with utter contempt.

## Bukhara to Guzar

Jasia and Alicja were looking forward to joining the young cadets in Guzar, in preparation for joining the Polish forces. With many other girls from the collective farm in Vobkent they travelled by arbas to the station in Bukhara. Alicja wasn't well and would struggle to cope with another long journey but there was no alternative. Kazia had made sure that the girls were getting closer to the Polish army by enlisting them in the cadets, she stayed behind with Janusz who was too young to join and she was also nearer to where her brother Walery was stationed.

The sisters witnessed complete mayhem when they arrived at Bukhara station, so many starving people lying on and around the platforms barely able to move waiting for a train to freedom. Many had been stranded and hunger and sickness had taken a huge toll. People were lying in the streets and on the railway concourse begging for food, 'many were skeletal covered in rags, their feet wrapped in newspaper or dirty cloths and held together with string, many were barefoot, very thin and almost yellow in colour, they were bloated, shapeless with sunken eyes and looked very old and shrivelled.'

They would have to sleep in the open air whilst waiting for the train and there wasn't any food. 'Those who haven't experienced starvation will never understand the desperation to put food in your stomach, to stop the gnawing pains, the contractions and the awful tiredness'. So many had eaten tree bark to prevent the agonising pangs of hunger. The girls found it frightening as they noticed, especially during the night, people wandering around stealing what they could, any piece of clothing, anything to exchange for food, they were so very desperate. Most of the deportees had by now bartered away everything they had for a piece of bread and had no choice left but to steal. The girls tucked their few belongings closer to them and settled down to wait.

The train eventually arrived and they scrambled on and sat on luggage in the corridor and after many uncomfortable hours they arrived at their next stop at Kogon, were given water and food and then continued through Karaulbazar travelling all night through the desert to Qarshi and arrived in Guzar in central Uzbekistan after 3 days travel. It was a relatively short journey, about 200km and the 7th Division of the Polish army was there looking very smart in their British uniforms but very tired and haggard, handing out food and water.

They were almost as haggard as the girls and all the sisters wanted after seeing them was to join the army. By now Alicja was becoming quite ill and was struggling with the exertions of travel and lack of food, Jasia, although a little stronger was also feeling the effects of malnutrition, the hard labour and the extreme climate.

The Soviets noisily ordered them off the train but Polish personnel stepped in to help and it was reassuring to see them, they were from the detachment of the Polish army unit and the Polish military hospital camped nearby, with a transport company and an army field kitchen. They advised them to stay where they were and to refuse to go to any village or collective farm, to ignore any instructions from the Russians and they would get them on their way as soon as possible.

People had come from all over Russia to join the army of General Anders and were always debriefed on arrival at their particular centre. The place and date of their deportation and the destination in the USSR were noted for the records and this information was sent to every Polish unit in Southern Russia where Polish people were assembling. Details were also taken of people they had met on their way and travelled with to gain as much information for their records.

Those who arrived at Guzar who were thought to have infectious diseases were quarantined at a medical unit and would later be sent to a camp hospital. They had their clothes collected and burned and were showered, deloused and some had their heads shaved. They were given sheets, blankets and fresh clothes which had been provided by the Red Cross and then shown to their living quarters at the Cadet School.

The name Guzar means 'valley of death' and from what Alicja remembers it looked and felt like a valley of death. Here nature conspired against life. It was a sandy desert, and from May the temperature could reach 103°F. The steppe would turn into a desert with dust so thick you couldn't see through it. The water would dry up and the local Uzbeks would leave the valley in the summer for the shade of the nearby hills. Many Poles died here on the threshold of freedom, from dysentery, typhus, malaria and other tropical diseases, it was too much for their grossly malnourished bodies, they were skeletal and exhausted.

This was one of the places where General Ander's army was formed in 1942. It was the Organizational centre of the Army and the Auxiliary Centre for Women's Service, a field hospital and the main camp for typhoid quarantine.

At the Cadet School the sisters were given food and medical attention and were able to rest, they were so relieved at not having to work in the fields for the Uzbeks. Soon after the sisters arrived Alicja contracted typhus. The living conditions in the labour camp and the Kolkhozy had been dire. Rats and other vermin were endemic in the huts and lice and fleas were something the families had to get used to. They continually scratched and were never able to sleep properly due to the parasites. They now had to contend with other creatures, plagued by huge black hairy spiders and scorpions they had to check their clothes and footwear each time they dressed. A bite could be fatal and Alicja did have one lucky escape.

Neither of the sisters gave up and somehow, like Kazia who had struggled with her heart condition, they found the strength to live through each day. They must have inherited some instinct for survival which saw them through everything. As a family they had promised themselves that they would never give up, if they did they would never be free, they would starve, be killed by their captors or risk being separated and never see each other again. They were finding it very difficult to live up to their promise.

Alicja remembered one day when her fever had passed she was allowed to leave her bed to go to the window to see Jasia, and when Jasia saw her big sister she burst into tears, Alicja didn't realise that she had lost most of her hair and looked like a skeleton having lost so much weight. The sisters were so upset because they couldn't even hug each other and they missed Kazia's support dreadfully. Jasia was so afraid her sister would die she looked so awful and she left wondering if she would have to make the rest of the journey alone.

The family were all separated at that time, Adam was in Iraq, Jasia and Alicja in Guzar and Kazia and Janusz in the Kolkhozy in Vobkent. At that point they didn't think they would ever see each other again and this caused great heartache but they persevered, they would find the courage. Eventually Alicja did recover well enough to be discharged from the medical station and went back to the Cadet camp and soon both sisters regained some of their strength.

Days at the Cadet school were filled with many activities, an early start at 6am in the morning and after breakfast exercises and then beds to be made, marching to be practiced and shoes to be polished. The girls took to the routine with energy and there was always laughter and at night time the sisters giggled and chatted with the other girls. The cadets would see on a daily basis lines of horses pulling carts stacked high with bodies on the way to the makeshift cemetery, it was an upsetting sight they would get used to, some of those on the wagons had been their friends.

They were being well looked after and had clean clothes and shoes on their feet. They had arrived at the collective farm in threadbare, filthy rags their padded clothing finally wearing thin and with sore, bare feet.

The cadets were excited to learn that General Anders was to visit their camp and they all gathered to hear him address them. He told them that very soon there would be a better life and they must be patient. Seeing him gave them the hope and courage they needed. General Anders was responsible for this exhausted tribe fleeing from Russia via the Urals and the Steppes, south and eastwards, through central Asia to the Caspian Sea. There were many, many thousands of them. This army of his was unique, not only was it formed in exile but it travelled with all its dependants, husbands, wives and thousands of children, many of them orphaned.

He must have been overwhelmed at the huge demands of the Polish

Exodus but he was determined to lead this group of his countrymen out of the USSR, onto the oil barges and decrepit ships to the safety of Persia. The sisters continued to work hard with the cadets but missed their family badly. They would quite soon be moved nearer to Port Krasnovodsk on the Caspian Sea and their thoughts were with Kazia and Janusz hoping they had been able to make their move from Vobkent. The sisters were moving further and further away from them.

The Polish authorities would be sending the cadets on to Krasnovodsk by military train and trucks, towards the Polish army post in Kitab, one of many scattered over southern Russia. Always moving the escapees closer to the main point of assembly, the Polish army in Pahlevi, westwards towards Persia and the cadets were made ready to move again, only waiting on the General's orders.

Neither Jasia nor Alicja were yet very strong physically, Alicja couldn't eat the food provided as it was very fatty and she now had yellow jaundice on top of the typhus. Corned beef and fatty soup and lamb given by the British soldiers caused havoc with their digestions which had only been accustomed to dry bread, no one could tolerate the rich food. Jasia would take her ration back and exchange it for fruit as her sister needed nutritious food but Alicja was too ill to be interested in food of any sort. Jasia later told her that she was in such a state she only wanted to die. Then she went down with dysentery and they both urgently needed a hospital bed and were moved to the Medical Station.

Their shrivelled stomachs would have to become slowly accustomed to richer food, any food. Their care at the medical station slowly revived them although the effects of starvation and disease would stay with both for some considerable time. It wasn't until 1955 after the birth of her third child that Alicja began to put on a little weight and start to regain her physical fitness. Her mental fitness never fully recovered and it would be the same for the rest of the family.

Many of the cadets had been ill from their enforced labour but were now ready to be moved towards Tehran. Care and proper diet at the Cadet School had given them strength, they would be getting closer to freedom at Port Krasnovodsk which would then take them to Pahlevi and even further away from the brutality of the NKVD. So many people died from typhus, dysentery and malaria on this route alone. Those who survived looked like living ghosts and remembering this brought huge sadness and tears to my Mother over the years, it was very difficult to see so many deaths when they were so near to freedom.

The sisters were happier now they were getting fitter and they had each other for comfort and confidence although Alicja was struggling to regain her full strength. To have your sister to rely on and to share the tribulations of the journey was a blessing. They missed their parents badly especially after having been so ill and they wouldn't have survived if they had been left to cope with this arduous journey on their own, many others had made this journey alone, their family members having died in the camps or on this journey and it was a huge test of character for them.

Guzar became one of the largest Polish cemeteries in the Soviet Union, the station at Kermine, a recruiting station 'was one huge refugee camp.' 'The local cinema was turned into a hospital for infectious disease and here without any medicine, surgical measures no food other than the occasional piece of black bread, hundreds of men lay on the ground suffering pain. In these conditions thousands died, their shrivelled remains put into boxes to be taken by strong men to communal graves dug at the town's peripheries. Once the ditches were full, the bodies were covered with quick lime and topped with soil.'

## Guzar to Krasnovodsk via Bukhara – March 1942

The orders from General Anders came soon after his visit to their camp and they were on the move again. They were fed and prepared for the journey but Alicja was still very weak and could barely stand let alone walk and couldn't carry anything, even the very little they had, so Jasia carried their few belongings tied around her back and she too struggled to get to the station but the cadets helped each other working as a team.

They were to leave by military train towards Krasnovodsk then transfer to wagons. When they arrived back at Bukhara station from Guzar, travel details were changing by the day, they were greeted with a long passenger train, not a cattle wagon as they had travelled in previously. At this time they hadn't heard anything from Kazia and Janusz and they were very worried as it must have been desperate for them left in Vobkent and they were moving further away from them. However, whilst the sisters were on the train crawling through the mountainous part of Uzbekistan heading towards Port Krasnovodsk, Kazia and Janusz were also heading in the same direction, but at that time none was aware of this.

Janusz would have had to join the cadets for him and Kazia to get out of Uzbekistan but he was too young and too short and hadn't so far been accepted but Kazia had other ideas and wouldn't be beaten. She put paper in his shoes to make him appear taller and at the next attempt of joining he was accepted. She had managed to get Janusz into the cadets by sheer perseverance and they could then make the journey towards the Polish Army and the sisters.

In order for the Poles to be able to leave Russian soil, General Anders had conscripted everyone, male, female, and even children into the Polish army, he had put as many as he could into a uniform to ensure they got out of the USSR. When the amnesty had been signed on 30th July 1941 he had been a prisoner in the Lubyanka prison in Moscow and was very quickly released on 4th August to officially take up his command of the Polish Forces on 8th August.

The cadets travelled by train from Bukhara and then army wagons through Guzar, Ashgabat, Turkmenistan, through mountains on the right side that divided the USSR from Persia and the sandy desert on the left, on the Trans Caspian rail route following the old Silk Road. Through Qarshi and Kasan, finally arriving at Port Krasnovodsk, about three days and 1,500km later. The train had moved so slowly and for some reason would often stop in the middle of the desert. They realised later that it was to take off bodies. Dysentery was raging and the toilet spilled into the carriage, conditions were awful for everyone and disease spread very quickly.

## Port Krasnovodsk to Pahlevi – March 1942

After almost falling off the train at Port Krasnovodsk, through sheer exhaustion, they suddenly found it very hard to breath, the heat was intense and many found it very difficult to stand, dizzy from hunger and exhaustion, they had no energy. Polish personnel met them with food and water and then showed them the tents on the nearby beach where they were to spend the night. They were tired and hungry but spent the night in a relaxed atmosphere and with the thought that freedom was so close they slept soundly.

The next day in a sandstorm so thick they could barely see, they made their way with the other cadets to the harbour, but not before cleaning the sand from themselves with greasy water, which didn't help at all, it just smeared the sand even further over them. They looked awful and laughed at their futile efforts! The sisters were so full of hope they didn't mind waiting a little time to board one of the boats that would take them to Pahlevi, with so many thousands of people it would take some time. They chatted and made new friends amongst the other cadets.

Some of those small boats that ferried the Poles across the Caspian Sea on the last leg of their journey to freedom were vessels of hope but were in a dreadful condition, some were made of only planks of wood and propelled by paddles and others were just empty oil tankers. They were badly overloaded without drinking water or sanitation but they would serve their purpose.

*Alicja & Jasia in Pahlevi c1942*

Whilst they waited the sisters noticed the people around them, the look in their tired eyes, staring and drained of any sparkle. I have photographs of my family taken in Persia and the striking feature is their eyes, I can only describe as empty of emotion.

Some people were so traumatised they couldn't raise themselves off the ground to board the boats although they so desperately wanted to, while others refused to give up the fight and kept going. The distances they had covered were exhausting for even the fittest of them, the weakest had a psychological mountain to climb and the ship would become a graveyard for very many.

Jasia and Alicja with the cadets, boarded one already quite full, so very many people already on board and so little space, but they managed to squeeze into a corner on deck as Alicja so desperately needed to lay her head somewhere. At this point she still felt so ill she didn't 'care if the ship sank'. She wasn't coping at all and it was lucky that the sea was calm. Jasia looked round at the sights that met her, sights she would never forget.

Most of the people on the boat were ill and there were many deaths over the course of the voyage, mainly caused by dysentery and typhoid. They were packed so tightly it was very difficult to lie let alone sit. People were only skin and bone, filthy in rags and crawling with lice, some almost naked, with the very weak trying to hold each other up. They were so very determined to see it through and get to Pahlevi and away from the Soviets.

What children there were amongst them were in an even worse state, naked and with lice under the skin. Tuberculosis was in children under 5 years of age, their stomachs blown up with their limbs and faces shrivelled up. They were so ill and weak and unable to even cry, they were mostly orphans with no adults to care for them. Alicja remembers a young girl badly emaciated waiting to board, holding her tiny sister very tightly, her sister so very thin, when she was approached she whispered 'I could only save my sister.' There were many similar heart rending stories but there were also tales of happier accounts, of parents finding their children, although very few.

The Polish representatives witnessed terrible sights, 'collections of skeletons covered in rags, feet wrapped in newspaper or dirty cloth tied with string, although many were barefoot. There was not a normal face to be seen, they were either very thin the colour and texture of yellow parchment, or bloated and shapeless like the face of a drowned man. Their eyes sunken and completely lifeless or glowing feverishly. They looked old and shrivelled although some of them must have been young'. And these were some of the fittest to leave their prison camps.

The sisters witnessed dead amongst the dying, with typhus, dysentery, malaria and frostbite and they were simply thrown overboard, their bodies pulled along by the ship's wake towards Pahlevi. There was only a handful of the thousands on board who could be called healthy. It was a distressing sight that stayed with the sisters for many years and they moved closer together, Alicja was struggling and Jasia was aware of the battle she was having and held her close.

The boats and small ships that ferried the deportees across the Caspian Sea on this stage of their journey were their last hope. Every available space was filled, terribly overloaded and a lack of clean drinking water and basic sanitation added to the huge death toll from dysentery and typhoid. The sisters remained on deck with the other cadets and many others, all so determined and the sea air revived them a little.

After 3 days they could see Pahlevi in the distance with a very long beach and the ship crossed the Russian-Persian border and anchored at the Port. The sisters disembarked and stumbled onto a beach covered in hot pebbles roasted by the sun. Some walked across barefoot before finding shelter from the sun under empty fish crates. They were exhausted by what they had endured in Siberia and the long journeys since had taken a huge toll.

From the heat, hunger and physical exhaustion Alicja was too weak to stand, she fell to her knees with the many hundreds of others and kissed the land of Persia, they were free and safe from the Bolsheviks. She sat and didn't move for some time and then cried, heart wrenching sobs which shook her exhausted body. Jasia looked on, tearful and quite lost and gently put her arms around her big sister and held her tightly, sitting together both sobbing quietly. They desperately missed their Mother and it hurt but they realised they were free, safe at last.

Other cadets had moved towards them and formed a circle around them, all hugely emotional, they sat together and wept. When they looked around them they couldn't believe their eyes at the beautiful sight that met them, a blue ocean so very calm and on the beach were palm trees. At last they felt really and truly free and were almost calm. The nightmare of Soviet Russia and their precarious journey was over for now and they saw in the distance tents stretching over a huge area.

They had made it, they were in Pahlevi in Persia, on the southern coast of the Caspian Sea, and as they made their way from the boats they saw before them a city of countless white tents. It was an oasis, with large walnut trees, vineyards and streams, the river banks covered with flowers and shrubs. The air was cooler from the mountains, but there would be danger from malaria as they were to find out.

It was here after their exodus from Russia, that they had found their first real shelter, courtesy of the Shah of Persia. Alicja was very weak but with enough strength to be happy. How had they found the energy to make the journey? From Kotlas in Russia to Port Krasnovodsk in Uzbekistan to Pahlevi in Persia, including the journeys in between was over 6,500km. A journey of escape few people make in a lifetime.

Their countrymen who had already arrived ahead of them shook their hands, hugged them and patted their backs and life was feeling a little bit better. A photographer nearby was recording events, a photographer by the name of Lt. Col Henry Szymanski, a US Army Liaison Officer. He was to take photographs of the true state of the malnourished refugees, which were classified until 1952.

Roosevelt and his propaganda team of communist sympathisers and journalists through the Office of War Information (OWI) and the Voice of America, (VOA) issued photographs of healthy looking refugee children, dressed in clean clothes and well nourished holding loaves of bread in baskets. His reason? To hide the truth of Stalin's crimes against the Polish nation from the world.

Many more would arrive, 'exhausted and in rags, impoverished, covered with sores, louse infected, without hair, resembling strange creatures more than human beings. They made their way with the last of their strength to the medical stations or the Recruitment Commissions where they would die from exhaustion, having wasted away on the very threshold of a new life'.

'Evacuation staff made up of Poles, British, Persian and Indian officers arrived in Pahlevi to find several boats ready to offload their cargo. They were grim faced as they surveyed the human wreckage being unloaded, their faces expressed pity and disgust that once healthy people had been brought to such a state of misery. Spontaneously the Polish officers knelt on the sands with the 'cargo' and silently thanked God for their safe journey and freedom. Emotion was strong and very many of them wept from sheer joy.'

They then watched the small boats continue their shuttles to the main boat to collect the corpses of those who hadn't survived the journey. Bodies were laid out on the beach and covered with sheets and those who had lost relatives walked down the rows hoping to discover their own parent or child, or sibling, it was heart rending.

When the British and Persian officials had watched the Soviet oil tankers, small boats and coal ships list into harbour at Pahlevi on 25th March 1942 they had little idea how many people to expect or what physical state they would be in. They had watched the ships arriving, over loaded and struggled to put a plan together to save a nation. Only a few days earlier they had heard that civilians, women and children were to be included among the evacuees and this was something they were not prepared for, they had no idea what to expect, it was mayhem, yet the organisation was slowly catching up.

Persia at this time was occupied by the Russian and British forces and relations were strained, the country was badly affected by political instability and famine and the Soviets and the British sent all the resources from Persia to the frontline of Europe despite Persia declaring its neutrality. This makes the compassion and hospitality of the Persians even more exceptional considering the conditions the country found itself in.

With the Polish refugees there was an immediate affinity from the moment they had arrived into this land. My Mother often spoke of the generosity of the Persians and how they made them so very welcome. The debt and gratitude felt by the exiles towards their host country is written of in most memoirs and the kindness of the Persian people is spoken of everywhere.

A makeshift city of over 2,000 tents had been erected along the shoreline of Pahlevi to house the refugees, it stretched for several miles on either side of the lagoon, a huge complex of bath houses, latrines, laundries, bakeries, sleeping quarters, disinfection booths and a hospital, provided by the Persian army. Unoccupied houses in the city had been requisitioned and even this was to prove not enough to provide for the many thousands of refugees coming through to the army bases.

Alicja and Jasia were so happy to be met by British troops, Polish soldiers in British uniforms and Polish liaison officers who reassured everyone. They had to walk through disinfection spray, which wasn't very pleasant, were showered, given food then issued with new uniforms of army cadets after their old uniforms were burnt. Whoever was healthier helped the weaker and the sick, many of whom had crawled on all fours to get away from Stalin's slavery.

They had been infested with lice, in terrible shape, hungry, broken and in rags, 50 died from exhaustion alone every day, 3,000 died within 2 months of arriving and the many orphans that arrived were moved into children's homes in Persia, mainly in Isfahan. Those with any infectious disease were quarantined in medical stations for a few days and Alicja who was still suffering from typhus would shortly be sent to the camp hospital.

Like in Guzar they were allocated their living quarters in tents, where they could lie down and rest, given sheets, blankets and fresh clothes if needed by the Red Cross. The sisters were beginning to relax although both still quite unwell and were missing their family so much.

No sooner had the cadets got ready for the night than came torrential rain and the tents pitched on the beach for their first night just couldn't keep the water out or hold up against the wind. They were absolutely soaked, but managed to get the tents back up with some help from the Polish officials and then fell back into them and slept like logs.

In the morning the sun was shining and everything dried out and all was well. Jasia and Alicja didn't yet know but Janusz was looking for them.

He had already arrived in Pahlevi a week before them and was quite established, wandering around the tents each day looking out for his sisters as each of the loaded transports came in. Kazia must have used every ounce of her charm and persuasion on the liaison officers to get him accepted into the cadets so quickly, unless he'd grown six inches!

When Jasia and Alicja bumped into him a few days later they couldn't believe their eyes, the three of them together again was wonderful. They embraced each other and wept, they couldn't speak, it was too much, too emotional. They sobbed and held tightly onto each other, but Alicja's legs gave way and she dropped to the ground overwhelmed by the sheer emotion of their reunion. It took some time to get their breath back, they hadn't known if they would ever see each other again. Kazia had separated them to get at least two of her children to safety with the cadets and had stayed in Vobkent to ensure she could do the same for her youngest child. My Babcia was my inspiration to write this story, as she must have been to her children, to encourage them to fight their way to survival.

Of course the first question from the sisters was 'where is Mammy?' Janusz said she was in Teheran in hospital, over 600 km away, sent there with the families of the cadets. He had come with the cadets to Pahlevi and started his search for them almost immediately. He had food, boiled eggs and some Polish wódka, the sisters had never felt so much joy, you can't imagine it. And how had he got the wódka? he'd bartered for it and also for the eggs from the Persians. The Persian people were very welcoming and offered them dates and nuts and raisins, pomegranates and boiled eggs. Some were able to eat these offerings but to many they were too rich for their malnourished stomachs.

Alicja forgot about her illness and rejoiced that they were out of that desolate land, really and truly out of Russia. They were in a Paradise, almost all together and heading towards a better life, just to be together would make it a better life. 'Stalin had tried to take away my family, the joy of my life.' It had been over two years since the Russians had stolen into their country and deported them to Siberia packed into cattle wagons, 'but my God it had felt like a lifetime, and the aching, mind numbing fear, no one truly understands how it feels to be free again.' – *My Mother's words.*

'There were no guards with rifles and dogs in Pahlevi, we could open and close doors ourselves, there were no locks, no feeling of fear, no having to look over our shoulders or watching what we said in case it might be interpreted as anti-communist! After two years of imprisonment and persecution in those gulags, in a land that was desolate and uninhabitable, digging into the ground and felling trees, working in snow up to our waists.

We had dug through permafrost and had mostly existed on weeds, black stale bread and water, working to the point of starvation and exhaustion, and the Russians came to Poland to help us! To save us from the Germans.'

'The utter joy and happiness, to smell and breathe freedom, light and air, gifts beyond imagining, it overwhelms you.' 'Oh God, those who didn't live through it can't possibly imagine, it felt like being reborn.'

In Pahlevi they were treated with kindness and understanding by the Polish, Persian and British officials. The Russians who were also in Persia were avoided at all costs.

The only aim in fleeing the USSR, was to enlist in the Polish Army, and head towards bases at Tashkent, Kermine, Samarkand and Ashkhabad for which the Soviets had allocated very little food and provisions for them. For the many hundreds of hungry women and children who were camped on the military bases there was nothing. Stalin had cut their provisions, his cruelty knowing no bounds, these people, mostly starved in his labour camps and gulags, were heading out of Russia towards the Polish army, to fight with the Russians! The Polish army in response to Stalin's petulance enlisted as many of the civilians as they could into its ranks, even children regardless of their age, to save the people from starvation but it was too late for many.

In Pahlevi, the sisters' training as cadets continued, they had been issued with identity cards and were now fitter after their rest and medical treatment and wanted to join the army instead of the cadets but when the sisters went to the Women's Volunteer camp they were told they were far too young. They had all been inoculated against various diseases, given more rigorous disinfecting procedures, fed good food and the liaison officers instilled them with hope. Their dream of joining the army would have to wait a little longer.

They sang songs of joy, part of their training, to let out the anguish and terror they still felt and instil confidence and morale. They knew, here and now, that Jasia, Alicja and Janusz and Kazia were safe. Adam was safe in Iraq, and they just prayed that the five of them would remain that way and although they were not yet all together, they very soon would be. Kazia was in Teheran and all the cadets were going to move there quite soon and the children were anxious to see their Mother, their rock.

Walery and Ziuta and their family were also safely in Teheran. the grapevine that had developed was amazing you only had to ask one person if they knew Walery Radomski and if they'd heard from him or knew where he was? If they hadn't they most likely knew someone who probably had. The power of the spoken word travelled well over such a vast land it was amazing, slow but effective.

## Pahlevi to Teheran – April 1942

Within a couple of weeks they were to be transferred in army transport wagons to bigger more permanent camps in Teheran, Mashmad and Ahvaz. There was a constant line of trucks waiting to transport the exiles by a very twisting and treacherous road from Pahlevi, over 600km across the Elburz mountain range. It was to be a hair raising journey and the road was open to traffic for only 5 months of the year as snow drifts, avalanches and floods made it impassable for the rest. On one side of the road there were deep ravines, which was really frightening with the drivers negotiating the hazardous bends at speed, and there had been an instance of a wagon toppling over the mountain.

They boarded the wagon and Alicja sat on the floor so she wouldn't be able to see anything of the route, she was terrified at the thought of going over the edge. Everyone seemed nervous but Jasia didn't seem too bothered, she had recovered better than Alicja and chatted to the other cadets and admired the beauty of the mountains and the villages in the valleys. Janusz had gone on an earlier transport with the younger men. The route via Qazvin was beautiful with scenes below them of olive groves and fruit trees.

Alicja remembers little of the journey only that they stopped during the night at Qazvin and stayed in an empty school, it was such a relief to stretch a little and have a drink and the drivers could have a rest. They made an early start next morning as it was still a long way to Teheran, but the road was better and Alicja didn't have to sit on the floor this time. The journey took them through the most beautiful scenery, past vineyards, flowers and rice fields, the tree-covered slopes of the mountains of Elburz.

The scenery changed as they wound their way between high mountains and over deep ravines with less and less vegetation and then just bare rocks. At last they came down to Tabriz, arriving later in the afternoon into Teheran itself and driving into Camp 1 which was run by the Red Cross. The Persian people had provided buildings and many other amenities for the sole use of the refugees.

Camp 1 consisted of two brick buildings within a brick wall enclosure on the outskirts of Tehran. In the larger of the buildings beds were arranged on platforms and families would hang blankets for privacy around their very cramped living quarters. As more refugees arrived 500 tents were erected around the main buildings with washrooms and showers and a field kitchen which provided 3 meals a day. At one time the camp held 7,000 refugees and the tents were replaced by mud-brick barracks which housed as many as 80 people.

Tehran also had 5 transit camps, administered, financed and set up by the Polish delegation of the Ministry of Labour and Social Welfare. One for the army and the others for the civilians in various parts of the city. Camp 2 was a collection of tents outside the city and this was the largest. Camp 4 was a deserted munitions factory, Camp 3 was situated in the vast garden of the Shah and was surrounded by water and trees, Camp 5 was in Shemiran.

There was also a Polish hospital in the city, an orphanage run by the Sisters of Nazareth and a convalescent home for sick children and a hostel for the elderly. The Queen Alexandra Royal Army Nursing Corps was also there to help the refugees. The Cadet School was financed by the Polish Government in exile as was most of the care for the Polish refugees.

People who were already in the camp came out of their tents, searching desperately for their relatives. And who should be there to meet them but Janusz with Marysia who had travelled on an earlier transport with Ziuta from Tashkent. But again no Kazia, where was she? Ciocia Ziuta told them that Kazia was still in Tehran Hospital, seriously ill. They were in this beautiful city of Teheran, happy at being reunited with Janusz and the others with the worst behind them, and they were greeted with this terrible news about Kazia.

Starvation had left a terrible mark on them all, but on top of Kazia's heart condition it had almost taken her life. She had ensured that the workers in the labour camp, Adam and Alicja and then Jasia had eaten, if only weeds and water and hard stale black bread, she had often gone without. They were now in a completely different land and the contrast was worlds away from Siberia but they were faced with losing their Mother.

Many refugees were taken to hospitals before being sent on to civilian camps to recover and the staff at the hospital in Tehran had a huge Polish contingent newly arrived from the USSR. It was run by Persians with help from Polish doctors and nurses and the Polish Red Cross who listed names of the evacuees and Pahlevi's processing centre then sent them on to other army or refugee camps to help other refugees link up with family members. It was well organised.

'Teheran was beautiful, the hospital was large and we were very well looked after, the roads and trees and cars, the limousines and the people beautifully dressed. I'd never seen such beautifully dressed women, lovely looking and the men quite handsome, after the rough and ready NKVD it was a delight'.

The Poles were welcomed by a people who were extremely kind and respectful of their situation who were also very generous towards them, especially with their time. They met them with smiles and gifts of food and clothes making buildings and facilities available for them. It was noticed by the Persian army that the Polish soldiers saluted them in the street, the British or Russians didn't show them this courtesy.

It was a city of hustle and bustle, shops were full of goods, the Persians carried baskets on their heads and sold all manner of goods, dried fruits, cigarettes, boiled eggs and much more. The Persians couldn't do enough for them and they were all very indebted to them but at this stage the family had next to nothing, having bartered away most of their possessions some time ago. Two years of living with the deprivation imposed by the Russians had not prepared anyone for the overwhelming sight of shops full of goods and the cleanliness of the town.

They were able to bathe and enjoy the fresh sea air and eventually enjoy the good food. To the wearied Poles, nothing more than skin and bone, a plentiful supply of fresh fruits helped with their physical recovery, however the climate, with its baking heat was giving rise to dysentery, typhus and scarlet fever. It's thought that between 115,000 and 300,000 had made it to Teheran from the USSR but were in such bad shape that as many as 50 a day died.

By the end of 1943 the Ministry of Religion and Public Education of the Polish Government in Exile established 6 kindergartens, 8 primary schools and several secondary schools and lyceums. Within a short time the Polish community had set up their own theatres and opened art galleries, formed study circles, ran their own radio stations and published Polish newspapers, gathering their people together to strengthen and maintain their Polish roots.

Life was getting better for them but a setback to the community was the death of General Sikorski in a plane crash on 4th July 1943. He had just visited the troops in the Middle East and the circumstances of his death left the Poles feeling the tragedy keenly. There were many questions about the security of the plane he was travelling in and suspicions towards the Soviets were high.

To many thousands of Poles liberty was almost within reach, or so they thought. Most able bodied men and women of military age had enlisted, as had those who had recovered and were later assigned to military camps. Thousands had travelled south to join the Polish army to fight with the Allies but their stay in Tehran would be short as the army quickly evacuated to Lebanon and this included the Polish forces being reformed there.

Stalin had by now put a complete stop on any others leaving the USSR, he now considered them to be 'Soviet citizens' and the last Polish deportees escaping out of the USSR arrived in Pahlevi on 31st August 1942. Most like those arrivals before them, joined the allied armies in the Middle East and the rest, mostly women and children remained in Iran for up to 3 years.

There were 25,000 Polish civilians living in Persia in 1942 and by 1945 about 4,500 remained in Isfahan and Tehran. In 1946 there were approximately 6,000 Poles in Lebanon, some including orphans were sent to Commonwealth countries, Canada, Africa, India and New Zealand as well as to Mexico, diverted there by Roosevelt.

In Teheran's Dulab cemetery there are graves of thousands of Polish men, women and children, it is the largest of several, row upon row of gravestones have the same date, 1942, the only footprint of this sad and forgotten journey. 'In Isfahan in the Roman Catholic church candles are the only flickers of remembrance of almost 3,000 Polish men, women and children who died on the point of freedom.' Teheran had been a beacon to almost half a million Polish citizens escaping the labour camps and gulags of Siberia and so few lived even after reaching safety.

In later years relatives would send letters to the caretakers of these unmarked graveyards asking that a candle be lit on one of the many hundreds of headstones. Letters would arrive to the Polish Embassy in Teheran inquiring about a parent or relative buried in one of the graveyards. Almost 3,000 Polish souls lie here, so very far from home, victims of a tyrant. I wonder if any candles flicker to this day in remembrance of those Polish men, women and children?

Statistics are few, but it is estimated that approximately half of the 1.7 ml people deported to Siberia were still alive at the time of the 'amnesty' but news had been deliberately kept from them and very many thousands had died not knowing. In general, the news of the amnesty had spread very slowly and many of the camp Kommandants either did not believe it or chose not to believe it. After so many lies over the years from the Soviets some Poles also found it hard to believe. To suddenly find that the Soviets were their friends and would be fighting on the same side was hard to take.

However, it seemed that the attitude of a minority of Soviets had changed and they allowed some prisoners to take their possessions and make their way to stations where transport would be waiting for them.

The Soviets and the NKVD did all they could to obstruct the refugees on their exodus out of Russia, Stalin's cruelty would sometimes specifically target Mothers and their children on their escape from Russia. There had been a convoy of 23-25 wagons of Polish Civilians travelling to Persia in the winter of 1941 which had been diverted to the sidings by the NKVD, ignoring the Polish soldiers who were waiting for Polish transports from the USSR camps. The station was Czkalow now called Orenburg, close to Totskoye. They were kept in the sidings for 3 days with the doors locked without food, water or fuel.

When the NKVD allowed the Polish soldiers to eventually approach and open the doors, the occupants, women and children were frozen solid. The group of Polish soldiers had a doctor with them, Dr Maria Chmurzyna, also a soldier who reported that the occupants, mostly Mothers and babies were dead in every wagon. A consequence of Soviet brutality and a wholly shameful and unnecessary act and to those Polish soldiers opening the wagons it must have been almost impossible to withhold their hatred and hostility towards the Bolsheviks with whom they were now allies! No Russian has ever been held accountable at the Nuremburg trials, for the crimes they committed against Polish citizens!

Shortly after they had arrived in Teheran in 1942, the evacuees had been asked by the Polish officials to write about their experiences under the Soviet regime in Siberia. This was mainly to collect information that would be used to help nullify any annexation of eastern Poland after the war. The exiles also formed the first large group of people in about 20 years who were exposed to life in the Soviet Union and allowed to leave. 'Testimonies may constitute a precious source of evidence enabling us to reveal to world opinion the truth about Russia' one official noted. Of the tens of thousands of handwritten reports collected about 20,000 ended up in the Hoover Institution, including many written by women, approximately 2,000. Children too young to write drew pictures.

However, many of the Poles so very grateful to have been safely delivered from their labour camps and gulags, were advised to keep silent by the Soviets and Americans and many complied, although had they known of the propaganda perpetrated by the Voice of America (VOA), staffed by communist sympathisers they may have declined.

Many others who followed in the last wave of liberation in August 1942 also kept silent about their treatment even when the Soviet Union was exposed as a murderous tyranny. Their history however is not completely lost, like the exiles who escaped from the grip of Stalin, their children especially have not been silenced and they continue to highlight the story of Stalin's exile of their families from the Kresy, in the eastern borderlands.

Very few of the evacuees who passed through Teheran during 1942-1945 would ever see their homeland again. This included my grandparents Kazia and Adam and her brother Walery and sister in law Ziuta, as their fate was sealed in this land of freedom in 1943. Stalin, Churchill and Roosevelt met in the capital of Persia, Teheran, to decide the fate of post war Europe. Their secret discussions assigned Poland officially to the zone of influence of the Soviet Union after the war.

Poland would lose its independence and territorial integrity and the eastern borderlands would be absorbed wholesale into the Soviet Union. The Polish Government was not consulted or informed of this decision until some time later. Polish soldiers, 48,000 of them, would lose their lives fighting for the freedom of the nations whose governments had secretly betrayed them in Teheran. The decision was made known to the world in Yalta, Crimea in 1945.

My family took away from Persia a lasting memory of freedom, friendliness and sympathy and their time there is shown in the many photographs taken in that generous and beautiful land, included in this memoir. My family never forgot the hospitality and friendship of the Persians and the Shah of Persia and the debt they owed to them. The country had stood as a beacon of hope and freedom to them on their journey of escape.

CHAPTER 7

# Sanctuary and Recovery

## QUEEN ALEXANDRA ROYAL ARMY NURSING CORPS – QARANC

Russian and Polish Prisoners of War and Refugees WW2 34th British Commonwealth General Hospital

An eyewitness account from the journal of Principal Matron Lieutenant Colonel Annie Hughes 1942 of Queen Alexandra's Royal Army Nursing Corps.

The history of the modern day QARANC can be traced back to the Crimea War. Florence Nightingale took 38 women to work as nurses and nursing attendants at Scutari Hospital from 1854 to 1856. She was recruited by the Secretary of State for War Sidney Herbert to lead the women in tending the wounds of the injured soldiers. He had identified the need for a nursing service because soldiers had little medical care and treatment and were dying from neglect as well as their horrific wounds.

Camel convoys were the chief means of transport in the mountains which were still covered with snow and with narrow, deep ravines on either side making the road difficult and dangerous, but the Royal Army Medical Corps units got through to Pahlevi and started to unpack in readiness. Before the day was out. Someone looking vaguely through the blizzard spotted three ships approaching – if you could call them ships, they were not fit for the use of human beings or cattle – across the Caspian Sea. The vessels anchored and rapidly disgorged their contents of humanity on the beaches. What a shock for everyone – this sight would never be forgotten! The smell was too awful to describe. There were thousands of both sexes of all ages, packed like sardines and they could not lie down or even sit. They were emaciated, being skin and bone only, filthy and lousy, the dead and the dying all mixed up together, sent over without food or drink, no sanitary arrangements and with the weak trying to hold each other up. They were dressed in bits of old, dirty rags, some almost naked, with no shoes and crawling with bugs. Practically every disease in medical history was evident there, typhus of the worst type, dysentery, malaria, tuberculosis, frostbite, some with limbs almost dropping off with disease. There were just a handful of the fairly healthy mixed up with the typhus cases. They had received no medical attention, the kiddies' bodies naked but covered with embedded lice under the skin. Tuberculosis was at its worst among children under four years of age, their little tummies all blown up, limbs and faces all shrivelled up and outlining only the bone formation and they were too ill and weak to cry.

My Mother Alicja was in tears telling me of the sights she had seen in Pahlevi, she couldn't have described it more vividly. My family had received medical attention along the route to Pahlevi and although in dire physical conditional they were not in as bad a state.

The bath unit and disinfector could not be used for all the cases, many being too ill and the numbers too great to be dealt with. Our chief anxiety was to get them to the hospital at Dosham Tapu for immediate treatment so we sorted out those able to make the journey. The language question was a drawback at first, having an all Indian staff and the patients Polish and a few Russians but this was soon overcome, being only a minor detail. Over one thousand were admitted to the hospital on the first day. We had only five hundred beds so the remainder as a temporary measure had to lie on folded blankets on the ground. The fatigue party put up more tents where the patients lay. With only four of us to cope with the nursing side we tried to get some of the not so ill to help with the washing and feeding. At first they refused, for after seeing so many of their compatriots die, they were terrified of catching typhus. This went on for four days and in the end they had to be compelled to help. We had to work day and night with practically no rest, taking only a hurried meal and when that was over getting back to find hundreds more lying on the ground waiting for attention. An improvised operating theatre was set up under canvas, with two pieces of board on trestles forming the table, instruments were few, field ambulances' equipment only and these were boiled in old tins on charcoal first to deal with the cases of gangrene and frostbite. This work was done at night as the numbers arriving during the day was so great and it took time to get them settled.

The hospital now had 1,500 patients desperately ill and dying. More refugees began to come over the frontier, so a camp had to be organised nearby to accommodate them. Often they had to look after themselves. This camp eventually held 25,000, a daily visit being paid by the medical officer to attend to those reporting sick.

This Indian hospital was called the 34th British Commonwealth General Hospital, I was told there was a 500 bedded hospital in the stores at Teheran Station waiting for a British hospital to come up the line if it was necessary but when headquarters in Baghdad heard what was happening they released this hospital to us. HQ then sent several officials over by plane, these including Sir Edward Quinan and Sir Henry Maitland Wilson the C in C. At nine o'clock the following evening Principal Matron in Persia arrived, also a matron from one of the large hospitals in Shaiba. We did not expect them and no preparations had been made for them. I could not stop to welcome or speak to them as there was so much work to do. These ladies immediately donned gowns, masks and gloves and worked alongside us throughout the night. The matron of the hospital had not been seen and did not know of the arrivals until we went to our Mess for a break and well earned cup of tea at 6am. It was during this break I was able to give details of what had been going on but we were almost too tired to talk. They remained with us and helped for a week. The Principal Matron sent a signal for immediate reinforcements and twelve QA Sisters arrived within 48 hours. The authorities were afraid of sending too many along at this time as it was too dangerous, the Germans were shelling Stalingrad and were expected over the Caspian Sea. The few Sisters sent gave us time for a short break and reorganisation of the hospital routine. The mountains surrounding the valley were from 5,000 feet to 180,000 feet high and by now it was beginning to get very warm. The brass hats visiting us were amazed at the amount of work being done.

Before the Principal Matron returned to Baghdad she informed me I had to take charge of the Teheran area and camps. This was a terrific undertaking and responsibility which rather took my breath away. I was now acting Principal Matron with the rank of Lieutenant Colonel and I got down to the duties. The previous Matron was posted to the Middle East.

Amongst the refugees we found Polish medical officers and some nursing staff from Polish hospitals and after feeding them up and giving them clothes they were put on duty in the hospital. Clothes had been collected from various people and even the Americans sent hampers over to clothe the women. This was a great beginning and we felt the work was progressing, they being able to speak the same language and looking after their own people. They turned out to be very good workers, several students working as nursing orderlies and grateful for being given the chance to help. A few weeks later more patients began to arrive, more beds had to be made, women and children from the camp helping to make mattresses with straw collected from packing cases. The hospital now had 2,000 patients.'

I found a few well educated women amongst the campers. They also came along to help in the hospital kitchens but before they were able to help, clothes had to be found as they only had dirty rags on. Some of these refugees were fully trained matrons and sisters from Polish hospitals who had been taken as prisoners. Their bodies were covered with weals, scars and cuts and they had sore feet from tramping many miles. The American Embassy in Teheran gave us wonderful assistance in getting things, as did the Indian Red Cross. As prisoners, it appeared the higher the class the worse the treatment given. These ladies had been made to clean lavatories, sweep roads and help the men to cut down trees.

One day I approached some of their medical officers and General Anders, asking them to give Red Cross lectures and this was done, with over 200 students. I had some of my RAMC lectures with me and these were interpreted into their own language. On examination they passed out with good marks and eventually they were dressed in khaki and given the same grading and pay as the soldiers. They soon picked up in health after receiving good food and treatment. As the men got discharged from hospital they reorganised a unit and started training again. How they dreaded this time. It was pathetic to see them go because the training was for active service.

I found a matron, a very experienced woman, amongst a batch of refugees. She had been in charge of a large medical training school in Kraków and had remained behind until her hospital had been evacuated. She had also been very badly treated. I took her under my wing as an assistant matron and trained her how to organise and run a field hospital. When the patients started to get their discharges in fairly large numbers, the Polish Government started to open up hospitals of their own in the Middle East. The Polish Matron was appointed their matron in chief and the nurses trained at 34th CGH also went.

The removal of the dead was a problem. The Nursing Sepoys (Indian) would not touch them, it was in their religion and considered unclean. The lower caste Indians called Sweepers had this duty to perform. There were hundreds of dead amongst the new batches arriving and due to the climate and diseases their bodies had to be buried within a few hours. Wild animals prowling around would often carry the bodies away. A large tent was erected to receive the bodies and this was guarded day and night. In the shadow of an 18,000 ft mountain the Polish refugees dug a large common grave, quite a number having to be buried as unknown.

More QA's and Indian assistant nurses arrived making the number up to 30. The Indian Government had sent sisters and nurses over to help. I was fortunate in having the loyalty of all my staff which included British, Indian and Polish, 170 in all and through good team work there was no illness amongst the staff. I think that working and sleeping in open tents kept everyone fit. The staff having been increased we were able to take proper off duty time with a clear conscience. This time was spent going into the city for shopping and sight seeing. In the early days the city was out of bounds to British sisters as we had been threatened with death, the Persians accusing us of bringing diseases to Teheran but as nothing happened they began to realise we would do them no harm and they would benefit from our shopping. The shops were full of wonderful things but much too expensive for us to buy though by this time our garments sadly needed replenishing. Stockings could not be bought for less than £5 a pair in Persian money, shoes being £6 to £20. After appealing to HG in Baghdad an Officers' shop was opened in the town to where British male and female uniforms were sent by plane. Even our shoes were past repairing.

German paratroopers had been seen coming down, some having been captured in the Caucasus so in July 1942 British and American troops began to arrive in the north to meet what they thought was going to be a grave situation. The enemy was advancing and was expected to cross the Caspian Sea or come over the mountains. Guns and bombing could be heard in the distance. The authorities thought the work as far as the Poles were concerned, had finished. So the 34th CG Hospital began to pack up. British and American hospital units began to come up the line. They were lucky in taking over a half finished modern German hospital that had every luxury. They were horrified to find that a large Indian Hospital was under canvas on the plain and remaining through heavy snows and heat but I would not change my life for the comfort of bricks. My British staff were redrafted to their units but the Indian nurses remained with me.

Refugees were still coming through at the rate of 5,000 a day, by 6th April 19,000 Poles had been moved and when the number reached 44,000 we thought the movement had finished. News came through that it was possible a second evacuation would take place later though by now only a skeleton staff remained.

Some of the new arrivals had walked across the country from Siberia, many high ranking officers amongst them. They were given no food but just turned adrift and told to make their own way. They had been Russian prisoners and the Russians were too busy defending their own lines. Only a few survived the ordeal, hundreds dying before they reached the frontier, all ranks helping each other along. It was hard to believe they were human beings. A few Polish women joined them on the walk, these women showing their marks of ill treatment. Most of the females were able to go straight to the camp. I found several pregnant and arrangements were made for their own women to deal with them.

The winter season was coming on with snow on the plains many feet thick, being crisp and hard to walk on and the air was like champagne. A fatigue party had to be detailed to go around periodically to knock the snow off the tents to prevent the weight from collapsing them. The winds in the Persian hills were bitterly cold. The hospital was now very busy. German troops continued to advance and Stalingrad was invaded. They were pushing down towards the Caucasus, hoping to penetrate to the river Araxes in the North of Persia.

Settled in once more my patients improved sufficiently for quite half their number to be transferred to the camp to be looked after by Polish nurses who had been trained in the hospital. At this stage it was feeding up that they wanted and their own cooks gave them the kind of food they were used to. Doing the rounds of inspection in the kitchens I was amazed at the queer concoctions though they smelt good. And how these poor creatures could eat, even those in the hospital.

General Sikorski and General Anders gave a banquet at their new Persian HQ to meet all the high rankers of their own army. The Colonel and myself were invited as honoured guests. It was a wonderful dinner all Polish and what intrigued me most was that they started their courses where we leave off, they ended with soup. This was the first time for me to taste Vodka but was not impressed. After this a letter in Polish was sent from HQ Evacuation Base, Polish Army in the East.

The Polish army had been greatly reformed having been put into khaki uniform given by the British Government. Even boys of 14 had to join up as they were needed for further fighting, their one aim being revenge. They certainly appeared very bitter. I met many of their great generals and leaders who were very appreciative of all that had been done for them and I received many letters from the men and women of Poland.

The unit was awaiting orders for the next move and one morning when I too was wondering where our next place would be, I met our Indian Colonel waving his hands over his head and in a terrific flap, they do get very excited when in a fix. The reason was that a ship had been sighted crossing the Caspian Sea. At first it was thought to be an invasion because no one expected any more refugees to come that way as it was too late to escape Russia, unless they tramped over the hills of Turkestan or the wharf at Krasnovodsk. Already 6 Germans had landed by parachute about 70 miles south of Teheran, 3 more dropped near Mosul and 3 landed in SW Persia so the military authorities blocked all frontiers leading into Persia and Iraq with troops. I think about 8 frontiers.

When the ship had anchored we saw it was a very small vessel of the type we call a cattle boat. It was very old and one wondered how it made the crossing as it was certainly unseaworthy. It just made it though actually, it was not meant to arrive. The sight of its cargo was again too awful to describe. It was supposed to have on board 1,000 babies from 3 months to 10 years old. There was difficulty getting to know their ages. The older children could not help us because they were strangers to each other and much too ill and weak to talk. With more than 200 dead and many more dying the stench was awful. They were naked and caked with filth, emaciated to skeletons and looked more like very old people. Their eyes could barely be seen having sunk so far into their sockets. They had blown up tummies, suffering from abdominal tuberculosis, typhus and dysentery. There was no one looking after them on the journey, no food and no one to say when they last had a feed. They had been in homes and orphanages, belonging to no one, some having been picked up on the streets in Russia where probably their parents had been killed. The older children look at us with fear and terror and it took some time to convince them that we wanted to help them. The OC and his staff were concerned because they were babies and felt it was impossible to do anything for them but when told they were in my responsibility they sighed with relief.

I recruited some kind motherly women from the camp and a few Polish nurses. There was also a Polish children's hospital matron amongst them. I felt the children would feel more at home with their own people. A large building in the grounds was turned into a suitable place, with mattresses on the floor. They were taken there after they had been cleaned up and given nourishing fluids. Old sheets were collected and torn up to cover their wizened little bodies. I did not think they would survive but given treatment and good attention from the very kind foster mothers it was amazing how they picked up and only a few died.

Then when the time came to get them up and teach them to walk the question of clothes was again a problem. Our Red Cross could not help us and I appealed to the American Red Cross. Through the kind and helpful wife of a British Consul within a few days large hampers arrived with lovely woollies, dresses and shoes, also little baby sets, all hand knitted, having been flown over from America. All had a good rigout and I don't think the little mites had ever seen or been clothed in such lovely things. Coats, shawls and bonnets also arrived and it was a pleasure to see their faces. All the Polish women and nurses had a good cry over such kindness.

The day arrived when we had to part with 500 of them. They were sent to India to finish their convalescence and to be safe. The very poor women, to show how grateful they were, made a rag doll dressed in Polish national costume and presented it to me. I loved this little doll, the gift spoke more than words, it was the thought. I had the children for roughly 6 weeks and here is a copy of the letter they sent to me after they had left.

The matron of the Polish Civil Hospital sends her deepest gratitude to the Matron of the 18th Indian Gen. Hospital for her kindness to the Polish children during their stay at the 18th IGH.

In spite of the lack of knowledge of the Polish language the Matron was always attempting to understand and assist the Polish children for which we are ever so grateful.

The Polish people shall never forget the acts of kindness displayed at the 18th Indian Gen Hospital. – *Signed H. Wydecka Teheran, Persia.*

The Poles recruited into the army, were assimilated into battle formations of the armies of the western powers while the civilians and children were placed in temporary camps in Iran, India, British East Africa the Middle East and even Mexico.

In all of these places were many of the families of the military settlers from the eastern borderlands of Poland, the homeland of my family.

From the middle of 1942 Soviet repression of the Polish representative units increased. On 5th January 1943 the Council of People's Commissars, without notifying the Embassy of the Polish Republic, issued a decree whereby they placed all the Polish centres under Soviet control. On the 25th April 1943 Polish-Russian relations came to an end. The Soviets began forcing Poles left on USSR territory, to accept Soviet citizenship, those who refused were imprisoned, many died, among them military settlers from the eastern borderlands, the Kresy.

I've included Matron Hughes' account in her own words, it describes perfectly the atrocious physical condition of the Polish refugees on their arrival in Tehran and is in complete contradiction to the reports and photographs submitted by the Americans. The refugees had suffered dreadful mistreatment at the hands of the Russians throughout their imprisonment in the labour camps and the OWI staffed by communists, with Roosevelts support, did their utmost with propaganda to present a very different story.

## Sanctuary on the Caspian Sea

It was now early summer of 1942 and the family were settling into Camp 1 in Teheran after receiving such a warm welcome from the Persians. They still hadn't had any news about Adam, and so desperately needed him, he and Walery had reported to the Polish army unit in Kermine, the nearest army HQ to Bukhara and he had been posted to Iraq. They only found this out later through Antoni, who had worked so hard to organise their journey from Siberia. Walery had been searching for them through the Red Cross and Antoni reassured them that they would soon meet up.

The day after their arrival in Teheran, Jasia and Alicja went to the hospital to see Kazia. She was very ill, but so happy to see them, her face lit up and she was so relieved to know they were safe. It was a hugely emotional reunion.

Hospitals had opened in Pahlevi and Isfahan with the assistance of the Red Cross and the Polish-American Relief Organisation. Included also were the Queen Alexandra Royal Army Nursing Corps. Acting Principal Matron Lieutenant Colonel Hughes, has documented in her diaries first hand detail of her care and that of her nurses, of the Polish refugees from Russia at the 34th British Commonwealth General Hospital in Teheran.

Five refugee camps had opened in Meshed and Achwaz, as well as hostels for the elderly and an orphanage and community centre. Yes they were all safe, but Kazia and Alicja were very ill. Exhaustion and the sudden change in living conditions caused diseases to break out, primarily dysentery and typhoid, and many people died so close to freedom. Grief touched thousands of people, those they knew and had grown close to on their long journeys, were dying around them. 'One day they seemed to be recovering and the next they had died. It was heart breaking, very hard to accept, people were groaning in pain, others had staring eyes were gasping for breath and others would never breath again.'

Perhaps the sudden calm after so intense a mental pressure and physical hardship had been too much to bear and the body so weak had given out. It was so very sad and it affected everyone hugely. Many hundreds of bodies were to lie in the Dulab cemetery in south Teheran having almost touched freedom. Soon the family had to choose what to do, where to go as the refugees were being moved constantly to make room for others.

Jasia reasoned that because Alicja was so weak after having typhus and yellow jaundice, and Kazia was still in hospital, they should both remain in Teheran and wait with Janusz until they knew more about Adam's movements. They all thought this was perhaps the best idea allowing them time to recover. The rest of the cadets were being sent to Palestine, as were the more able-bodied men and women of military age to prepare for active service with the British forces in Palestine.

So with Jasia on her way to Palestine, Kazia, Janusz and Alicja stayed in Camp 1 in Teheran waiting for news of Adam. Ziuta and Marysia also stayed with them, both recovering from typhus and dysentery, before Marysia too could also join Jasia and the cadets in Palestine. Walery and Włodek had by now joined the forces in Iraq having travelled there from Kermine.

After much liaison with the Red Cross Adam had found out where the family was and reassured that they were safe and recovering from their trauma felt sheer relief. For the time being, recovery from illness was the priority for them all and it wouldn't be until a few weeks later that he would be able to travel to see them on leave from Iraq. For now he relaxed knowing they were safe and being cared for.

The family slowly recovered and regained their strength and looked forward to their reunion with Adam, life was becoming more relaxed and being together helped their recovery. When Adam arrived from Iraq it was a very emotional reunion. He stayed for two weeks and it was wonderful to be together and the family began to breath a little easier. The relief they felt at being free was overwhelming, sometimes they forgot and the tension hit them and they would gasp for air. They were all having difficulty getting used to these new circumstances. There were no guards with barking dogs intimidating them but everyone was still edgy, expecting aggressive orders from Soviet guards. It would take some considerable time for them to adjust, they knew they were free, but it was difficult to believe that freedom was really theirs, the restrictions of the labour camps had left a huge mark on them.

In January 1943, the Soviet Government sent a communique to the Polish Government based in London informing them that all Poles remaining in Russia who had originated from the provinces now under Russian occupation, including the eastern Borderlands my family's homeland, would be considered Soviet subjects. Stalin was determined to hang onto his Polish labour and dominate Poland with communism.

The Russian authorities had offered no assistance whatsoever to the Poles left in the labour camps. Many through age, exhaustion, infirmity or lack of dependents, had been unable to leave, not fit enough to make that most arduous journey to join the Polish army. They were condemned to endless captivity. In Kazakhstan alone 120,000 people can trace their Polish origins and there many survivors remained, often in abject poverty.

Day by day Kazia was slowly recovering and the day of her discharge from hospital arrived. Alicja remembers the day she went to collect her as a very happy one, just being together gave them all confidence, being apart had greatly unsettled them. Kazia, Janusz and Alicja, were in Camp 1, in Teheran for now, but for how long no one knew as the authorities were moving people all the time to make room for those Poles still arriving from Siberia. Many thousands were still making their escape from Siberia towards the Polish Army very many walking the 3,500+ km and very many dying on this perilous trek.

There wasn't enough space for them all in the Teheran camps so after receiving medical attention many refugees were sent to the British colonies, some to India and some to Africa. Many of the orphaned children were sent to Isfahan, further south in Persia where schools were being organised for them. These young children were in such a state of shock, having lost their parents, some their entire families, they were almost comatose. Some had siblings to help them bear the awful situation but many were totally alone in the world. How would they cope with this trauma at such a young age?

Wherever the Poles were sent, schools were immediately organised so that children wouldn't miss too much schooling and they hadn't had any schooling to speak of whilst in the Russian labour camps for the past two years, except for having to learn Russian and being schooled in the communistic ways of their Russian masters. Parents did their best to make sure this didn't happen, reinforcing the Polish ways and identity in the barracks. They were determined their children should remain Polish, and they mostly succeeded.

Kazia and Alicja were recovering well getting quite fit after their illness and Alicja had even put on a little weight and was beginning to feel happier. She had got a job in the camp sewing with Ciocia Ziuta, which was wonderful because she was earning some money and she and Kazia would go to the shops and buy some material to make clothes. They had arrived in Guzar and Pahlevi in rags, without shoes and had been given clothes by the Red Cross but they needed to make their own and to be able to rely on themselves. Working and earning some money would help their confidence greatly.

They heard from Adam, who had been very ill with typhus In Iraq, he sent them a letter and photograph of himself with Jasia, she and the rest of the cadets had stopped there on the way to Palestine and completely by chance, they had found each other whilst wandering around the camps. The family always seemed to be able to find each other when many others only faced disappointment!

Strange and wonderful things did happen whilst the Poles were escaping the Russian labour camps. On one of the trains from Swierdlowsk near the Ural mountains, they had noticed a young girl approach one of the men waiting to get into the wagon. She said "Daddy, is it you?" The man didn't pay any attention, lost in thought, but the girl persisted, and the man then looked and recognised her and burst into tears. They hugged so tightly and she told him that her mother and sisters were further down the line in another wagon. They had been separated many months ago and never thought they would see each other again. Very few families survived as a unit, and this was one very lucky family, as were my own family.

It was now 1943, they had all been found, although not yet all together but they knew where each other was and it seemed like a miracle. They were on the move again as the authorities were more actively sending people to Africa, India and other Commonwealth places for safety until the war was over. Kazia didn't want to go to Africa, she didn't want to go to any of the places they were offered, so she instead chose Isfahan further south in Persia. If they stayed there, they may be able to go back to Poland, she thought?

All their meagre belongings were collected and they made ready for another journey, waiting with many other families at the gates of the camp. They boarded buses which were quite comfortable after the trucks they'd travelled in from Pahlevi to Teheran and the roads were in better condition along the edge of the Great Salt Desert. It was very dry, they didn't see any vegetation, trees or people for very many miles and the villages were very few. It was just desert for most of the 448 kilometres journey and enduring the very high temperature was very difficult.

The journey lasted many hours and they were desperate for food and water. They had stopped along the route at various shelters, hamlets and shacks and had found shelter to rest for a while, but there was no food and very little water. Only occasionally did they see an oasis and took on as much water as they could. The route took them through Varamin, Kashan and Qom and was a very slow journey.

When the buses eventually rolled into Isfahan they were completely taken aback at the beautiful surroundings. Trees and flowers bursting with such vivid colours. Homes were surrounded by very large gardens and they were to spend the night in the courtyard of a large building which they learned later was the palace of the Armenian Bishop.

Next day they were all allocated their living quarters and happily settled in. Many buildings had been made available for the refugees and after a week or two of rest and finding their bearings, Ciocia Ziuta got a job in one of the schools as a carer and Alicja got a job in a hospital, in charge of the stores. She wasn't in this post for long because the manager heard that she had been in the Girl Guides in Poland so he offered her a job as a secretary of all the Scouts and Girl Guides in Isfahan, she had the necessary experience and it was a job she would enjoy.

Of course it was a much better job and as well as a secretary she was also made a Cub leader. She thoroughly enjoyed the job, her Cubs were called Krechowiecy, after Adam and Walery's cavalry regiment. Life was very pleasant in Isfahan, the old capital of Persia, as it was known then. It had once been a major empire with settlements dating back to 4,000 BC, a monarchy ruled by a Shah from 1501 until the 1979 Iranian revolution when Iran became an Islamic Republic.

Time had marched on, it was now 1944 and Kazia, Alicja and Ziuta were all busy and enjoying their jobs and making friends. Janusz was happy at cadet school but Kazia was not very well, the climate was making it very difficult for her, Isfahan was very hot, it was 35 degrees and it didn't agree with her heart condition and the ailments she had succumbed to along the many arduous journeys. She had difficulties breathing and the stress on her heart was beginning to tell, maybe because of the height above sea level.

Adam was soon to be discharged from the army, he had developed a stomach ulcer and hadn't fully recovered from the debilitating typhus and wasn't now considered fit enough for military duty. In the end he was to be discharged as being unfit for service and he was hugely disappointed at his inability to be with the troops to see active service and fight against the Germans, he would at least be able to serve at the military unit.

Like his fellow deportees, he had been able to control his feelings towards his new ally, Russia, although with some difficulty. He had somehow contained the hatred he felt towards the Bolsheviks for invading his country, transporting many hundreds of thousands of his countrymen to Siberia and trying to crush the Polish spirit. In this last case, Stalin had been unsuccessful! Instead, taking the lead from General Anders, all the Poles recruited into the Polish army from the labour camps and gulags, had sworn loyalty to their former captors and like him only wanted to fight the Germans.

In Isfahan there was an Anglo-Polish club where many Poles and British airmen who were stationed there would meet. The Poles had been well fed and clothed by the British Army and were beginning to relax and were ready to enjoy some socialising, especially the younger ones. Film shows were held there with concerts and meetings and one evening at a film show a young airman asked to be introduced to Alicja.

His name was Taffy and he started talking to her about where he lived in Britain although Alicja didn't understand much of what he said, her English wasn't yet that good. He walked her home that evening and she really wasn't very impressed by him. One afternoon Alicja and her friend Irena were in the club with two other airmen and Irena introduced Alicja to them, one was called Harry and the other Bill.

After that initial encounter they met occasionally when Harry and Bill were off duty and they would have a game of cards. The airmen were wireless operators and their job was to send weather reports to the Forces. They also helped Alicja and Irena to learn English and Alicja and Irena continued to socialise with them and the other Poles and Airmen.

Soon it was Christmas 1944 and the family had a very quiet, and reflective one. Their thoughts were of home and Wigilia, which the Poles celebrate on Christmas eve. It is the most important culinary event of the year. At one time dinner consisted of 12 courses, representing the 12 Apostles, but today it is far more modest. Even to think about those 12 courses was too much for their recovering appetites, but mouths watered thinking about the Uszka (little ears) with the barszcz (beetroot soup), fried carp with mushrooms and sauerkraut, gołąbki (cabbage parcels) pierogi, soused herrings and of course the poppy seed roll and cheese cake. It was something else to focus their minds on and look forward to in the future but what wonderful memories. Janusz did manage to barter for a bottle of Zubrówka and they quietly celebrated their freedom.

There was an English mission in Isfahan run by a lady called Mrs Mentle, and she had organised a party for the English airmen with their guests for Twelfth Night. Alicja and friends met at Irena's flat and Taffy had assumed quite wrongly, that Alicja was his girlfriend and that he was taking her to the party, which was a huge surprise to Alicja, but she reluctantly went along with it as the party had been prearranged.

The group arrived at Mrs Mentle's and it was quite a large place with plenty of room for dancing. There was a gramophone and lovely records were playing and couples were dancing, mostly to Glen Miller tunes. Alicja loved dancing and Taffy just sat there, hardly speaking to her and didn't even ask her to dance. She later learned that he couldn't dance and Bill had taken him to another room to teach him a few steps of tango. He was useless, so in the end Bill asked her to dance and they danced together for the rest of the evening. Alicja was never sure where a Lancashire mill lad had learned to tango! But she was pleased as they had a lot of fun and she was beginning to relax. Bill was also more talkative and easier to get on with.

Once the dancing was over, they all started the walk home. Taffy tagged along with them still thinking Alicja was his girlfriend, yet making no effort to talk to her! She was now confused and obviously out of step with the mind of a Welshman! Bill was walking behind them and she thought, 'I'm not walking with this dummy', so she called to ask Bill if he was going the same way and stepped back in line with him and they walked together the rest of the way. The night was so beautiful, a full moon was shining and it was starting to snow lightly, and she'd shaken Taffy off. Bill walked her home and then went on to his station.

She and Bill became quite friendly and met several times at Mrs Mentle's but soon after that he was posted to Teheran. In the meantime Adam was notified that he had to go back to Teheran to join his army unit, and Janusz and Kazia were to go there with him, to Camp 3, which was much better equipped to deal with the many people needing medical assistance. It was a place with many green trees and bushes and a little stream, and this would better suit Kazia's health and she would be nearer to medical aid.

Alicja was still at her post as a secretary in Isfahan when she heard that there was going to be a nursing course in Teheran so she decided to go with the family as Ciocia Ziuta thought they ought to enrol. The course was to be held at the Polish Red Cross HQ and Alicja hoped that Bill would find her. She liked him, he was good company and very loving and attentive.

There was another journey to pack and prepare for and within a few days they were waiting for the transport at the edge of the camp to take them to the station. They travelled by bus through Qom, Kashan and Varamin arriving back in Tehran at Camp 3. It was 1944-45 and the time had gone very quickly for them. They often thought of Poland and their home in Równe but at this stage could not see any way they could ever go back.

Alicja and Ziuta's nursing lessons started shortly afterwards and they were quite enjoying school again. They were informed that when they passed the exams they would be posted to the Middle East, Egypt, Palestine or even Italy. When Kazia found out she wasn't happy with this and she wouldn't hear of it as they had been separated many times already and she couldn't bear another parting, so she persuaded Alicja to take a job as a typist in the camp where they were living. She had already spoken to the Camp Overseer about Alicja and hoped he would be helpful. Jasia was with the cadets and settled and Janusz was at school and Kazia wanted and needed Alicja near to her.

As she had passed a typing course previously when they were in Camp 1 in Tehran she was confident. She went to the Camp Overseer and introduced herself and all she had to do was type a letter of application and she was offered the job. She was quite happy to be a typist in Camp 3 if it meant staying close to Kazia, and not put any unnecessary burden on her, her Mother needed her support and she reluctantly gave up the nursing course.

While she had been on the nurse's course Bill had been looking for her in Isfahan, as she hadn't let him know where she had moved to and he had to look for her over a huge area that was Persia but in the end quite easily found out where the family had moved to from the Red Cross.

Adam, who had just re-joined his army unit in Teheran, was informed that he now had to go to Egypt to be formally discharged. All this would take time and they knew they would all be leaving Teheran fairly soon for a journey to Lebanon and another refugee camp. 'We were being moved all the time but we never knew when or where to.' It was quite unsettling but they were at least being looked after well for which they were so grateful.

The authorities had a massive job on their hands with all the refugees still coming through to Pahlevi from the USSR labour camps. Room had to be made for all those who were arriving in such great numbers and the medical stations were almost overwhelmed. Those people would need the care and medical help that the family had been given to recover from the horrendous situation they had been forced into.

The Polish representatives had witnessed terrible sights alighting the boats in Pahlevi, 'skeletons covered in rags, feet wrapped in newspaper or dirty cloth tied with string and many were barefoot. Their eyes sunken and completely lifeless or glowing feverishly. People had been almost dying on their feet, they were so emaciated, only skin and bone filthy and crawling with lice, trying to hold each other up' and so very determined to see it through to Pahlevi away from the Soviets. There were many deaths, mainly from dysentery and typhoid.

In the meantime everyone in the family was occupied, Kazia now recovered had a little job sewing, Alicja was typing and Janusz went to his school lessons and Ziuta was working in one of the hospitals. They had acquired a dog they called Ass and were living in tents and they knew they would soon be on the move again. Events always moved fairly quickly, there was never enough time given, not much warning, just time to pack and wait for the next transport to the next camp, which they heard would be in Beirut in Lebanon.

*Alicja & Kazia – Isfahan c1943*

*Jasia & Adam – Palestine c1943*

# CHAPTER 8

# A New Life

It's 1945 and the family had learned of their next destination and from Teheran where they had been since early 1943 they had to pack quickly and immediately move all the way to Beirut in Lebanon, a journey of around 1,800 km. Firstly by train from Teheran to Arak, staying overnight, then by army lorries to a camp in Baghdad where they stayed only for a few days as the intention was to move them on to the next destination without too much delay. Before they were moved from Teheran, Bill had to leave for Iraq but before he left he had asked Alicja to marry him. He must already have asked her half a dozen times and each time she had said no. At that time she had seven 'boyfriends,' just friends really that she had met in the different camps on their travels, all of them in the forces in Palestine, Egypt and Iraq. Each one of them was writing letters to her and they were all Polish.

You can imagine her predicament. She was seeing Bill, an Englishman, so very loving, declaring his love for her and refusing to take no for an answer. She continually said no because she couldn't bear to leave Kazia. After so many separations and such hardships she would find it extremely difficult. She was only 21 and trying very hard to adapt to a new and very different life and also trying to absorb all that had happened to them.

The next time Bill asked her to marry him they were having a day out in the mountains at Demavent, where the Shah of Persia had his summer residence. It was Bill's last day in Teheran and it was a beautiful day. They had their favourite place to sit, a tree stump by a little stream and it was a very calm place and so peaceful, they sat listening to the sounds of the stream which was slowly running by and watched the sun and the shadows shimmer on the water. It was very romantic and Alicja felt it was an ideal place for a proposal. As they sat there, Bill was telling of his love for her, asking her to marry him again because he knew he would have to leave Teheran with the RAF very soon. He didn't know when or where he would be posted to and he was anxious for an answer, the right one!

Alicja had slowly stopped writing to her other 'boyfriends' and had continued seeing Bill, and on this his last day of leave in Teheran, she finally said yes, she would marry him, he loved her so much. But was she doing the right thing? She had wanted to say yes, but there was so much else to think of, her family and their future was still so unsettled, they had been reunited for such a short time and she would have to leave for England and they would have to stay behind.

Bill left Teheran a much happier man as he headed off with all the other airmen for Habbaniyah in Iraq. Alicja missed him after he left, but he wrote every day and as soon as he got to his camp in Habbaniyah, he wasted no time in applying to the RAF authorities for permission to marry her. The Lancashire lad who could tango had claimed his girl and wanted to make her officially his without delay!

It was going to take a long time for the formalities to be arranged and agreed and in the meantime they were getting on with life and preparing for more travels. They were used to packing up by now and were ready for the transport for the next stage. It was a long journey but they were by now fairly well recovered. The Red Cross had to make room for the other refugees coming into the country from Siberia and were moving many of those who had recovered and able to journey onto other areas. They were taken to the main station in Persia for the first leg to Arak and then by large army lorries to Baghdad. From Baghdad the journey continued on by train moving towards Lebanon and crossing the Turkey-Syria border to reach Aleppo in Syria. It wasn't very safe for them to be transported at that time because there was much unrest in those countries. British and French troops were in Syria in May 1945 at the time of the Levant crisis where there were nationalist protests against French occupation which was opposed by Churchill. He sent in British troops and a ceasefire was enforced, the French withdrew and Syria gained full independence. The family eventually got through the borders after some delay in sorting out the papers and permission to cross.

Aleppo was the second city of Syria, today the scene of civil unrest between President Assad and rebel forces, a civil war raging. There have been many previous conflicts with the Syrians, against the Persians, Greeks and Romans until Arab Islamic conquest in 636 AD. Since the 3rd millennium BC Aleppo was a flourishing city, a meeting point of many commercial routes in the north. A centre of trade with France, Turkey, England and Holland, it now lies mostly in ruins, bombarded by heavy weaponry, the ancient mosque and minaret devastated by artillery.

When they reached Aleppo British soldiers were waiting with hot drinks, for which they were extremely grateful as they hadn't had anything to drink for 24 hours. There were also Polish soldiers in British uniforms looking happy and confident, it was so reassuring to see them. They had waited for them despite the delays until the middle of the night. In Aleppo they had to transfer from the passenger train to the goods train for some reason, and this was to be the last part of their journey. They spent a nervous night in Aleppo, very much aware of the unrest but knowing there were British soldiers on hand to protect them they were reassured.

From Aleppo all the Poles were allocated different places which meant separations from newly made friends. Alicja, Kazia and Janusz were to go to a house in a village on the top of a mountain, it was beautiful, right by the Mediterranean in a village called Ghazir, just outside Beirut. It was lovely, but Kazia wouldn't be able to make the walk up and down the mountain, her health was still so precarious but they would have to manage for the time being.

It was nearly Christmas 1945 and Adam was now officially demobbed and was coming to join them. Jasia was coming from Palestine and Bill had got leave and he still had to officially ask Adam for Alicja's hand in marriage. When Bill and Alicja were apart waiting for official permission to be married he wrote her countless letters, sometimes two a day, and she still has them. It was going to be a very memorable Christmas, as it was their first together as a family for three years. It was to be a quiet Christmas though, as they were still unsettled and unsure of the future. After Christmas Bill would have to go back to Iraq and Jasia to Palestine, where she was at teacher training college and was also still a cadet, but for the moment it was a happy time and they were able to celebrate.

Lebanon was a beautiful country. The name means white, a reference to the snow-capped Mount Lebanon, its beauty took everyone's breath away. The youngsters would walk along the Serpentine to the sea coming back up the steep incline with the cedars in the background, it was rather exhausting but they were young and enjoyed it, they had physically recovered well.

Bill had got permission from Adam to marry Alicja, although her parents did have their doubts, it was now a matter of waiting for permission from the RAF and also from the Archbishop of the Catholic Church to be married in a Catholic church. This was necessary because Bill wasn't a Catholic at that time, so they had to wait for the necessary authorisations.

It wasn't until many years later that Alicja realised the historical importance of the countries they had journeyed through, there were many other things to think about and her concentration then was purely on getting through one day at a time! Whilst she had appreciated the beauty and the wonder she had not been aware of the significance. They had set foot on some of the oldest continuously-inhabited cities in the world, dating back to earlier than 5,000 BC. A once in a lifetime holiday in better times.

Bill was still writing her two or even three letters every day, keeping her up to date, she though wasn't a very good letter writer, so didn't write to him as often. How he found the time to write so many during such times!

Soon after Christmas Adam had asked permission from the authorities to move them from the house on the mountain to nearer the Serpentine because Kazia was having terrible difficulty walking to the shops and church. In the meantime Alicja was the main shopper, the 'little donkey' bringing the shopping home and caring for her mother Kazia.

Within a short time they were offered a place with an Arab family and Kazia was much happier because walking to the shops was much easier and she didn't feel so isolated. Her heart condition was so bad she had difficulty breathing, and walking any distance especially uphill wasn't helping her. That Kazia had survived so far was a wonder, she had incredible strength of mind and tremendous will. My Babcia Kazia has been my inspiration, my muse, she has left an amazing impression on me and I had to record her and the family's story. I also inherited her sense of humour which had served her so well during a horrendous time.

It was now 1946 and they were looking forward to planning the wedding. As Bill's parents were in England they were not able to come; it would have been impossible for them to travel. Bill eventually got permission from the RAF to be married and they also had approval from the Archbishop to be married in a Catholic church. This all took about six months, but the time flew by.

Now it was time to arrange the date and the Polish priest who was to marry them arranged the ceremony for the 9th July. Kazia and Alicja went to Beirut to get some material for her wedding dress. It was very lovely heavy crepe, which the tailor would make into a most beautiful gown designed by Kazia, who had trained in Warsaw as a tailor in her teens after WW1.

Bill's parents had made their intentions clear to him, they were not happy he was marrying a 'foreigner' and a Catholic and would not give their blessing to the marriage. Kazia and Adam, although liking Bill, weren't sure about him either feeling they hadn't known him long enough. They also weren't happy about it being a 'mixed' marriage, but especially concerned that Alicja would move to England. The family had not long been reunited, their futures so uncertain, they had no idea where they were to be sent next? Back to Poland under Communism and possible arrest? It was a huge concern to them.

The Poles in the Middle East would eventually be given the choice by the authorities of settling in England, America or Africa or going back to Poland. Like many thousands of other families mine had lost absolutely everything in their homeland, there was nothing to go back to. My Dziadek Adam and Wujek Walery feared that they would be arrested again by the Soviets having fought in the 1920 Polish-Russian war against them, the

Russians never forget, their record keeping and memory being meticulous and a score to settle top of the list.

Not many years later it became known to the family that former military deportees, especially from the eastern borderlands and servicemen who had returned to Poland were treated extremely harshly by the Soviet dictatorship in post-war Poland. Without trial, many were imprisoned either on trumped-up charges as spies or 'enemies of the people' and sent to gulags, some just disappeared and others were executed, as in the case of Witold Pilecki, a Polish war hero who was an embarrassment to the Soviets.

Alicja's parents, although uncertain about the marriage gave their blessing to the wedding and Alicja was busy learning English as communication was still a little difficult. Despite all reservations the wedding was set for the 9th July at 6pm and Alicja seemed in a state of bewilderment. She was seeing everything through a very thick fog and it just didn't seem real, so much had happened over such a short time for her to absorb.

Jasia and their cousin Marysia, also a cadet, were coming from Palestine and preparations were going well but as the date approached the priest informed them that the wedding would have to be on July 10th instead. The wedding rings had been engraved for the 9th, so they had to stay like that although that wasn't important.

Two days before the wedding Bill and his best man Eric arrived from Habbaniya and Jasia and Marysia arrived the same day from Palestine. Two of Alicja's best friends were present, Nusia and Irena. Walery and Włodek were in Iraq with the British forces and weren't able to get leave to be with them for the day of the ceremony and Ziuta was with them and couldn't attend either.

The day of the wedding came, lovely, hot and sunny. Whilst waiting to go to the church, the family and their guests sat under the lemon trees and grapevines on the terrace at the house they had rented. They were excited but also a bit nervous, Alicja's parents hadn't envisaged their daughter marrying in the Middle East but in a small church in Poland! It wasn't a big wedding as it might have been back home, a fairly big event with lots of family but it would be one to remember in a most beautiful country.

All the Polish refugees were being supported by money from the Polish authorities to cover their living needs and had income from jobs they had. They didn't have much, having lost everything, the Osada in the country and the apartment in Równe, the Russians and Ukrainians having taken all their possessions. 'Friends' and families of the NKVD had not wasted time moving in. But they were free, and it was such a lovely day although they sometimes couldn't help but think of what they had lost.

There were about 20 of them in the party. Alicja's friend Irena, was her maid of honour and dressed her to be ready at the church for 6pm. When Bill came to the house to meet them he was quite nervous, it was so different for him coming into a foreign family and their customs, although he liked the family very much, he felt a bit lost but he did look very smart in his RAF uniform.

It was only a short walk to the church, and it was a beautiful evening in Ghazir when Bill and Alicja walked slowly up the hill towards the church. She was carrying flowers and holding onto that calmness, she was only 22 and Bill, who was 26, was stricken with nerves. They chatted, and then entered the church. Alicja thought there would only be her friends there, she hadn't wanted a big wedding but she was quite popular within the Polish community and was also in the church choir, so word had got round and everyone seemed to know about her wedding.

The church was full, mostly with Poles from all the different refugee camps they had been in, friends from Persia, army personnel. There were also Arabs from the village who had heard that a Polish girl was getting married and were curious about a European wedding. It was a wonderful surprise, and she was so happy. Bill was still very nervous, yet surprisingly Alicja now seemed quite calm as they stood together with Adam for their wedding vows.

They were married in a French church, by a Polish priest, in an Arab village, Ghazir, not far from Beirut. When they came out of the church Janusz took photographs, some of them showing her parents looking quite serious. It was early evening and warm and they walked the short distance home meeting Kazia and Adam on the doorstep welcoming the newly-married couple home with bread and salt, as is the Polish custom. The guests arrived soon afterwards and they had a drink, probably a very generous shot of wódka if Janusz was pouring and some wine. It wasn't a lavish wedding, but supper was delicious. In later years at each special occasion or get together, they always called Janusz's shots of wódka, a 'Polish measure.' Janusz had a very good arm! And this talent seems to run right through the family.

With the help of Jasia I've been able to put together a few details of the wedding supper. Alicja also recalled that Kazia cooked everything on two primus stoves, very primitive, but there was nothing else. They had very little to their name, but were in a very safe haven, and of course they had each other and they held on tightly to that.

How Kazia was able to prepare such a wonderful feast was a lovely surprise but she had always been so resourceful. There was barszcz (beetroot soup), mushroom pierogi, (meat parcels), herrings with apples, beetroot salad, fried chicken, meat loaf with stuffed eggs and rice, meat balls and rice, mizeria (cucumber salad & soured cream) gherkins, olives, pitta bread, pancakes and oranges, dates and grapes. Most of which the family enjoy to this day.

She must have sold her soul, what a banquet! And what a wonderful recovered memory. It had taken a few phone calls with Ciocia Jasia but we had got the wedding menu in the end. They would have had something very similar back home in Poland.

Although it was a happy occasion the wedding photographs show everyone in a very serious mood, under the surface they were still feeling the effects of their experience in Russia, and would suffer flashbacks for many years to come. The family was to be separated yet again as Alicja was going to England with Bill, and this was heavy on her parents' minds. It was very difficult to hide their worries.

Later in the evening when most of the guests had left, Bill and Alicja danced on the terrace under the vines and stars, to some lovely music, mostly tango. It was a reflective, quiet moment, but there was a slight problem – they had no bed for the night. The Arab landlord had double-booked their room and there was only one other room for the whole family. They didn't find out about the double booking until later in the evening so it was impossible to make other arrangements. That night Bill slept on the roof garden with Adam, Eric and Janusz and Alicja slept downstairs with her sister, Marysla and Kazia. So their wedding night was a little different, but still memorable!

They were happy and it didn't really matter as it was such a minor thing in the circumstances. After that they made other arrangements and it was only for a few nights after all. Bill was then taken ill with papadach a tropical disease with a very high fever and was due to go back to Habbaniyah. So only a week after the wedding they were to be separated. With Bill and Eric his best man, back on duty Alicja was left without her husband, she was however with Kazia, Adam and Janusz, her sister Jasia and cousin Marysia had gone back to Palestine to the cadets.

Soon after the family moved house again, nearer the centre of Ghazir, closer still for Kazia to get to the shops and church. The family lived quietly, shopped and saw friends and waited for their future to be decided. Bill continued writing wonderful letters that kept Alicja going. He had to wait for all RAF formalities to be completed for taking her to England as his wife, and they had to cover quite a lot of officialdom before that happened. Alicja was feeling very guilty, sad and apprehensive about leaving her family and also very anxious about what to expect in England, meeting Bill's family, it was almost too much for her.

At last in October, Bill came to collect her, all formalities now concluded. He stayed overnight and the following day they would leave for Cairo. She packed her suitcase and had to say goodbye to her family. It was very, very hard because she didn't know if she would ever see them again. They all cried, it was heart breaking and her parents were distraught. It was an incredibly sad goodbye. She never knew how she managed to leave them. She and Bill reassured them that they would do all they could to help them to get to England but it didn't stop the tears, they were desolate.

Bill and Alicja travelled from Ghazir by taxi to Beirut and from there took another taxi to Haifa where they stayed overnight at the YMCA. Next day they took a taxi and then a train to Jerusalem, where they stayed for two days and were able to see something of the city. They didn't see very much or stay very long because of the rebellion, with terrible unrest at the time and they couldn't move around freely and Bill had to report to camp. They left Jerusalem heading for Cairo by train, which was a very long journey and although they were very newly-wed their start to married life wasn't very romantic. The journeys they had to take were long and uncomfortable, over 250 km so far and it was all very tiring, with trouble spots along the way. Alicja was also so sad missing her parents, knowing they were inconsolable after losing her so soon after their reunion following the trauma and hardship of Russia.

After a journey to Cairo of 280 km they took a taxi to the hotel, the Hermitage House, and at last they could rest on a comfortable bed. After their rest they took a shower and went down to the dining room to have something to eat. It was lovely food, and it was the first time they had eaten fresh dates from the tree. They spent six lovely weeks in Cairo at the expense of the RAF, waiting for a boat to take them to England as Alicja wouldn't fly, she was still in such an anxious state.

It was very hot during the day, so they went out in the evenings to open-air cinemas or to the Gropis café in Cairo, where they danced among the palm trees in the gardens, getting back to the hotel in the early hours of the morning. They had to be cautious because of the tensions in the Middle East at that time, it was quite frightening as troops were on the streets in large numbers, on high alert, and they could feel the anxiety in the ordinary people. Tensions had escalated after the bombing in July of the King David

Hotel, which was the administrative HQ for the British forces in Palestine. The Irgun, a militant Zionist movement were apparently responsible.

This had been in response to a raid on the Jewish Agency by the British authorities on Black Sabbath. The British had confiscated incriminating information about the Jewish Agency's involvement with violent acts and this information had been taken to the King David Hotel. The Irgun were determined to destroy this information and planted explosives in milk churns in the basement. To avoid suspicion they had dressed mostly as Arabs and the guards were easily overcome. The explosion caused the collapse of the southern wing of the hotel, causing many deaths and injuries to those who were in the road outside. Despite this state of unrest Alicja and Bill made the most of their extended honeymoon.

### Thoughts of a survivor

Jan Wojcik, a well known journalist and the 'Voice of Solidarność,' during his last broadcast on Radio, said: "I was forced to leave half a century ago and it is where I left that most essential part of my being, "my heart. Poland is inside me". After 50 years of wandering he went back to his birthplace, Volhynia.

"There had been a delightfully developed Osada in which had stood my home, surrounded by a garden and fertile fields" he wrote. "Nothing, but nothing, remained of any of this. Everything had been razed to the ground. Even trees and forests had been put to the torch so that no one could ever recognise his roots, and wouldn't dare put a claim to it."

They craved the very roots,
Desired the furrows groove swallow the top soil deep
So that nothing, no surface remained,
No linking with the past –
No past – no history of her and of this nation
Whose prediluvian line was nurtured here
Through countless generations.
They sought to smooth over the marks, The tiniest traces of dust.
Disfigured, drove, dispelled,
Divided the heart from the head. But one granule they quite overlooked, The grit of the Land itself

*– Feliks Konarsk*

*My cousin Marek Skocyzlas, son of Alicja's cousin Marysia, made a claim in his Grandfather Walery's name for the return of the lands of his Osada, but was unsuccessful.*

Married life began with a mixture of conflicting memories and yet more unrest, but Alicja and Bill knew it would only get easier from here on and were looking forward to married life. Tensions would however be fraught in the early days in England.

## Sunny Beirut to foggy Blackpool

At the beginning of November 1946 Alicja and Bill were to journey to Port Said to board the ship Durban Castle which was bound for England, it was a passenger ship converted into an army carrier. They left Cairo by train for a journey of over 200 km travelling alongside the Suez Canal. When they arrived in Port Said in the early evening of 1st November, Alicja saw in the distance a very big ship anchored some way from the shore, and while they were waiting for their papers to be checked, she wondered how they were going to reach it and get on board. It was such a long way out and she was beginning to feel very nervous. It was already dark when the time came to board the ship and they were told by the sailors that they would have to walk on pontoons all the way up to it. The military and their wives were lined up in their hundreds, the women very wary and mostly young brides of the English servicemen.

The group started to walk towards the pontoons and stepped on, putting one foot in front of the other very carefully, not daring to look between the gaps. When they got to the end of the pontoons which seemed to take for ever and was very difficult to stay on as it wobbled so much, they had to climb up ladders on the side of the ship and seeing the waves lapping between the ladders and the pontoon was very frightening. All this was happening in the dark and although the ship was lit up to give them some light to see where they were putting their feet, it was moving all the time, even while they were boarding the steps and they were all very relieved to eventually reach the deck.

There were hundreds of people on board, many of the newly married included women from Greece, Egypt and Poland and other Europeans and their military husbands. Everyone was allocated cabins, and Alicja was to share one with two other military wives. Their husbands were in separate cabins and had to sleep in hammocks. Alicja saw Bill only on deck during the day as they couldn't even have meals together. All the Servicemen were down below deck and were only allowed to see their wives during the day on the decks. The journey was terrible, it lasted nine days, and throughout all that time Alicja was seasick and couldn't eat anything. Every time she walked into the dining room and saw the waves through the portholes she immediately had to go back to the cabin, she just couldn't face any food and Bill fed her on dry cream crackers when they met on deck. It was a horrible voyage, very miserable, nothing but the high seas all around them. Alicja wished she'd never come, and there was no way of getting off. It seemed a very stormy crossing to her, although Bill thought it was calm! Perhaps if they had been together it would have been easier to bear.

Six years after that day in February 1940 when her life had changed forever, she was going into the unknown without her parents travelling to yet another country not knowing what to expect. She would be meeting Bill's parents and wondered what they would be like, it was all very difficult to deal with on her own. She was still only 22 and desperately missing the family. On the last day of the voyage she felt the ship stopping and she looked through the porthole to see land, green grass and trees. 'You can't imagine my joy to know that I would be able to put my feet on firm ground again'. Alicja thinks she had breakfast that morning, but doesn't really remember, she was too happy realising she was to be on land again.

They left the ship that morning, November 9th 1946, and Bill was with her when they disembarked at Southampton. After they had collected their luggage they went to a little café and for the first time in her life (but not the last) she had English fish and chips, which were delicious after all that time at sea. It was her first big meal since Cairo not having had very much to eat on board the ship and it was so tasty. Mum would always enjoy fish and chips.

They now had to take the train to Blackpool in the North of England, via London and travelled almost all night arriving at Blackpool North Station at 5am in the dark, in a very thick, cold fog. Alicja had never seen anything like it. It was so depressing, unwelcoming, grey and damp and she thought to herself that she would have gone back if she could and what a contrast to the beautiful countries she had just left. They took a taxi to Bill's parents' house, and arrived in the dark. A tall, white-haired woman, his mother Alice, opened the door and Alicja thought, 'she looks nice, I think I'll be happy here.' She embraced Bill, the son she hadn't seen for five years, and Alicja was just standing there in the hall waiting whilst they hugged before Bill introduced her. Alice just said hello and that was all, there was no welcome for their son's wife, no embrace, no friendliness, no warmth on her part. Alicja was away from her own parents, missing love and warmth in a strange country, just a young woman but there was very little welcome for her and she'd had such hopes. It was decided fairly amicably and after the children were born, that it would be better for William to find them a separate dwelling and Alicja was to stay in London whilst he looked.

Alicja was with her sister in London for several weeks before Bill found a house for them, he had worked very hard to find somewhere as he wanted his family back as soon as possible. She came back from London with the children and they moved into their new home in Lytham St Annes and they couldn't have been happier. It was heaven being on their own with their two babies, they didn't have much furniture but they were happy. There was a cooker and Alicja could cook some nice meals, they had somewhere to sleep, there was a garden, she had a very loving husband and knew that together, they would get on with life and work towards their future.

All was not milk and honey in this new land, there were many difficulties to deal with and it was hard to adapt to a very different life, mixing with people when shopping for essentials for example, trying to converse in English, which Alicja still wasn't very good at. People weren't openly hostile towards her but nor were they very welcoming, just accepting of the situation. The Government had written to all the Polish servicemen (1946) in Britain advising them to go home to Poland, seemingly not knowing of the reception and the reprisals their allies would face from the Soviet dictatorship! The Unions were also hostile, making it extremely difficult for Poles to get any work despite the country being in a state of devastation and in need of labour to help with rebuilding!

The English also had to adjust to a different life. After a devastating war they had to learn to deal with people of many nationalities now living amongst them. It was a learning experience for them all. Many refugees would find it extremely difficult after arriving in England, alone, still in a state of shock and perhaps bereft of hope, they would search crowds for any sign of the family they'd lost in their exodus from Russia, scrutinising faces in churches, shops, on the bus and the street for any recognition of family or friends, hoping to be reunited with just one familiar face. They would search for many years.

As the years have gone by I have realised from growing up with my amazing Polish family just how very badly they have been treated, by both Stalin and the Western allies. It has made me quite angry, especially since their treatment has been ignored from 1940 to this day. I've used my displeasure proactively to try and bring my family story to light and hope that they and the many hundreds of thousands of other Poles deported by Stalin to Siberia, get their deserved recognition one day.

CHAPTER 9

# Family Reunited

Stalin had achieved his aim, he had taken Poland and tens of thousands of veteran Polish troops lost their homes in the Kresy and other regions of Poland to the Soviet Union. This would have an effect on many of the service men, their relatives, wives and children, spread across the landscape of the war and those left at the mercy of the NKVD in Poland.

Churchill explained his actions at Yalta in a 3 day Parliamentary debate beginning on 27th February 1945 which ended with a vote of confidence. He was openly criticised and MPs strongly voiced loyalty to Britain's Polish allies, with 25 MPs drafting an amendment protesting against Britain's tacit acceptance of Poland's domination by the Soviet Union. The amendment failed and one MP resigned his seat in protest at the British treatment of Poland.

Churchill did however say that '...His Majesty's Government will never forget the debt they owe to the Polish troops and I earnestly hope it will be possible for them to have citizenship and freedom of the British Empire if they so desire. We should think it an honour to have such faithful and valiant warriors dwelling amongst us as if they were men from our own blood' (Sword, Davies and Ciechanowski 1989) This became known as Churchill's pledge, it caused concern in the Foreign Office and came across to the Polish allies as empty words, which they turned out to be!

In July 1945 Churchill and the Conservatives unexpectedly lost office to the Labour Party led by Attlee, the British people choosing the path of Socialism. The editor of the Daily Worker couldn't help himself by crowing that the Communist Party had eight 'cryptos' (informants) among the huge influx of new labour MPs. The balance of opinion within the Labour Party and the Left towards Poles and the Polish question was now very different. Although Attlee did eventually expel some of these 'lost sheep' from the Party, it was more pro Soviet than the anti Bolshevik Churchill and was much less favourable towards the exiled and displaced Poles.

Nothing better represents this attitude than the shameful exclusion of the Polish Forces from the Victory Europe Parade in May 1946. In fact there were strong feelings within the Labour Party and their Trade Union paymasters that as few Poles as possible should remain in Britain and that everything should be done to ensure their removal, including negotiation with the Commonwealth countries. Attlee had tried to re-interpret Churchill's pledge as having been merely an aspiration!

The Polish Government in exile had moved from Paris to London in 1940 and the British Government, press and the community had been largely sympathetic to the plight of the Polish people. However, in 1941 when Germany invaded the USSR and Stalin was forced to switch his allegiance to the Western Allies British-Polish relations were badly affected.

The British Labour Government wanted to maintain cordial relations with Stalin and ignored the Poles' outstanding war effort, their loss of land and belongings, population and family and tried to persuade the Poles in the UK to return to their homeland. Most Poles quite rightly felt betrayed and refused to return to Poland for a number of reasons, Soviet repression of their citizens in particular.

My Dziadek Adam and Wujek Walery could not return to their homes in the Kresy. It wasn't safe to do so, they had fought and won against the Bolsheviks in 1920 and for this reason alone they would have been sent back to Siberia, or worse. It was Stalin's reason for deporting the peoples of the Kresy in the first place! To return to Poland as ex military men meant practically committing suicide, they would be special targets for the NKVD, as 'potential nationalistic organisers/agitators', accused of spying and jailed. They would be prosecuted in phoney trials and even murdered, as many returnees were. Word had began to trickle to the Poles in England from their relatives, of the fate of those who had taken the risk to return home.

The London Poles began to get a bad press inspired by the barely suppressed pro-Stalinism of many Left liberal intellectuals and Trade Union activists. The Daily Worker, the British Communist Party's newspaper (later the Morning Star) called the Poles 'Fascist Reactionaries', 'landlords' and 'Jew baiters'. Words such as 'unrealistic', 'intransigent' and 'unrepresentative' began to be used by the Left. Pro-Soviet propaganda was increasingly written by sections of the press and accusations of right wing fanaticism against the Poles began, including organised marches against them by the Left. A hostile attitude the Poles were to endure for some considerable time!

The Unions were very open to Soviet ideology and an easier target for the KGB than the Labour Left Wing were, as they had the real power within the Labour Party being their paymasters. Jack Jones, leader of the TGWU the most powerful Trade Unionist and a hero of his day, was a paid up 'useful idiot' of the KGB who would rope in anyone who would be of potential help to their cause and the lure of post Soviet ideology is still strong within the Labour party front bench to this day, Corbyn, MacDonald, Abbott and others.

The Polish contribution to the war effort had been outstanding, they had formed the fourth largest Allied force in Europe and were the largest non British group in the Battle of Britain, yet despite being on the winning side the Poles saw themselves being as severely treated as defeated Germany. The loss of the eastern borderlands, the Kresy, was a huge blow to many Poles mostly from those 'lost territories' of the east.

They had been forcibly exiled and it wasn't safe to return, as a consequence the total number of Poles including soldiers and their dependants who arrived in the U.K. through the process of forced migration is estimated at 200,000. My grandparents Kazia and Adam like those other 'displaced' Poles, considered the Communist regime too dangerous to return to and we grandchildren were very lucky to be able to grow up alongside them embraced in their love and Polish traditions.

The Polish troops became an unwanted post war expense for a British Government feeling the financial strain of the post war economy. It became a regular subject in the House of Commons during 1946 and on 20th March the Sec of State for Foreign Affairs Ernest Bevan acknowledged the Polish achievements, 'as a major ally in the field, Monte Cassino and the Battle of Britain, Squadron 303 with the most kills and instrumental in cracking the enigma code .........'

And said further, 'I feel sure that the House would wish me to pay tribute to the magnificent services which these forces as one of our first allies in the late war, have rendered to the common cause throughout the whole long struggle. His Majesty's Government and I am sure the whole House are conscious of their debt to these men and are determined to deal justly by them.'

He also said, 'While we will not use force to compel these men to return to Poland, I have never disguised our firm conviction that in our view they ought to go back in order to play their part in the reconstruction of their stricken country.' How very noble, 48,000 Polish military died for the allies and freedom!

And that the British Government considered it was the '...duty of all members of those Polish forces to decide how to return to their own country.' Words spoken by another of Stalin's idiots! This was in complete disregard to the complexities of any returning Polish citizen to Stalin's terror and revenge which the British Government was aware of, but they were in thrall to Stalin and his ideology and musn't upset him!

Bevan, later in reply to Anthony Eden regarding the future of Poles in Britain, said 'We are extremely anxious that the Polish troops should return to their own country, subject to that we cannot relieve ourselves of responsibility for those who feel in their conscience that they cannot go back.'

Those Poles who had been exiled to Siberia, berween 1940-1942 were in danger if they were sent back, many of them had already been assigned as 'enemies of the people' by Stalin for their fight against the Bolsheviks in 1920, there was no free Poland to return to. The Commonwealth countries were far more obliging to the Polish troops and Polish refugees than the country the Poles had fought on behalf of. One of the last directives from Bevan in relation to the Polish troops was 'speaking on behalf of the British Government I declare that this is in the best interests of Poland that you should return to her now…' what gratitude.

There were Polish troops still in Italy, having taken Monte Cassino and in Northern Europe, the military cadets were in the middle east and the majority of these Polish troops were not convinced. Having been deported by Stalin in 1940, fighting with Stalin and the Allies from 1941 they were now in the hands of ungrateful allies, communist MPs and Unions.

The problem of registration, supervision and settlement of the Poles imposed a great burden on the Aliens Branch of the Home Office and Police Forces throughout the U.K. In the end the Government passed the Polish Resettlement Act of 1947 which provided 'certain Polish Forces' with an Assistant Board to meet their needs.

My Grandparents Kazia and Adam and the family of Wujek Walery were housed in Resettlement camps, Pulborough in Sussex being just one of several. Most of the accommodation was in military units in 170 camps all over Britain, many in airfields vacated by British and American troops.

Polish Pharmacists and Doctors were given temporary registration to practice in Britain. These measures identified the Poles as a special case which caused ill feeling not only in the Government but in the wider public domain. Large numbers of Poles, after occupying resettlement camps of the Polish Resettlement Corps, later settled in London and industrial areas of the north. Many were recruited as European Volunteer workers others settled in the British Empire, forming large Polish communities in Canada, Africa and Australia. Some also settled in Mexico and the US

I didn't understand why my family had little respect for Churchill and Attlee and the post war Labour government. My Ciocia Jasia filled me in when I was about 16, telling me about the secret deal in Teheran, then Yalta, the V.E. day celebrations and the efforts to send the Poles back to a Communist state. The underhand ways of the Unions to block Poles working here and I also did some research and I realised why they felt this way.

I understood completely why most Poles had little respect for the post war politicians and government, I understood the huge injustice felt by them. The Polish had been betrayed not once or twice, but several times and I can only describe that as shameful. The fact that the deportations in particular are still ignored and many Polish achievements glossed over, condemns the British establishment. They betrayed their Polish allies and ignored their many sacrifices for this country.

The vast majority of Poles in the U.K. and across Europe post war had rejected their homeland under the Soviet puppet state and Communism. They chose to remain in the West where they could continue the political struggle for an independent Poland whilst maintaining their language, culture and traditions. My Grandparents missed their homeland dreadfully and thought they might return one day but their family was now in England and they made their lives here.

The Polish Re-settlement Act of 1947 was the first ever mass immigration legislation offering British citizenship to over 200,000 displaced Polish troops, it also supplied a labour force to meet the demands of a war-torn Britain as there was a lack of manpower for mines and agriculture. However, the Trade Unions agitated for Government legislation to forbid employers from taking on Polish workers. 'Foreign labour can only be employed when no British labour is available and willing to work' so jobs remained vacant and a ready workforce unused!

Jack Jones was a full time District Secretary in the Coventry TGWU branch overseeing union organisation during WW2 and according to KGB files he was 'first cultivated by the Soviet Union as an agent in the aftermath of the Spanish Civil War'. Given the code name Drim (Dream) the 'agent' enjoyed Soviet contributions towards his 'holiday expenses' and he was regarded by the KGB as a 'very disciplined and useful agent'.

His influence and that of the other communist Trade Union leaders would have a large impact on the jobs market post WW2. Labour had sold out the Poles just as Churchill and Roosevelt had. They had been determined not to let the 'Polish problem' get in the way of their partnership with Stalin. The 'Polish problem' so reminiscent of Stalin's NKVD Order 00485 back in 1937, on the 'Polish Operation 'signed off by Nikolai Yezhov in the period of the Great Purge.

Members of the public wrote to their MPs complaining about the Poles. 'It is time they were back in Poland, I am sure you will act sensibly and order them to return.' What a contrast to Churchill's rhetoric in the House of Commons, his pledge to the Polish people that 'his Majesties Government will never forget the debt.'

The Polish refugees would have an enormous job on their hands to find work and generally fit into a post war England. They had the Unions and the Civil Service to contend with from the beginning. Numerous organisations and Politicians, local and national, were keen to repatriate the Poles as soon as possible and forced repatriation was used in some cases despite knowing what was happening in Poland under the harsh Soviet regime. No-one returning did so without consequences.

Many Poles did go back only to be branded as traitors and their fate would be death or imprisonment, back to the gulag or labour camp. Those for whom homesickness was a huge motivator to go back were never heard from, there were no letters or calls although censorship would have prevented this. The British Government knew exactly what was going on in Poland but the truth was kept secret for political expediency. Why break a rule the U.K. and the US Governments had used throughout the war! Stalin, or as Roosevelt referred to him, Uncle Joe, was looked upon and promoted as the saviour of the eastern bloc, not it's oppressor.

These men and women had helped to win a war which they had fought from the beginning to the last and yet lost their freedom and country. Normal people living their lives had lost absolutely everything, except their names and spirit. Their treatment by the British Government and public was beyond contempt. It must have been so disheartening to those Polish refugees.

Despite the almost unsurmountable odds they would face over 200,000 of those Poles had chosen to remain in England and Scotland to where some had been demobbed. They would soon be joined by their dependents from wherever they had been left. The largest number of Poles were those who had escaped from Siberia, Arkhangelsk, Kazahkstan and other USSR zones with the Polish Army in 1941-42. Many were in displaced camps in Africa and India and some were in Mexico, spread across huge areas of the world.

My Mother Alicja had married an RAF serviceman in Ghazir and had arrived in England in 1946, she was living in Blackpool with her in-laws who were making her life unbearable. They were very unhappy that their son, had married a 'foreigner' and they treated her quite badly. My Ciocia Jasia had arrived before her and lived in London at college with friends. My Grandparents and Wujek Janusz were still in Ghazir, in Lebanon just waiting to join them with Kazia's brother Walery and his family. Permission to settle in England with my Mum, who had British citizenship would take some time and travel documents would also be needed.

Alicja eventually got news of her parent's move to England in January

1948 and was 'as excited as a child,' she hadn't seen them for almost 16 months and had desperately missed them, they were due to arrive in February and would soon be followed by the other family members, Walery, Ziuta, Włodek and Marysia.

As Adam and Walery and their families had been considered 'class enemies' by the Soviets it was an easy decision to make to come to England and not return to a Communist Poland. From 1945 up to 1953 Polish underground leaders that were still in Poland post war, had been sentenced to death and then executed for 'sabotage', and some 20,000 others were murdered. Former deportees and other 'undesirables' were also treated most harshly. England would be a safe haven, there was 'no future in Poland unless you were a Communist' my Dziadek used to say.

The family arrived in Liverpool from their temporary home in Ghazir, Lebanon, where they had been since 1945 after a very long journey from Port Said in February 1948. Alicja and Bill had waited at the docks for hours, looking out for them. The seas were very rough, too severe for the boat to dock for a day or two, so they had to come back, which was very frustrating. They did spy her parents and Janusz waving his scarf like mad and the excitement Alicja felt she would never forget. They were so close to reunion, it seemed so long since she had left them in Ghazir. When they were eventually able to disembark there was the formal process of registration and passport checks to go through.

Bill and Alicja waited in a reception area for a long time as there were many hundreds of refugees to be processed, so they tried to be patient until the family suddenly appeared, and she could not describe her emotions. It was so very intense that they could barely talk. They held onto each other so very tightly, oh how she had missed her family, her mother especially. It was so good to see them and to introduce them to their 6 month old grand daughter, Teresa. There was much to be joyful for.

The reunion, however, was very short lived. Adam, Kazia and Janusz had been allocated places at a camp in Five Oaks, near Brighton, and were to travel there by train. The family spent the short time together catching up on news and holding onto each other before they were called to be taken to the station with the many hundreds of others, for travel to the various Resettlement camps.

They stayed at Five Oaks camp for a few days to get over their journey and were then placed in Pulborough, registered with the West Sussex Constabulary on 19th February 1948.

They were interviewed and issued with Certificate of Registration (Aliens Order 1920) documents and recorded as Adam Góral born 26/5/1894 born in Daleszewicje, Poland, ENA9012204 (A12295), Polish Armed Forces 1941-1944

Kazimiera Góral born 23/2/1899 in Wróblewo, Poland ENA9012203, and (A128294), Janusz Góral born 6/1930 in Równe, Poland ENA 9012205. Then issued with clothing and food coupons on 4th March 1948. Clothing was issued by the Assistance Board, West Chiltington Camp 1/3/1948 and 4/3/1948.

They were to stay there for several months and were then moved to other camps, usually unused army barracks, in Horsham, Ely, which was surrounded by beautiful forests and reminded them of their Osada in Poland, and then they were moved onto Kelstern in Lincs. They would be moved again over the next 18 months eventually being registered at Monkmead Camp, Billingham, Sussex.

Alicja, Bill and Jasia visited the resettlement camps and the whole family were able to gather to see them in Lytham and London. Their registration cards record visits to and from Lytham St Anne's from those camps up to December 1950 and visits to and from Victoria and Brixton in London up to 1958. Each visit to and from was stamped by the Metropolitan Police or Lancashire Constabulary. They were finally exempt from registering their movements in 1961.

The only way to accommodate the large numbers of refugees was to place them in camps that had been recently vacated by the American and Canadian troops. There were many camps in the UK, most had been built in the early 1940's in rural areas, often in the grounds of large country estates, as well as military Hospitals, Army bases and Airfields. A Polish Resettlement Corps was raised in 1946 as a Corps of the British Army into which Poles were enlisted for the period of their demobilization up to 1948. The camps were given up by the MOD for housing Polish families and they were administered by a number of organisations and local authorities.

On arrival at the camp, travelling in army trucks, the Poles were very aware of the barbed wire that surrounded the camp and the tall watch towers which reminded them of the Labour camps they had been imprisoned in. Soon after arrival however the barbed wire fences and watch towers were taken down. They were registered and given I.D. cards and assigned to their Nissen hut. Everything had to be provided as the displaced Poles had very little, only what they stood up in and very few belongings. My Babcia still had the photo albums taken with her from Poland safely packed in her bags.

Their worldly goods amounted to very little.

The hut was furnished with beds, bedding, chest of drawers, chairs, and a table with some cutlery and plates. The sleeping area was sectioned off with a curtain so there was some privacy. In the centre of the camp was a cookhouse and communal mess room which catered for everyone to begin with but in time as more facilities became available, pots and pans and ranges, people cooked for themselves and were given their ration books.

Most of the buildings were Nissen huts made into hostels for single working men and a handful were Polish boarding schools run by the Committee for the Education of Poles. There were also a number of Polish hospitals. As people were finding their feet many moved out of the camps in search of work and accommodation. A large number emigrated to the USA, Australia, New Zealand, Canada and Argentina. Families were moved from camp to camp and by the 1950's the 200 plus camps had dwindled down to about 50. Northwick camp closed in 1970.

People in the camp came from many corners of Poland and from every walk of life. Factory workers, foresters, farmers, lawyers, doctors, nurses and teachers. There was a purpose built sick bay staffed by Polish nurses and doctors and those with serious illnesses were sent to the Polish Hospital in North Wales. In the early days language difficulties made finding work difficult but men and women found work in the canning and other factories.

Most of the Nissen huts didn't have internal plumbing and water had to be fetched from cold water taps and toilet and washing facilities were in separate blocks and there was a huge coke filled boiler house at the far end of the camp. For those who could not look after themselves communal meals continued until 1969 but many of the residents were self sufficient although they were some distance from any shops and this was a problem. One enterprising Polish man acquired a van and sold Polish sausage, sauerkraut, gherkins and lots of other Polish foods. Another sold bedding and clothing and the residents were soon able to become self reliant. Local buses were laid on once weekly and people were able to travel further afield. They all pulled together, helping each other through any difficulties.

By 1949 there were 16 Nursery Schools and 34 Primary Schools with over 2,000 children spread over the camps and hostels throughout the UK. The Committee for the Education of Poles in Great Britain administered the education of Polish Children. As in Tehran and Lebanon, schools always sprang up to educate the children whose education had been interrupted by the war and very many had missed out. To the Poles it was very important for the children to continue their education wherever they were and whatever the circumstances.

The Committee also concerned itself with the education of the adults and teaching them English to enable them to get by and find work. The children found it much easier to learn a new language than the adults although they persisted. Some children went to local English schools but most attended the camp schools. Some went onto secondary and some to grammar schools where it was strictly forbidden to speak Polish amongst themselves which was quite unfairly punished as some children still found it difficult to fully communicate in English. Kazia and Adam were only ever able to learn the very basics but managed to get by. Most of their time would be spent with their countrymen and family.

There was a Polish boarding school for the many orphans of the war and for those whose parents were too ill to look after them. Many Poles were still suffering the effects of starvation, typhus, dysentery and malaria they had caught in the labour camps as well as from psychological effects. There were two fee paying boarding schools and the Poles in Great Britain were successful in establishing 4 faculties at British Universities, Medicine at Edinburgh in 1941, Architecture at Liverpool in 1942, Veterinary studies at Edinburgh in 1943 and Balliol College in 1944.

Over the next few years more families arrived at the camps, many having travelled half way across the world, fleeing their imprisonment in Siberia through the Ural Mountains, Kazakhstan, Uzbekistan, Persia, the Middle East to Africa and India, arriving in England in the late 40's and early 50's. By the 60's people were leaving the camps as they became more prosperous and found homes and work further away. Many settled in the Midlands and London, were allocated Council houses and some of the buildings on the camps were later made into residential homes for elderly Poles.

Alicja's parents came to live with them in 1951 when they were able to leave the resettlement camps and Alicja and Bill started decorating the house in preparation, putting lino on the floor and varnishing the floorboards. With rugs on the floors it was looking much nicer. They were so excited and were ready to welcome them. I was 4 by then and my Babcia and Dziadek lived with us until I was nearly 8.

My grand parents found it quite lonely in Lytham as they didn't speak English very well and consequently found it very difficult to mix. Most displaced people coming to England after the war had headed to the capital, and small Polish and Jewish communities were springing up. St

Anne's was only a small town and there wasn't a Polish community for them to become involved with. They were still young enough to be more active and needed something constructive to do.

My brother Tony and I were at convent by then and although Adam and Kazia enjoyed taking us to and from school and teaching us Polish, it wasn't keeping them busy enough. Adam had his garden and Kazia busied herself in the home whilst Bill and Alicja were at work but it wasn't really enough, they needed people of their own age. They needed to be in a Polish community, and it wasn't long before they left to go to London, where the Polish community was growing. Alicja understood their needs and with sad hearts she and Bill saw them off to London.

My grandparents first lived with Ciocia Jasia and her husband Bolcio in Victoria from 1953-54 and then later in Brixton, helping to raise my favourite cousin Alec whilst they both worked.

My Ciocia Jasia had been in England before the rest of the family, in September 1946, and she had lived and worked in Everleigh, Wiltshire, as a teacher in the Polish Refugee camp. She then moved to Guildford after finishing her further education course. She had met her future husband Bolcio (Bolesław) in Guildford. He was a university graduate and physical training instructor who had taken part in the 1936 Olympics in Berlin, a footballer in Poland and a veteran of the Battle of Monte Cassino.

They married on 23rd July 1949 and settled in Victoria, London, their son Alec was born in 1950. In 1954 they moved to Brixton and later on to Streatham in 1962. In 1963, without any indication of ill health, Bolcio died of a coronary at the age of only 49.

My Wujek Janusz also shared the house in Brixton, putting down roots in a new country was expensive, so sharing costs, especially the purchase or renting of a house, was quite common. He later moved to Forest Hill, sharing the lower part of a large house with Kazia and Adam. He had by then married Pamela and had two young daughters, Anita and Krysia.

Adam was a devout Catholic and dedicated his life to charity, helping to raise money for the poor and starving in Africa. He was also active for the local Polish community and helped to raise funds for the purchase of their own church in Balham which to this day is a thriving Parish and has a meeting place for the Osadników Kresowych. This society is made up of the surviving relatives of the families of the eastern borderlands, survivors of Stalin's deportations. The president of this society is Ryszard Grzybowski, a friend of Jasia's, who is a leading member of this society; I met him at her funeral in December 2011 and have met him several times since at various Osadnicy events with other children of the Sybiraks.

When Bolcio died Kazia and Adam moved back to Streatham to support Jasia and Alec always on hand for whoever needed their help. In their later years they moved to a Polish home in Corby and later to Antokol in Sidcup.

Jasia remarried in 1966, to Bruno Misik, an artist, who spent a lot of his retirement renovating the Stations of the Cross at Balham Polish church. He died in 1990 and Jasia then devoted more of her time to the Polish community. She was a most colourful personality, some acquaintances likening her to Zsa Zsa Gabor the actress, having a very strong Polish accent and always being so beautifully dressed. She became a stalwart figure in the Balham Polish community, running social clubs for the elderly and lonely and a charity for Polish orphans in Warsaw (Pruszków Charity) for which she collected generous amounts of money by advertising in the Polish Press.

Jasia moved to Balham in 2000, where she cared for her then partner Stanisław Raymond, another veteran of Monte Cassino who had suffered serious head wounds and in later years developed dementia. This all took a huge toll on Jasia's health, and after Stan's death in 2009 her own health deteriorated dramatically and she battled hard over the next two years. In December 2010 she was diagnosed with secondary lung cancer and struggled with the considerable pain it caused her.

My Mother Alicja stayed with her several times 2010/11 and was there in November 2011 when she died whilst a carer was tending to her needs. The family knew it was inevitable but it was still an awful shock, as Alicja's little sister was such a vibrant person. I took it badly, as we had been very close and she was also my godmother. Alicja and Jasia had cared and fought for each other throughout their travels to and from the USSR. Kazia and Adam, Walery and Ziuta, Włodek, Janusz, Marysia and now Jasia, were all gone. Alicja was now the only one of the family left who had survived the wartime hell created by Stalin. She suddenly felt quite alone and is today at 97 imprisoned by Alzheimers.

The children of Sybiraks have organised several Facebook sites to exchange information of our parents' experiences of Siberia 1940-1942 and other USSR states. It is our endeavour to keep the memory of what happened alive by exchanging detail and supplying historical data to those who are trying to trace family members. Very many grandparents and parents had been unable to speak of their ordeal and for their children who only know a very basic amount of detail these sites are invaluable.

I have two friends with a Polish father and they know very little about their history from WW2 as their Fathers were unable to talk about it. My friends don't know their real names or where in Poland they came from and their fathers both died without sharing any information. Do they have family in Poland? Without a name or place of birth or area where they grew up or came from, which labour camp they were in, where they fought? They cannot trace their origins. A very large part of their heritage is missing. One of them is actively researching through the Polish history Facebook sites as there is more information available now than ever before.

There are also commemorative events that are organised by the site organisers and my cousin Alec and I have met members of families that were in the same Osada back in the eastern borderlands and the same prison camp as our family. It is hugely emotional to meet these people who shared so much with our family. I belong to Kresy Family and Kresy Siberia and several other of these history sites and I'll list them all at the end of the chapter for information.

After his arrival in England my uncle Janusz had gone to Glasgow to continue his education with a group of the cadets before moving in with Jasia and Bolcio in Victoria around 1951. He studied restorative dentistry but gave this up to move into the better paid hospitality trade in the hotels of London, the Berkeley, the Bedford and then the Savoy where he worked until retirement at 65. He met many famous faces here, the most memorable being the Queen Mother.

Marysia had come to England in 1946 with Jasia as cadets and later settled in West London with her parents Walery and Ziuta and her brother Włodek. They had arrived in 1948. She married Wieslek in 1950 and later with their three children, Marek, Ania and Ewa, they moved to Brockley. Marek has lived and worked in Warsaw for many years and has three children, Adam, Marcin and Izabella. He is a grandfather to four baby girls. Stella, Augustyna, Janka and Jadwiga. The twins Ania and Ewa live and work in Kent.

It wasn't until some time after their arrival in England that Wujek Walery and Ciocia Ziuta had devastating news about their younger son Zbyszek, who had joined the Polish underground in western Poland at the outbreak of war. He had been shot by his 'best friend' in a terrible drunken, accident on returning to barracks after seeing Ciocia Genia in Lublin,. His friend had demanded to see Zbyszek's pass on entry to the camp and Zbyszek's reply was "but you know me, I've just shown you my pass," but his friend fired at point-blank range and killed him.

He was only 23 and he had survived the desperation of war only to be shot by his best friend! The exact details are unclear, and why his friend was drunk and on duty will never be known, the family was shattered. It isn't known what action if any was taken by Wujek Walery and Ciocia Ziuta, or what happened to the young man who fired the gun.

Those who stayed behind in Poland, Kazia's sister Gienia and her daughter Halina had survived the war with Genia's husband Władislaw in Lublin. Halina married Wiesek Morawiec, and both worked as doctors in Stalowa Wola. Wiesek died at quite an early age and Halina who was a specialist in rheumatology suffered from dementia in later life, and died recently, 2020. She lived in Stalowa Wola. They had a son, Maciej, who practises law in Warsaw and regular contact is maintained between him and myself and my cousin Alec via Facebook.

After Gienia died, Halina found a letter from Sofia her Babcia, whilst sorting out her belongings, The details are quite vague but it describes Sofia's experiences and survival during the Russian occupation and later behind the Iron Curtain. I don't yet have access to this information from Maciej so it isn't known what happened to Sofia or how she had managed to survive on her own during such harsh times, as she had been elderly during this period. Gienia had related some of these details to Jasia in the phone calls they shared over the years, but these details are vague as she had to be so careful in her contact with family in England. She was lucky to be able to get permission to visit her sister Kazia and the family on two occasions.

Conversations had to be short and they were not able to discuss personal details freely as there was constant surveillance in Communist Poland. Whatever was spoken was spoken in secret and quietly because there were situations when so called friends would report you to the Police, and even if you didn't say what this 'friend' had reported, you were still arrested.

Thrown into a padded cell where a suspect could find themselves banged up for months in solitary confinement on the whim of a reckless neighbour, then put into the interrogation chair where a suspect could be grilled to the point of insanity. The fake delivery vans patrolling the streets would snatch a suspected dissident off the streets. Spy cameras would be hidden in belts, ties and buttons and instruction manuals on how to destroy people's reputations were eagerly read by the Secret Police. This was happening when deluded English Lefties would take their holidays across the 'paradise' of eastern Europe. Only the Stasi in east Germany would outdo the NKVD?

Under Communism everything had to be shared, one family member could easily be turned against another, as loyalty to the proletarian class, the state, was all that mattered. In eastern Germany a third of the population were informants to the Stasi. I'm not sure of the corresponding figures for Poland's secret Police but I don't think they compare. The older Poles were open of their contempt for Communism and shared this with their children despite the penalties.

Specific relationships family, religion, culture and art were considered by the Soviets to be the 'base' of society, and were to be broken by the Communists as they associated with the old 'capitalist order'. Individualism, loyalty and truth would all be ruthlessly stamped out. It was a brutal practice. Tens of millions of people were murdered by many Communist regimes in many countries by Lenin, Stalin, Mao Zedong, Pol Pot, the Kims and the Castros.

The influence of the USSR post war spread to their satellite states of Poland, Hungary, Czechoslovakia, Romania, Bulgaria, Albania, E. Germany, Iran, Azerbaijan, Austria, Korea and Afghanistan, who all 'benefitted' from military, economic and political aid from the USSR. It is still interfering in European democracies, in the U.S , Montenegro, Ukraine and Syria to name but a few.

I didn't intend to go into an expose of Communism but my Dziadek's words from many years ago suddenly reverberated in my head. He always told me how the theory of Communism was brutal in practice because it was brutal in theory. It touched more than a billion people and killed millions. Stalin, my Dziadek said, 'was a brutal dictator, no different from Hitler or Lenin.'

Stalin continued his violent dictatorship, to abolish the so called bourgeoisie of the eastern borderlands, eliminating those people who would not easily relinquish their property, culture and beliefs, family and God. By fighting for their livelihoods and their country and believing in their God, my family were considered 'class enemies of the proletariat' and had to be eliminated. Stalin was fighting against a 'class' not individuals and was intent on discarding those individuals from Poland en masse, for the sake of the collective, or was it revenge for the Bolshevik war!

My grandparents loved their country but were never able to go back, it was too dangerous. They had heard what had happened to those who did return, especially those like them who had been exiled in 1940 and who had fought with the Allies.

They are my reason for writing this memoir, it is in their honour. I cannot ever imagine what they experienced during their time in the Arkhangelsk labour camps, or the precarious, long and exhausting journeys to reach freedom but I remember their courage, love and humour.

***The many historical sites I've referred to relating specifically to Polish heritage are:-***

- Sons and Daughters of Displaced Poles
- Silent Heroes of the Forgotten Holocaust
- Polish Culture
- I Love my Polish Heritage
- Shallow Graves in Siberia
- Unravelling Your Roots
- Poland's Long War
- Sybiracy
- Polish Media Studies
- Encountering anti Polonism

*They are full of information and views and data is exchanged tracking down family members long thought lost.*

# CHAPTER 10

# Journeys in Detail

One of the aspects of my Mother's journeys that gave me the biggest headache was researching the routes she took from her home in Poland, to Russia and onwards, as I've detailed below. It took some considerable time as I was determined to see how far the family had travelled, especially their many journeys from the Labour camp in 1942 through to their journey's end in England. The fact that they were in a dreadful physical condition needing to stop at various points along the route to Uzbekistan for medical aid, didn't take away their determination to get to the military points the Polish army were assembling at in the Middle East.

My Mother remembered the final stop in Russia and the names of camps they were in which helped me to track down the areas and train stations and with some encouragement she began to remember a little more. That it had all happened so very long ago was difficult for her and at 97 with Alzheimers she remembered very little although she hadn't forgotten the hardship and trauma of the camps, 'I remember but it doesn't hurt my head so much.'

It has taken time but I now have the completed journeys illustrated as accurately as I can, checked with my Ciocia Jasia, against the routes of a friend from their Osada, Danuta Gradosielska who had kept a diary of her deportation and some research from Mum's notes. They travelled through 5 time zones, on the Trans-Siberian, Trans Mongolian and Trans Manchurian railways.

I marvel at the spirit and determination of my family to have survived not only the deprivation of the Labour camps but the arduous journeys taken over so very many km to reach safety and freedom and to begin their recovery.

## February 1940 – The Kresy, Poland

10th February 1940, their last night at home, arrested by the NKVD at 5am with a decree of deportation read out to them, they're told they were 'a threat to public order' and the family were then taken to the outskirts of Równe for the first stage of their deportation to the USSR. Transport had been ready and waiting for some considerable time.

## Journey 1 – Równe to Gorki, Moscow Oblast – 2300kms

From Równe, the train heads out through Lubormika, Zdolbunow, Iwanko, Szepetowka, Orzenin, Korosten, Owrucz, River Prypet (scene of the Chernobyl explosion) Gomel, Brynansk, Orzel, over River Don, Karaczew, Alexandrowka, Rybna, Holworsk, Woskriesensk, Oriechovo, Pokrowa, Pietruszki, Untow, Wladimir and Gorki, a journey of 17 days in temperatures of minus 30 degrees.

### USSR – Journey 2 – Gorki, Moscow Oblast, to Sharya, Kostroma Oblast – 690kms

They left the train at Gorki to travel onto Sharya, another 2 day's towards the labour camp. They stayed overnight in an empty and very cold Orthodox church and early next morning set out for the train to Sharya. On arrival at Sharya, they had to walk towards the labour camp, Poldniewica, Gorkowski Oblast, in very deep snow. It was about 20 km away and they were very tired as they had very little sleep. The other labour camps they are moved to whilst in the Archkangelsk region are Duraszewo only a short distance away, approximately 10 km and Darowatka, in the Gorkowski Oblast about 20 km away. I've been able to find two of the labour camps on map Specposiolki w Obwodzie Wologodzkim 1940-41. Duraszewo I'm assuming is not very far away and in the same Oblast but have not yet been able to locate it.

### Poldniewica, USSR – December 1941

In mid 1941, after the news of the 'amnesty' was known to the prisoners many just left from their camp, Derawelka, eager to get to the Polish army, whilst many others gathered at camp Poldniewica about 20 km away to plan their escapes. They would have to wait for their official 'amnesty' papers, without which they would not be able to claim food at stations along the journey, the papers would also 'guarantee' their safety up to Uzbekistan.

They left Poldniewica camp in late December 1941 almost two years after arriving there, on hand made sledges staying with local Russians, they would have frozen without their help, it was bitterly cold. There was a railway line between Poldniewica/Poludnevitza and Darowatka which would make the journey out of the camps easier for all those heading towards Kotlas.

### Journey 3 – Labour camp to Kotlas, Arkhangelsk Oblast – 457kms

Early next day they had a lift in trucks from a group of Russian soldiers they had come across purely by chance. There was much movement of troops across Russia at that time after Hitler's attack on Russia and the troops helped the group of 15 to Kotlas station. It had saved them many days walk in very deep snow.

The journey from Kotlas, took them through Kirov, Zuyvka, Molotov, Kama, Shalya, Kuzma, Hropik, Swierdowsk, Czelyabinsk, Kartal, Aktybinsk, Shalkar, Oktiabinsk, Aral Sea, Samarkand and then onto Tashkent, a journey through the Ural Mountains, the Kurgistan Steppes, Kazakhstan and Uzbekistan. It took about 6 weeks with many stops for aid at the medical stations set up along the route by the Polish army.

### Uzbekistan - January-February 1942

They left the train at Tashkent, a group of about 30 people, and were diverted to a field to wait for over 2 days and nights without food or water. They were terrified as there were no Polish officials there to help them as there had been at points on the journey so far. The Uzbeks told them they would soon be moved. This was just another diversion by the NKVD together with the Uzbeks who had stopped them here to send them onto Bukhara, to a collective farm to work for them.

### Journey 5 – Tashkent to Bukhara – 570kms

From Tashkent they boarded a train for the journey to Bukhara. They had been met by Polish officials who told them they would very soon be moved towards the army and to go with the Uzbeks for now as there was little alternative. There were so very many Poles fleeing the USSR and the Polish officials were almost overcome with the numbers.

### Journey 6 – Bukhara to Vobkent – 35kms

From Bukhara they travelled to Vobkent in yak drawn wagons by Uzbeks to a collective farm. It had been an exhausting journey of hunger and of a hell unimagined with the Soviets generally disrupting the evacuation. Refusing to allow access to trains to help their exodus and diverting many of the transports towards collective farms, Kolkhozy, for the labour they still required. Stalin's grip was tight and would continue to be throughout their journey to Persia. Adam and Walery had heard via the grapeline that if a family member was in the army, in a uniform, it would help the other members of the family to leave and join them and the Polish army in the Middle East. They both left with this in mind, Adam was then posted to Iraq and Walery to Uzbeksitan, the families were now on their own. The stay at the Kolkhoz was thankfully short, circumstances moved very quickly and the sisters Jasia and Alicja would soon leave the kolkhoz to join the Polish cadets in Guzor. Walery had found the family as he had been assigned to an army base in Uzbekistan and had been searching for them. He told his sister Kazia to get the children into the cadet school and into uniforms urgently, as the borders would soon be closed. He knew how Stalin worked and he was right, Stalin would close the borders to the Poles in August 1942, keeping them in the USSR.

### Journey 7 – Vobkent to Bukhara – 35kms

The sisters leave Vobkent and head back to the station at Bukhara in arbas to board a train to Guzor.

### Journey 8 – Bukhara to Guzor – 217kms

They travelled from Bukhara to Guzor arriving at the Cadet school after a day, they were deloused given basic medical attention and issued with cadet uniforms. The 7th Division is here and despite their haggard faces the Polish soldiers look very smart in their English uniforms. The girls are happy and eager to join the cadets.

### Journey 9 – Guzor to Bukhara – 217kms

The cadets then had to travel from Guzar back to the station at Bukhara as plans were changing all the time which was quite confusing. The new Polish army was constantly on the move. Stalin was cutting off supplies and the NKVD continually intervened to hamper the journeys. Alicja had typhus and Jasia had dysentery, both were very ill and Alicja would need hospital treatment.

### Journey 10 – Bukhara to Kitab – 275kms

Next journey after Alicja had partly recovered, was by train from Bukhara onto Kitab where some of the army units were assembling. General Anders was ensuring that all the Poles leaving the USSR were being moved to be safe and closer to the Polish army, away from Stalin's clutches. General Anders visited their camp in Kitab and instilled much needed confidence in the cadets.

### Journey 11 – Kitab to Port Krasnovodsk – 1,595kms

From Kitab another train journey through the mountains of Uzbekistan to Port Krasnovodosk (now Turkmenbashi) a gruelling journey and both girls were quite ill Jasia with dysentery and Alicja had typhus and yellow jaundice. It took several days with stops at medical stations for treatment and to recover. March 1942 – Mum's notes say she thought 'it was August' but I haven't been able to match this up.

### Journey 12 – Port Krasnovodsk to Pahlevi across the Caspian Sea – 200kms

At Port Krasnovodosk they waited for two days and nights in a sand storm, amongst many people in terrible condition to cross the Caspian Sea, a 2 day sail. Some of the boats were just fishing boats and not in good condition but the sisters were able to get onto a larger more stable one which was very over crowded.

### Persia (Iran)

In Pahlevi after a crowded but calm journey they were de loused again, their physical condition was awful, they were scratching and desperate to be clean. Given new uniforms and medical assistance from the Red Cross and the Queen Alexandra Nursing Corps they were sent to tents on the beach before being moved to a Camp in Pahlevi.

### Journey 13 – Pahlevi to Tehran – 680kms

Janusz was looking for them in Pahlevi, he and Kazia had arrived a week earlier and she had been sent on to a hospital in Tehran. After a week they were moved to a larger refugee Camp 1 on army transport passing thru Tabriz, the Elbrus Mts, Qazvin and finally into Teheran. Whilst here they heard that 'permission' to leave the USSR had been withdrawn and many thousands of Poles were left in the Siberian wilderness. They had not been able to leave as the Kommandants of many camps had kept the 'amnesty' from them in order to retain their labour. They were in Teheran for about 1 year recovering and working before being moved to make room for other refugees coming through from Pahlevi's refugee camps. Alicja had yellow jaundice and was too ill to move to Palestine with Jasia in Autumn 1942 and she stayed in Tehran with Kazia and Janusz. Adam visited on leave. Alicja, Kazia and Janusz leave Tehran in Autumn 1943.

### Journey 14 – Tehran to Isfahan – 448kms

Autumn 1943, from Teheran they were moved onto Isfahan through Qom and Kashan to another refugee camp and were there for possibly 1 year when Adam was recalled to his army unit in Tehran.

### Journey 15 – Isfahan to Tehran – 448kms

Alicja meets William in Autumn 1944 in Isfahan, she and Ziuta enrol in a nursing course at the Red Cross HQ in Tehran. William is posted to Tehran and Adam has been recalled to his unit so the family all move back there through Kashan and Qom. They were also moved to make room for other incoming Polish refugees from the USSR.

### Journey 16 – Tehran to Ghazir, Lebanon – 1840kms

Another move came for Adam to be formally discharged from the army in Egypt in 1945, due to ill health. From Tehran they travel in army lorries through Arak, Ahwez staying there over night, to a camp in Baghdad for 2 nights. They cross the Turkey-Syria border into Alleppo, transferring from a passenger train to a goods train. They were allocated a house in Ghazir and William proposes to Alicja before he is posted to Iraq. Alicja and William are married in July 1946 in Ghazir.

### Journey 17 – Ghazir to Beiruit – 26kms 1946 –

In 1946 the family is allocated other accommodation and will shortly move from Ghazir to Beirut. William collects Alicja on 1st October for their journey to England. They take a taxi to Beiruit after a very tearful goodbye to Alicja's family, they didn't know if they would ever see each other again.

### Journey 19 – Beirut to Jerusalem via Haifi – 433kms

2nd October – From Beirut a taxi to Haifi staying over night then train to Jerusalem the following day. They stay a couple of days in Jerusalem at the YMCA.

### Journey 20 – Jerusalem to Cairo – 740kms

3rd October – From Jerusalem a long train journey ahead through Palestine and into Cairo where they spend 6 weeks

### Journey 21 – Cairo to Port Said – 203kms

5th October – A honeymoon in Cairo and a wait for a boat to take them to England from Port Said.

### Journey 22 – Port Said to Southampton – 5,762kms

1st November - Leave Cairo and journey along the side of the Suez canal reaching Port Said early evening. They board the Durban Castle and arrive in England on 9th November and then travel by train to Blackpool, Lancashire – 423kms

### Journeys from Poland to Russia to Uzbekistan to Iran to Lebanon to Jerusalem to Cairo to England 1940-1946

*I've worked out distances at approximately 23,000km over a period of 6 years. There will be some journeys not accounted for and I've checked dates and places against family photo's, my Mother's notes and information from Ciocia Jasia and others.*
*It's as accurate as I'll ever get.*

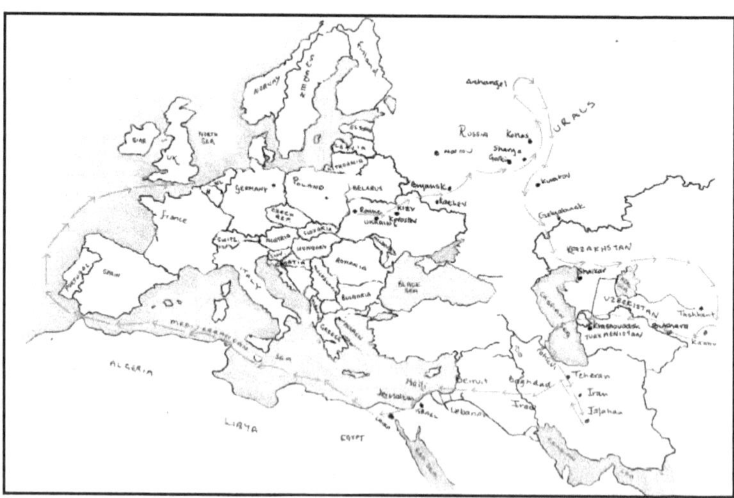

CHAPTER 11

# Personal Recollections

Adapted from notes made of conversations with my Dziadek, Adam and Babcia Kazia, in their attempts to dispel the myths surrounding their beloved Poland and to educate me about my heritage.

Many look upon Poland as a backward nation that was defeated in a matter of days by overwhelming and efficient German troops, that Poland's army and air force were destroyed and that Poland capitulated within a very few days. The truth is very different.

Polish forces did not collapse, they fought for 35 days, the last battle of the campaign was on 5th October five weeks after the German attack, they were overwhelmed by a far greater force. Poland's losses were 67,000 killed and 134,000 wounded. The Germans expected to have a quick and easy victory but the Polish authorities had immediately begun organising Armia Krajowa to continue the fight, it was the first and the largest Resistance army in Europe. Poland's fight then continued on the 17th September when they had to contend with Stalin's invasion from the east on his excuse of 'coming to save Poland from the Germans.'

Poland did not surrender. It's Government continued to operate in exile throughout the War, first in France until it fell to the Germans and then in London until its dissolution in 1990. It also had an excellent intelligence service, Armia Krajowa. Before the war the Poles delivered models of Germany's top secret Enigma encryption machines they called 'bombas' to British and French intelligence, enabling the Allies to read key German communications throughout most of the war. It was not Turing who cracked the Enigma code as is commonly believed, it was Polish mathematicians, although he was able to build on the Poles' initial expertise and mathematical genius.

Poland held out in 1939 against the Germans, alone, almost as long as France, Holland and Belgium held out against the Germans with major British help in 1940. If not for the Soviet invasion on 17th September the Poles would have held out longer if they'd had the promised help from France or Britain, which did not come until much later.

I speak with pride about Poland's contributions to the Allied victory in WW2, their incredible efforts have been overlooked by the Allies since the end of the war, their exclusion from the celebrations on V.E. Day an insult, to which there has never been an official apology, although I believe former PM Tony Blair did acknowledge the exclusion. My family lost everything, almost their lives and I include many thoughts from Sybiraks who survived, especially from Sybiraczka Alicja, my Mother, and my grandparents in the main part of this memoir.

Alicja Góral, is 97 the only remaining member of a family who survived the deprivations of Siberia whilst very many didn't. Their graves are scattered along the routes to Siberia, the Russian plains, the Siberian wilderness and along the paths to freedom from Kotlas to Tashkent. There are also graves in the cotton fields of Bukhara where they were again forced into labour by the NKVD for the Uzbeks, the NKVD who trailed the escaping Polish exiles, sabotaging their escape efforts.

I spoke with my Mum very many times over the years before she was lost to Alzheimers, we had many nazdrowje's and she opened up a little each time. She didn't talk about this period of her life very much as it 'hurts my mind' and she gets emotional because she can't remember what she wants to say and I cannot anticipate it. She desperately wants to remember something specific and can't. 'What's the matter with me' she asks? I'm too upset to say, seeing her struggle with her memory, my Mother who was so strong throughout my childhood is now so reliant and vulnerable, sometimes impatient for memories of her homeland.

She remembers something, she is 'in a new place' maybe 1946 England? A young woman in a new country away from her family for the first time since their exile. She says she 'felt foreign and didn't belong'. 'I didn't feel at home at all, I didn't feel like my children were truly mine, it's very difficult to explain.' Maybe she means bringing up children who speak a different language which was perhaps a little alienating, especially to begin with. Although my brother and I were learning Polish from both Mum and our grandparents and were fluent pre school but she said she 'felt alien.'

I asked if Babcia and Dziudziu felt the same and she said yes they did 'they didn't feel as though they belonged here,' they were viewed with suspicion for many years.

Mum couldn't ever explain why she had never felt at home, she has been here since 1946 and was perhaps reluctant to mention the hostility. As children we knew of the hostility and were bullied at school because of our 'foreign Mother.' I wish I'd had this particular conversation many years before but at least I'd had the foresight to ask her to write her memories down 20 years ago after my Father had died. I thought it would fill her days and that it might have been a release for her. I was wrong, as she remembers Siberia and it still causes her stress. Sadly she can't remember her home in Poland, except for 'the bridge over the river.'

After WW2 many Poles in England as registered refugees, were given a hard time by the Labour Govt and the Communist supporting Unions, despite having been a major ally of the British and USA. Manual labour was needed to rebuild the country and the Unions put up many barriers to foreign refugees. Many Polish servicemen had been asked to leave the country by PM Attlee, although the Polish Resettlement Act of 1947 gave them reason to stay in England and make their homes here but many left for what proved to be more hospitable countries in the Commonwealth.

I've included personal recollections from individual Polish refugees in England, in their own words with some amendments for grammar.

**Michał** was born on 12th August 1927 in Boldury in the Tarnopol region (now deep in the Ukraine). He was the eldest of 6 children and in 1935 his family moved to another farm between Tarnopol and Wołyn where his father built a house. They were there in 1939 when war broke out.

The beginning of the war brought great tragedy, his Mother died on 1st September in the evening of the outbreak. His grandmother stayed with the family but his grandfather had to go away, it was the last time they saw him, murdered by Ukrainian bandits. Michał remembers that it was a beautiful autumn that year. In the 2nd week after the outbreak on the road between Beresteczko and Racichów many people were fleeing east from the Germans. In the evening the German planes started shooting into the crowds with machine guns and there was nowhere to hide, only open fields on each side. This happened every day until 14th September.

'Then the Russians arrived from the east and the refugees turned round and started heading back west. It was a terrible winter in 1939-40 and on the 10th February in the middle of the night we heard tremendous banging on the door. My father opened it to an NKVD Soviet agent who entered with a gun and several other Red Army people. They scattered about the house and two surrounded my Father and put their guns against him. We started crying uncontrollably it was so frightening, I'll never forget it, the picture of my father surrounded by those ready-to-kill soldiers will stay with me forever. We were told to take as much as we could as there's nothing where you are going.'

The family were taken by sledge to the station 24kms away, as they were leaving 'our big dog howled terribly and one of the Soviets shot him dead.'

They were put into cattle wagons and their long journey to Siberia began, they travelled for 22 days and the journey finished where the track ran out at Kotlas in Siberia. 'We endured 18 months at the labour camp before the 'amnesty' of July 1941 when we made our way south towards the Polish Army in Tehran'.

The family were separated by the end of the war and in 1947 Michał came to England spending his first few months in a re-settlement camp near Winchester. Finding work was difficult due to the Unions being dominated by communists who wished to please Stalin's whims, making the employment of Poles difficult but many firms sought to employ them.

The family were active members of the Polish community and lived productive lives in England.'

My mother Alicja, had a break down in her late 30's and my Ciocia Jasia and Wujek Janusz suffered mental health problems. There would also be flashbacks for them over the years, impossible for them to ignore. My grandparents Kazia and Adam suffered quietly although Kazia especially could laugh when remembering the Bolsheviks, she somehow coped. Adam involved himself in the Church and raising money for overseas children.

I know from speaking to family members of survivors and friends, that some knew next to nothing about their parents or grandparents, who had never spoken of what had happened to them. They're not aware of any living relatives they may have in Poland and children of Sybiraks who are researching their family history have little to go on. These days there are many research points as the history of Poland's WW2 is recorded in many areas.

**Stanisław** was born in 1936 near Wilno in north east Poland, his father was in the Polish army when Germany invaded Poland, the Russians invaded shortly after and very soon occupied the local area. On 10th February 1940 all 8 members of his family were deported by rail in cattle trucks through the depths of Russian winter to frozen Siberia. The privations of the journey led to the death of his youngest brother shortly after their arrival in Siberia.

There his parents had to work outdoors cutting trees, the older children attended the Russian school and the younger ones stayed in the camp.

The 'amnesty' of June 1941 enabled the family to leave the camp in late 1941. He remembers the arduous journey south after their release. 'my father was very good with his hands and built 3 sledges, my mother pulled one, my father pulled one and my eldest brother who was 12 pulled one. My sister who was 10 walked as there were 3 younger siblings.'

They managed to get to the station and then travelled by train to Uzbekistan which took several weeks, a journey of over 3,000 km, to meet up with the Polish army. His father joined the army and the family were supposed to remain and work in the cotton fields for the Uzbeks in return for subsistence. After 3 weeks his mother decided conditions were so bad that they should leave and follow the army. Obstructed by NKVD agents at train stations, Stalin needed their labour, they were luckily rescued by some Polish troops who grabbed them on board the train. This was extremely fortuitous given the terrible conditions other fleeing Poles experienced in Uzbekistan having got stuck there.

'There were some transports organised and we left Uzbekistan in 1942 for Persia, that's when we met my brother (must have been separated) and from then on we moved to one of the British colonies called Tanganyika in East Africa'.

Six years later the family sailed for England and were reunited with their father. Life was in Nissen camps in the Cotswolds and he finished his education in Northamptonshire. He met his wife at the Lifford Park school.

The family settled in England, some of the children going to University, one to Cambridge and some siblings eventually moving to Canada. Stanisław and his wife entered into the English and Polish communities and helped those Poles who came into England post 2004 needing help with the English language.

Like many refugee Poles he has sent parcels of food and clothing to various cities during post war Poland and even up to the 60's through various crises which occurred under communist rule in his homeland. He has not yet visited the area of his former home which is now in Belarus.'

Very many survivors were unable to speak of their ordeal, it was very firmly buried. My Mother only gave me a very basic outline to work on, it was far too painful to recall much detail but what she gave me was the backbone of the story.

Many young Polish people came to Britain after 2004 when Poland became a member of the E.U. and settled in Birmingham and increased the number of Polish Delicatessens popular with English customers as well as the Poles.

These new arrivals are unaware of the earlier wave of Polish refugees post war [they were not informed in their schooling under Communism] predominantly servicemen and their families, who had spent some years in Soviet labour camps and post war in resettlement camps within the British Empire recovering from their ordeal. There were also very many thousands of orphans.

Together with other groups of Polish people in London and Leicester, Birmingham etc, these people established thriving communities and only those who arrived as children or young adults survive to this day.

Those that I know of, include my Mother Alicja, family friends Danuta and Ryszard from the same Osada and labour camp and Halina a very dear friend of Alicja's.

Many of these refugees fought in the regular Polish units or resistance units against Germany in WW2 or were from families where their father fought with the Allies in the war. Some were from families who were exiled to deepest Russia or Siberia on the orders of Stalin, for their fathers' participation in the Bolshevik War, or simply viewed as 'enemies of the state' as my family were.

Others were from families whose members were forced into labour by the Germans in factories or on farms in Poland, Germany or occupied France.

Their lives had been greatly impacted by WW2, many arriving in England by troop ship, as my Mother Alicja did with her husband who served in the RAF or on large merchant ships after 1945. Some arrived during the war by small boat or aeroplane to join the Allied cause, many fighting in the Battle of Britain.

These Polish refugees have spent a large part of their lives in England, some were born in the re-settlement camps. They all found employment and became productive and law abiding members of British society and they have all mostly kept strongly to Polish traditions as we as a family have done. Even extending to the generation of grandchildren and even great grandchildren.

Most of the newly arrived Poles lived in army camps, renamed as re-settlement camps spread throughout England and Wales. They remember their experiences of WW2, the deportation to Russia and relatives dying on the 2,000+km journey. The NKVD coming in the middle of the night, giving them only half an hour to pack. The extreme hunger in the camps and many thousands who died from starvation, typhus and other diseases.

The older refugees had to come to terms with having lost everything they owned, their property confiscated by the Soviets, taken over by 'neighbours' or burned to the ground, their livelihoods lost. They had to realise that although they had gone through terrible hardships they were 'compensated' by living in a free England. Many were never reunited with relatives or knew what had happened to those left in Poland. My Babcia Kazia never found out what had happened to her Mother Sofia, who would have been in her 60's at the outbreak of war.

Their country had been decimated, 20% smaller than in 1939 and the loss of the Kresy was a great blow to many of them. Many Polish refugees were from the 'lost territories', the eastern borderlands and in their eyes they felt they had been as badly treated as Germany and yet they had been on the winning side!

The severing of diplomatic relations between the Polish Govt in exile and the Soviets in 1943, meant that all future discussions regarding Polish matters took place between the representatives of USA, GB and USSR, without Polish representation and Poland was handed over to Stalin

On their discharge from the forces, there was provision of free passage and 56 days pay and allowances plus a war gratuity for the years of service and rank in the Polish forces while under British Command. My Dziadek was registered as being in the Army from 1941-44. Large numbers of Polish servicemen did return to Poland, approximately 105,000, their fate mostly unknown although many were put on 'show trials' in their now Soviet homeland, imprisoned or murdered.

The Polish re-settlement Act of 1947 was passed to meet the needs of the Poles and their dependants, either as a cash allowance or maintenance in the re-settlement camps. Health needs were met and registration was given to Polish Pharmacists and Doctors to practice in Britain. These measures identified the Poles as a special case which caused some ill feeling in the Labour Govt and wider public, in a post war England suffering many shortages and rationing. Ignoring the fact that Poland had more than shared the efforts put into winning the war against the Germans.

**Mieczysław** was born on 15th September 1923 in Dermanka in the Wołyn region of eastern Poland (now Ukraine) he had 4 sisters and his father was an Osadnik (military settler) who had been appointed a forest ranger. The war put a cruel stop to all his ambitions when the Red Army invaded in September 1939 and occupied the area.

On 10th February the whole family were deported and he remembers the words of the soldiers who came to his home in the deep of the night, 'you've got 20 minutes, get something to eat, get something to keep you warm.' He recalls they were taken to the train station about 22km away and packed into cattle wagons, about 50 people per wagon, they didn't know where they were to be taken. They travelled for about 2 weeks and kept alive by only a bowl of hot soup served once a day. At the end of the train journey they were put onto sledges, some walking at the side, on the journey to the camp which was to the west of the Ural Mountains, Derowetka (my family were also in that camp) in the Arkhangelsk region and here they lived in barracks with a number of families sharing each hut. Living conditions were very crowded, they worked in the forest cutting trees and wood from 7am to 7pm. Each worker received 400gms of bread a day, 200gms for those who stayed in the barracks.

After the 'amnesty' in June 1941 Mieczysław was allowed to leave to join the Polish army. It was a complicated journey, many families were diverted by the NKVD to further forced labour picking cotton for the Uzbeks. Transport was later arranged taking them to the port of Krasnovodosk on the Caspian Sea and across to Pahlevi in Persia. By February 1942 he had joined the Polish army and much of 1942 and 1943 was spent training in Egypt. Late in 1943 the army embarked for Taranto in southern Italy and he fought throughout the Italian campaign, including Monte Cassino and was with the troops when they took Bologna in 1945.

Only 3 out of 7 of his family survived, his mother and father died in Russia and also two of his sisters. His other 2 sisters spent 5 years in India. He arrived in Liverpool with his army unit in September 1946, 'it was horrible, the terrible rain after the sunshine of Italy and sometimes so foggy.' His sisters soon arrived from India and were located in a resettlement camp in Lancashire. He met his wife when visiting them and got married in Preston. The family moved to Birmingham where job opportunities were better but they experienced some 'hostility and snubs from the locals and landlords.'

The family settled and became productive and enjoyed being members of the Polish community.

**Zofia** was born in 1928 in a small village near to Drohiczyn in the Polesie region. A child of Osadnicy, military settlers, who were given land on the eastern borderlands in recognition of their participation in WW1 and then the Bolshevik War. Life she remembers was very good on the land and her father had been made mayor of a town close to the farm.

'It all came to an abrupt end when war broke out with the German bombs and then the Russians harassing the Polish population'. The fateful day of 10th February 1940 arrived which severed their connection with their homeland. In the depth of that very cold winter they were only given 20 minutes to pack and told they were to be sent to Siberia. They were taken to the train station and put into cattle wagons. The journey took about 3 weeks and they were only given 1 bowl of weak soup a day. Zofia was just 11.

In the camp people were allocated various jobs in the forest, cutting down trees, cutting logs, loading and transporting them to the railway line. Hard labour, disease and starvation were the norm. One day someone turned up at the camp and asked them 'what are you doing here, don't you know that there's an 'amnesty.' Russia is at war with Germany.'

This was excellent news but logistically, organising the now free Poles scattered all over the vast Russian steppes and getting them to the Polish army, was a formidable task. It was the autumn of 1941 and their journeys in the trains and trucks in the freezing temperatures would be a constant worry as was finding food but they eventually arrived in Bukhara in Uzbekistan. Her grandmother was very ill from lack of food and died from starvation.

The family then became separated, her father left to join the army and typhoid struck her mother and brother and disease and starvation continued. The family somehow made it to Krasnovodsk on the Caspian Sea but were too late for the boat so had to go back to Bukhara and she joined the scouts. They eventually did get onto a boat bound for Pahlevi and then onto Tehran. After recovery they were sent onto a camp in Kampala where food was plentiful and nutritious. Her father had arrived in England in very bad health, it was now 1948 and Zofia and her family were sent to England by plane.

They were in a resettlement camp called Daglingworth near Cirencester then moved onto Northwick camp near Moreton-in-Marsh. They were finally reunited with their father and brother who was in the RAF.'

She ended up as a teacher and like all post war Poles settled and worked, married and had families and became involved in the now growing Polish community. They were well adjusted and fully integrated into their new country, determined to make the most of the opportunities offered to them. Like all Poles new to the country, they made a meaningful contribution.

It was hot in Pahlevi when Paulina and family landed after 3 days, and it was now August 1942 and her father was taken straight to hospital in Tehran. 'We were all washed down and given clothes and then transported to Tehran.' Her mother was also ill and was taken to hospital, Paulina went to look for her father but she was exhausted and collapsed and the medics took her into the hospital. She finally found her father, his face was yellow and he was very ill but he recognised her.

Her father left hospital and joined the army, she, her mother and sister went to Ahwaz and from there to India. 'Once there we were divided into groups and we went to east Africa to Masindu' and in the camp her mother and sister fell ill with malaria, her mother was reduced to 42kg and they received much needed medical help.

When the war had finished they wanted to go back to Poland but her father didn't think it was a good idea as they had nothing to go back to. They went instead to England and to a resettlement camp in Cambridge and her sisters to special schools to learn English and get qualifications quickly.

The family lived and worked in Cambridge for a time and then the Midlands. She and her future husband had 7 children and kept strongly to their Polish traditions taking a very active part in the Polish community.

**Michalina** born 30th November 1926 in Ciepliwoda, her parents had moved there as military settlers after the Polish-Russian war of 1921.

Life was turned upside down in February 1940 when her mother turned up at the school accompanied by a Russian soldier and tearfully told her she had to leave school because the family were being deported. That evening they were told to pack and were taken to the railway station, packed into cattle wagons with many other thousands.

Into the bitterly cold snowy weather they travelled for about 3 weeks, travelling mainly at night stopping in the middle of nowhere. They eventually arrived at a camp at Gorodok Poldniewica in the Vologda region, where my family were also taken to. They were to find out that previously the occupants had been the Tatars, deported there many years ago by the Tsar and had all died. It was winter when everything was frozen and bitterly cold, they were given a bread allowance and the amount depended on how much work they did.

Her father was skilled at making furniture and he organised a group of men with similar skills and they were able to earn some money and also work indoors away from the severe frost. Until illness struck, the family lived as well as they could but her father and mother, 2 brothers and sister-in-law got ill with typhoid which was terribly painful.

At the 'amnesty' in 1941 they were able to leave the camp. Many young men left to join the army but her remaining family needed money for food and found work on a farm and were given meat in exchange. Her mother spent time preparing food and in November 1941 they left travelling south east to Uzbekistan. It took a month travelling only by night. Reaching Uzbekistan they had to work in the cotton fields for 9 months in order to subsist, waiting for transport to the Caspian Sea. Michalina contracted malaria and was very weak and ill for many months. By August 1942 the order came to take them to Persia and they were taken by train to Krasnovodsk on the Caspian Sea. 'We were terribly thirsty and some boys were selling water like gold dust, but we had little money so we only had one small bottle between 4 girls.'

When they landed at Pahlevi, it was beautiful, clean beaches and clear water. They were stripped of their clothes which were burned because of infestation, their heads were shaved and they all had a bath. The men's trousers they were given had to be tied on to them as they were far too big, they had lost so much weight.

They spent time in hospital in Tehran to treat malaria and then moved to a transit camp in Ahwaz. They were there for 2 years until moving to Palestine with the cadets. Here the climate suited her better after suffering for so long with malaria.

They were eventually transported to England, from Egypt to Liverpool and were put in an American ex army camp in Foxley. After education and taking their A levels, finding jobs was the next thing, some found work in factories and some of the girls went to Wales to work as nurses.

**Jan, Julian, Jadwiga, Bolesław** all born between 1919 and 1927 in central Poland or in the eastern borderlands of Poland. Children of military settlers and living on the Osada's of the Kresy region. Exiled to Siberia by the Russians or to France and Germany by the Germans to work as hard labour. Taken by their oppressors and given very little time to pack before being loaded onto trucks or trains.

After the 'amnesty' they were free to go if they were on Russian soil, as they couldn't go back to Poland they headed south to join up with the Polish army in Tehran. Many spent time there recovering and working for up to 3 years, before being sent onto Lebanon to make room for other refugees.

They eventually came to England and were in resettlement camps before finding work or education. In the case of some of the refugees in earlier arrivals, they had travelled onto Blackpool to join the Polish Air Force base training there before fighting in the Battle of Britain.

There was no returning to their homeland. All property, farmland had been burned to the ground by either the Germans or the Russians. The lands of the Kresy razed into a wilderness. The messages coming from Poland and other Poles was that life under the new regime was not good, although this was not generally known to the wider British public.

I've included some personal recollections more specific to living under the Soviets after they had taken over the eastern borderlands, from those who lived through it. Recollections from individual Sybiraks, who had settled on the Osada's and worked the land after the 1921 Bolshevik War. Single military men in their 20's without a roof over their heads on an empty grassland with no farm buildings, agricultural implements or life-stock, who were faced with farming the land from scratch.

These recollections are mostly in their own words with some amendments for grammar and they give an insight into how the Soviets were 'welcomed' into Poland, who played an active part in the deportation of the settlers, who took over their empty properties and who collaborated with the Germans and the Russians, in the lootings, killings of entire villages, and the genocide by the UPA.

The majority of Byelorussians were quite friendly, benefitting from work on the settlers' Osada's, as did many of the other ethnic communities. The problems occurred from the communists within the Jewish, Ukrainian and Byelorussian communities once the Soviets arrived in the Borderlands.

Helped mainly by these communists, livestock and cereals, potatoes, almost everything from the land, farm buildings and homes were taken by the 'Soviets' from the Polish settlers.

The make up of the communities was reflected in the schools within the Osada's, Polish, Byrlorussian, Tartar, Jewish, Lithuanian and Ukrainian. There were scout groups and many other multinational social gatherings.

**Janina** from the Osada Krechowiecka, from where my own family lived, says 'there were only 9,000 military settlers and many civilians including their families, up to 4500 and 1 in 5 of those settlers deported were from military families. On 10th February 1940 the number of families taken was 26.790 made up of 139.286 people. Before the war there was much help between the many different groups but then the conflicts began.'

**Maria** from Osada Budowla, 'the Bolshevik agents under orders of the Soviet command, incited the killing and beating by the Byelorussians and brutal executions, people and children buried alive and Polish soldiers shot.'

**Dr Wladysław**, from Osada Bortnica, '1941 German units heading eastwards towards Russia on the Dubno-Rowne Road began imposing a new order with the Ukrainian militia with repressions of the Jewish population of Dubno and other nearby towns and repressions against Poles with massacres of 50 people by Ukrainians. By 1944 the Red army had crossed into Dubno with heavy battles through January and February and all Osadas were razed to the ground to hide that Poles had lived there.'

**Bronisława** from Osada Mackzkowce 'the Ukrainians began to strut about sure of their importance and the Jews were building numerous welcoming triumphal arches without hiding their feelings, they joyfully embraced the units of the Soviet Military as they thanked them for saving them from the Polish capitalists and bourgeoisie'.

**Felicja**, from Osada Ostrowska from the book, Leaves in the Wind, 'Communist Poland never allowed it to be admitted that the borderlanders were deported, nothing was said about the misery and the many deaths, starvation and abuse.'

**Wanda**, from Osada Pilsudczyzna 'the population was mixed Polish, German and Ukrainian. After the deportations the Ukrainians who had also assisted in the deportations, became very haughty to the Poles, their brutality was at its height following the Germans heading eastwards towards

Russia in 1941. Gangs of Ukraianian militia robbed and murdered the Poles. Hipolitowka was encircled by them and houses doused with petrol and set alight. All perished, with the escapees mowed down by machine gun fire. One uncle saved relatives but was murdered, mutilated with his eyes put out and his chest slashed. One uncle's body was never found.'

**Stanisław**, from Osada Ulanowka 'there were many refugees from the west, petrified and in a daze. Explosions were heard from Brzese, from bombs and anti aircraft fire, villages were alight. Soviet army entered and the Germans withdrew. Jews were welcoming the Soviets with arches and the Byelorussians and Ukrainians were 'settling old scores'. Arrests began and many settlers were imprisoned. Agitation had arisen with various groups coming together, stripping their 'liberated country' naked.'

**Zofia**, from Osada Adampol 'as soon as the Soviets arrived the local population who had seemed well disposed towards us changed. They felt that they had Soviet backing and harassment began as well as robbery and arson attacks. Settlers were shot and it was even worse at night. Food, possessions, many things were taken leaving nothing to feed the family.'

**Waclaw** from Osada Kuchczyce, '... those perfidious Belorussians and Jews began constructing arches of welcome for the encroaching Soviet army, some Jews put red arm bands on their sleeves and having been assimilated into the NKVD, denounced Polish patriots to the Soviets. They would have the same punishment meted out to them by the NKVD'.

**Zygmunt** from Osada Chrynow, '...that very next morning Poles were murdered by Ukrainians in the church at Chrynow and in many neighbouring civilian villages such as Kalusow. I can remember a frightened woman running down the country lane calling out to me, 'they are murdering' ....... Among those killed were my uncle Ignacy, his daughter Stefania and my godmother and once the Ukrainians had discovered them in the attic, the neighbour and his children. Also murdered in the church were the priest, Eliza and others..... In July 1943 in the village of Kalusow the Ukrainians herded together all the men and women in the barns where they were killed.'

**Halina** from Osada Niechniewicze, 'the most worrying concern was weapons, which Mother had hidden away and for which the Soviets constantly searched. With a sudden rattling on the door in the middle of the night which would alert everyone, we children would cry and Mother would be put up against a wall and threatened with a rifle. Very often those involved were not Soviet soldiers but Belorussians. ...on 10th February 1940 at 2 o'clock in the morning we were all roused and started crying, in strode two NKVD men and 4

Belorussians, one of them read out something in Russian which none of us could understand. One of the locals asserted that we were an undesirable element in the locality and were to be resettled in some nearby province. It's more than evident that local peasants knew exactly what was in store for us'.

'Soviet troops confiscated everything, horses, cattle, sheep and our supply of food. There were constant checks and searches for arms. What an army they were. Hungry, clad in tatters and with outright threats and petty annoyances from 17th Sept to 10th Feb when we left. Most were Byelorussians to whom my parents had shown great generosity and they took everything they could carry from the house and farm buildings and were involved with the Soviets on 10th Feb to arrest us. Although four of them helped us to take bedding, clothing and footwear and carried them out to the sledges.'

**Edward** from Osada Kuchczyce, 'In Lachowicze I bumped into a Jew from Kleck who delivered apples to the station and gave him a little money to take me back with him on his cart. In my conversation with him I had to be very careful because a large number of poor Jews were committed to communism and in the towns the majority of commissars were Soviet Jews. Lots of people who had been sympathetic towards communism had the scales taken from their eyes as they realised they had fallen into a trap. There were quite a number of people mainly Belorussians and Jews who had constructed welcoming arches for the invading Red Army and for some their reward was deportation to Siberia and Kazakhstan.'

**Wladysław** from Osada Budowla, '17th September arrived and the road was filled with tanks, lorries pulling trailers, horses being ridden without saddles, in such a manner was the entrance of the Red Army while at the same time Belorussians prowled through the villages. They sported red arm bands on their sleeves and the rifles and boots confiscated from the Polish soldiers who had retreated from the Germans. These peasants claimed to aid in 'the liberation from the Polish masters', in fact anarchy reigned and news broke that 11 settlers from Lerypol had been murdered and buried in the forest by Belorussians from Ogrodniki village.......'. The Byelorussians who stood up for the Poles were threatened with murder and many settlers from Osada Budowla and Osada Lerypol, approx. 25, were also murdered.'

**Zofia**, from Osada Nowosiolki, 'the military settlers were drawn from a wide disparity of social class yet lived in amity quite well. The relationship between the settlers and the indigenous people was more than acceptable, one must nevertheless admit that among the locals there was an element hostile to the Poles, especially towards the military families. There was destruction of crops and animals, frequent threats of murder which later proved too true, encouraged by Bolshevik propaganda among Byelorussian communists.'

**Alicja** from Osada Chrynow, 'We reached Poland in 1946 and only two of my mother's brothers Piotr and Julian were awaiting us. My grandparents, her sister Weronika and brother Felix were murdered by the Ukrainian UPA units in July 1943.

And from **Christine**, a personal account of her father Wladyslaw who lived in Hraine with his godparents, wife Janina and two sons, who came home in April 1943 after fighting with the partisans. He had heard the stories of Ukrainians murdering Poles and of villages being burned

'The UPA began their murders in the village of Hraine which was mostly Ukrainian and ¼ Poles. It was brutal. His sons Julian 8 and Roman 5 were beheaded as were all the children in the village. Women were nailed to barn doors, it was horrific and his godmother was tied to a chair and daggers were thrown at her. His godfather with his hands tied behind his back was made to kneel and had his tongue nailed to the table.

Some of the villagers had their hands tied with ropes and the UPA on horseback pulled their limbs apart. People were burned alive, cruelty beyond belief. Wladyslaw had been hidden by a Ukrainian friend and a cousin, from the killers in a pile of manure, he escaped to the woods and never came back.'

All the properties vacated by the deportees were instantly taken over by former 'neighbours' from the Byelorussian, Ukrainian and Jewish groups. My family had barely got onto the sledge taking them to the station when their property was seized.

**Zofia**, from Osada Chlewiszcze 'the 'Soviets' were constantly searching homes, taking possessions, hay, potatoes, cereal, furniture. They would just arrive and take what they wanted as the Soviet admin had been established so quickly. Arson and raids began on the farms and settlers' houses, with arrests and burning down of farms. A general election was held and all settlers were collected and taken to vote as Soviet citizens,'

The Germans and Soviets incited the UPA, to a point, to murder the Poles although historically the Ukrainian UPA wanted 'their land' back and needed very little encouragement, lauded by the Ukraine to this day.

The common theme throughout these recollections is the way the mostly communist element turned against the Polish settlers, after having lived and worked amongst them for so many years. It seems obvious that the intent of that element was to 'settle old scores' in order to 'get their land, back'.

These many recollections were from the Polish refugees living in England who would eventually become British citizens under the Aliens Registration Act of 1929. Before then they had to register in a Police station every time they moved houses, or visited relatives, or changed jobs and this continued until 1962.

I have detail of the movement of my own Grandparents from 1948 to 1962, logged in their Aliens Pass Books.

They had gone through very similar hardships and made England their home, made an immense contribution to their own and English communities and were also sending parcels to their own families and orphanages in Poland until the 1990's.

They had suffered for Poland, been happy in Poland and helped their homeland whilst living in England. Most of the Poles here after the war have been happy, making new lives for themselves, they are grateful to England. They began here in resettlement camps, and set up Polish schools. The risk of returning to Poland was high, conditions for families were difficult under Soviet rule.

'I felt a stranger there, you could feel the atmosphere of occupation' said relatives upon visiting their sisters who had remained in or gone back to Poland. Family members would be imprisoned by the new Soviet regime for the most spurious of reasons. Many returnees were accused of being spies and arrested, went through sham 'trials' and sent to labour camps or gulags, those who had been Partisans as very many had been, met worse fates.

Kazia and Adam, my Babcia and Dziadek, died in England within a year of each other in 1983 and 1984. It's a long time ago but I will never forget them. Their homeland Poland had been chilled to the marrow by Stalin's invasion and taken over by Communism, they could not go back. They were in Lebanon in 1946 with their son Janusz, waiting for permission to join their daughters Alicja and Jasia who had earlier travelled to England. Alicja with her English husband and Jasia to Teacher Training College.

In England, the Attlee Government was hesitant to allow more dependants into the U.K. and was writing to Polish servicemen asking them to go home! By early 1947 however their prospects looked brighter with the Polish Resettlement Act, the first ever mass immigration legislation of a British Parliament. They would soon be able to make arrangements to join their daughters. They arrived in February 1948 having waited 18 months for permission.

They had heard of the difficulties of returning to their homeland, from relatives of those who had been met with aggression from the Soviets. They would be treated as 'dissidents' as Adam was ex Military (British Army 1941-44 and Polish Cavalry 1915-1921). Being deported by Stalin in 1940 to the USSR would also be a black mark against them, their future in Poland would be dire.

Dissidents, were classified as the Polish' intelligentsia', or what remained of it. Stalin had murdered most of them shortly after he invaded Poland, Teachers, Professors, Lawyers, Doctors, Military, Students, Priests, actors and many others. They would be deprived of their professions, forbidden to study or to travel. If they joined the Communist Party they might survive in the most menial of jobs, porters, railway workers, cleaners in schools and apartment blocks, porters in stations or be left to their own devices. Most likely they would be 're-educated' in another gulag.

They would be treated as criminals for uttering the wrong word, reading the wrong book or newspaper, simply for thinking freely. My grandparents would not have survived under Soviet control, it had been difficult in the labour camps and having fought against the Russians in the Polish-Soviet war (1919-1921) my Dziadek would most likely have been sent to a gulag or worse. My Babcia would probably be sent with him and I would never have known my 'dissident' grandparents.

The Secret Police were in control, even the trees in the parks were bugged, seems ridiculously extreme but this was Stalin's Communism, this was now Poland, ally of the UK and USA, sold out to Stalin. Files were kept on 'dissidents' and those of 'interest' and the NKVD policed the border between what was permitted and what was forbidden they saw enemies everywhere. Any deviance from the 'norm' was quickly dealt with.

People would inform on a person of 'importance' a neighbour even. Friends betrayed friends although the situation was not as brutal as in East Germany where the Stasi, 12 times bigger than the Gestapo and 35 times bigger than the NKVD was in complete charge. WIth an army of informers at their disposal to keep notes on 6 ml people, files which stretched 125 miles! It seems quite incredulous but that is Communism.

Loss of personal freedoms with no individual liberties, where the government controls everything and where all goods are 'equally' shared by the people, although from conversations with friends of mine who have lived through Communism, the practice is very different. Most goods are shared by the controlling totalitarian government employees and little gets to the ordinary people! When the ordinary people queue for hours at the shops the shelves are bare, cleared by those on the other side of the counter!

It took another war to eventually defeat Communism across Europe, the Cold War instigated by Stalin in 1947 which created tension between democracies of the western world and Communist countries of eastern Europe. It wasn't until post 1989 that ordinary people eventually overcame the unfairness of the regimes, the corruption of the few, the persecution by the few and the growing riches for the few.

The ignorance about Poland in WW2, especially in the media, about her role as an Ally and her Resistance is astonishing. When it comes to the question of Polish conduct under powerful, brutal, German and Russian occupations, it is treated as a sideshow to Jewish suffering, overlooked.

The world of WW2 was one in which it was easier to hide the truth, London and Washington have obscured the facts for very many years, of the Polish citizens exiled to the wastes of Siberia, 'advised' not to talk about it when they were safely in Iran! After so long it is unforgiveable that the truth is still hidden and in many cases misused by revisionists to spread misinformation.

With the children of the Sybiracy becoming more involved in their family history and with the writings of just one prominent historian, Norman Davies; who has written comprehensive books on this maligned and misunderstood country; one by one the planks are being knocked down but it is a battle for the truth.

My Mother Alicja is 97 and suffers from Alzheimers and her moods are unpredictable but she was happy when I last saw her. It took some time to decipher what she said due to her speech as she told me she remembered how 'we survived the camps, we got out, we got out as a family, all of us, safely, we were so lucky, I am so happy, life is wonderful'. You can imagine the impact it had on me, there were much needed tissues to hand.

My family was very lucky to have found refuge in England. They missed their homeland dreadfully but they had survived the labour camps and the long, arduous journeys from the USSR towards the Polish Army, as a unit and they lived out their lives as free people.

*Alicja is my darling most loving Mother,*
*together with Kazia, my inspiration for*
*setting pen to paper to record the family story.*
*This is for her, for Babcia and Dziudziu,*
*for Ciocia Jasia and Wujek Janusz,*
*for Wujek Walery, Ciocia Ziuta, Włodek,*
*Zbyszek and Marysia,*
*the Góral's and the Radomski's,*
*my family, they are not forgotten.*

Teresa Radomska 2021

Poland 1916–1940

# The Radomski Bloodline

Radomski Family 1930

# CHAPTER 12 – Radomski-Góral bloodline

Władysław Radomski - 1917

Adam Góral - 1917

Tolus Radomski - 1917

Adam Góral
& Walery Radomski - 1917

Walery Radomski 1919

Ziuta Radomska - 1919

Tolus, Bronia, Kazia, Walery,
friend - c1917-18

# CHAPTER 12 – Radomski-Góral bloodline

Walery, Kazia, & Bronia
Radomscy – 1918

Kazia & Adam Góral – 1920

Władysław Radomski – 1920

Ziuta & Kazia – 1919

Walery Radomski – 1918

## CHAPTER 12 – Radomski-Góral bloodline

Jasia Góral - Równe 1935

Góralowie - 1936

Parish Church - Równe

Adam, Gienia, Kazia & Janusz

Ziuta & Marysia Radomska - 1937

# CHAPTER 12 – Radomski-Góral bloodline

Osada Krechowiecka – 1937

Janusz – 1938

Równe 1937
Kazia with Ala, Janusz and Jasia

Ala, Halina, Jasia, Janusz
Osada Krechowiecka 1938

Janusz & Adam Góral – Równe 1936

Janusz with Kazia – Równe 1936

Ala & Janusz Góral – Równe 1938

Równe 1939
Kazia & Adam with Janusz

Ala Góral – Równe 1938

Ala Góral – Równe 1938

Jasia - Palestine 1944

Ala - Teheran 1943

Teheran 1943

Jasia & Adam - Palestine 1943

Ala, Jasia - Pahlevi 1942

Ala at the sick bay – Teheran 1943

Kazia, Ala, Janusz, Adam – Teheran 1943

Ala & Kazia – Isfahan 1944

Kazia – Isfahan 1944

Mosque – Isfahan

Jasia – Nazareth 1943

Jan, Kazia, Adam, Ala – Teheran 1943

Janusz – Teheran 1943

Ala, Janusz, Ziuta, Kazia, Marysia – Teheran 1943

Isfahan 1944

Adam, Włodek & Walery – Teheran 1943

Ala & Bill – Isfahan 1944

Ala & Kazia – Isfahan 1944

CHAPTER 12 – Radomski-Góral bloodline

Ala – Teheran 1944

Ala – Teheran 1944

Ala & Bill – Teheran 1944

Ala, Janusz, Kazia – Isfahan 1944

Ala & Jasia – Gazir 1945

Ala & Jasia – Gazir 1945

Ala & Bill – Gazir 1945

Bill – between Khanaqin, Iraq and Kermanshah, Persia 1945

1st Xmas together since 1942 – Ghazir, 13 Dec 1945

The Wedding – Ghazir, Lebanon 1946

Passports & Certificates of Registration for Adam & Kazia Góral

Alien's Order A128295 & A128294 – 1948

Necessary paperwork for our grandparents to enter England

Jasia - 1949

Kazia & Adam - 1948

Janusz - 1949

Bolesław, Jasia, Ala, Janusz - Kew Gardens 1949

Jasia & Bolesław - Victoria, 1949

Janusz, Jasia, Bolesław - London 1949

# CHAPTER 12 – Radomski-Góral bloodline

Bill, Ala & Walery – 1951

Bolesław & Jasia – Wedding, Victoria, 1949

Walery – 195?

Bolesław & Jasia – Wedding, Victoria, 1949

Marysia, Wiesiek – Wedding, Brompton, 1950

Lytham St Annes 1952

Alec - Lytham, 1952

Alec & Janusz - Victoria c1952

Alec & Jasia - Victoria, London 1953

Teri, Alec, Tony, Chris - 1956

Alec, Tony & Teri - Victoria, London, 1952

Kazia & Adam with Ala & Grandchildren - 1956

Brixton - 1957

Sisters Kazia & Gienla - Brixton, 1957

Wiesiek, Marysia, Wlodek, Walery, Gienia, Marek, Kazia - 1957

Janusz & Pam Reception - Chelsea, 1956

Janusz & Pam Wedding - Clapham, 1956

Halina & Wiesiek Morawiec - c1959

## CHAPTER 12 – Radomski-Góral bloodline

Adam - c1963

Jasia & Bruno Wedding 1966

Janusz - Bedford Hotel c1965

Jasia & Bruno Wedding 1966

Alec - Wedding 1972

Adam & Kazia - 1976

Adam & Kazia - Streatham c1976

Ala with Adam & Kazia - c1979

Alec & Hazel - Wedding 1972

Ala 1985

Janusz with
Queen Mother -
Savoy Hotel c1982

Pamela, Ala & Jasia 1980

Ala & Bill

Adam & Kazia - c1980

Ala, Janusz, Jasia

Ala & Chris 1992

Anita, Tim, Hazel, Alec

Ala, Stan, Jean, Janusz, Jasia

Jasia & Stan

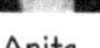

Anita

Tony & Chris

Ania, Anita, Ewa, Hazel

Wiesiek & Marcin

Jean, Jasia, Ala

Jasia & Ania

Alec, Hazel, Chris

Ania, Wiesiek & Ewa

Ala & Teri

Janina & Wiesiek

Lynsey

Hazel, Ania, Alec, Anita

Chris & Jana

Ania & Ewa

Nicola, Ala & Nella

Ania, Alec & Ewa

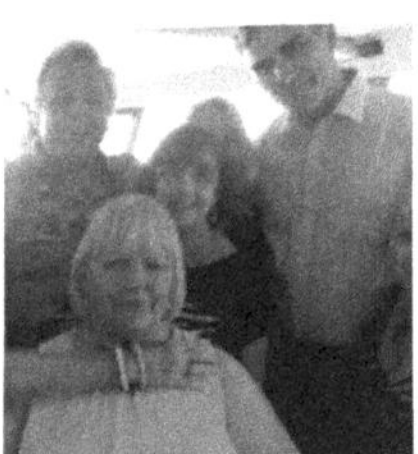

Alec, Ania, Hazel & Ed

Steve, Ania, Marek, Tony

Ewa, Ania, Anita, Krysia

Lynsey & Anthony

Tony & Hazel

Anita & Wiesiek

Nicola, Natalie, Margaret

Emma & Daniel

Krysia

Ala & Halina

Chris, Anita & Margaret

Tony with sons Will, Jon & Dan

The
2010s
A social revolution.

Margaret & Teri

Tony & Anne

Alec & Marek

Alec & Anita

Chris & Jana

Natalie & Ala

Ala 95th

Alec, Ala & Teri

Maciej

The
2010s
A social revolution.

Will & Trinia

Ania & Alec

Tony & Anne

Alec & Chris

Nicola, Ala & Natalie

Ala

Alec & Teri

Halina & Ala

Chris, Hazel, Ania, Teri, Nicola, Ewa, Natalie - at The Polish Embassy in London 2018

# *Siberian Exiles Cross Awards*

## *A very proud day for the family*

Today we are at *The Polish Embassy in London* for the Presentation Ceremony with family members.

Alicja Góral-Hartley has been awarded the Siberian Exiles Cross. Her sister, Janina Góral-Dyki-Misik, has also been awarded posthumously.

The sisters along with their parents Kazia and Adam and brother Janusz were deported in cattle wagons from Równe to a labour camp (Gulag) in northern Siberia on 10th February 1940 on Stalin's orders.

The cross is awarded in order to recognize and commemorate the sufferings of Polish citizens deported to Siberia, Kazakhstan and Northern Russia from 1939–1956 against their will.

*The cross memorializes their devotion to the ideals of freedom and independence against Communism.*

The application took over a year to process and we are grateful to Elzunia Gradosielska for locating the forms for us and Rysiek Grzybowski for his assistance in preparing the applications.

*Teresa Radomska has documented Alicja's story of events in* "Midnight Train to Siberia" – ***available from Amazon***

Ala

Ewa & Teri

Teri, Ala 95th & Tony

Jasia

Alec, Chris, Marek & Adam

Halina, Teri & Ala

Chris & Alec

Ewa, Chris, Teri, Ania, Marek, Ewa, Adam,
Alec, Elzunja, Danuta, Ryszard

Marek

Krysia

Marek, Adam, Izabella, Marcin

Ed, Alec, Marek,
Anita & Ania

Ania

Lynsey

Ivy & Nella

Ed & Anita

## CHAPTER 12 – Radomski-Góral bloodline

### The Production Team

Chris

Alec

Natalie & Ala

Teri

# Family Radomski – formerly Bielawski

Walerian Bielawski was arrested and imprisoned in Częstochowa during 1863 uprisings. Escaped prison and moved to Radzymin 30km NE of Warsaw, changing his name to Radomski. Died age 49 had 2 sons & 4 daughters (eldest Wladyslaw)

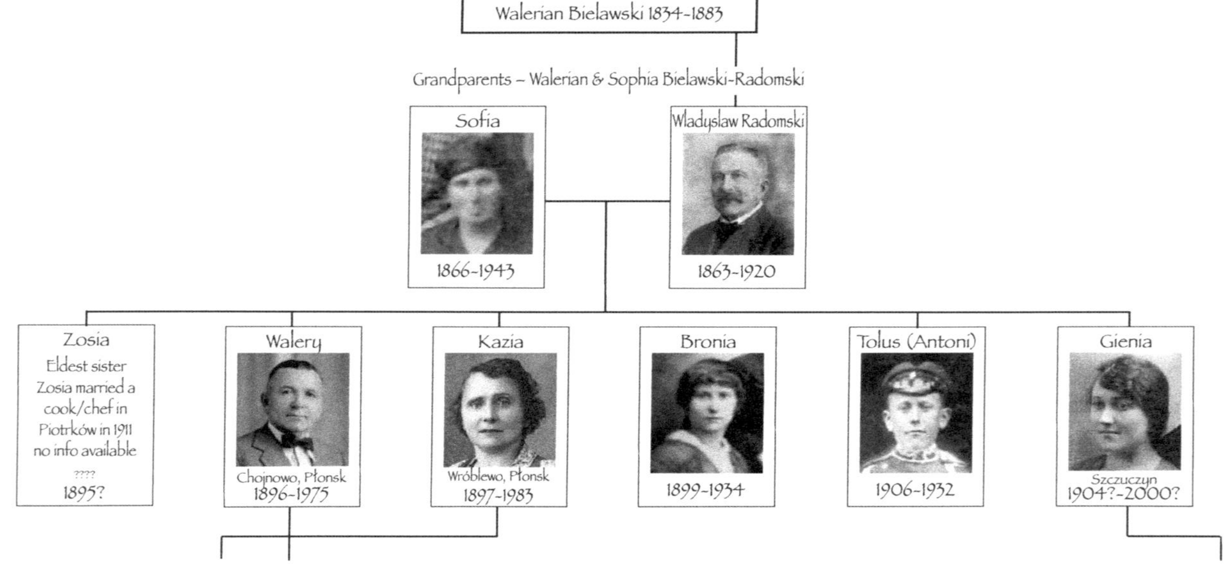

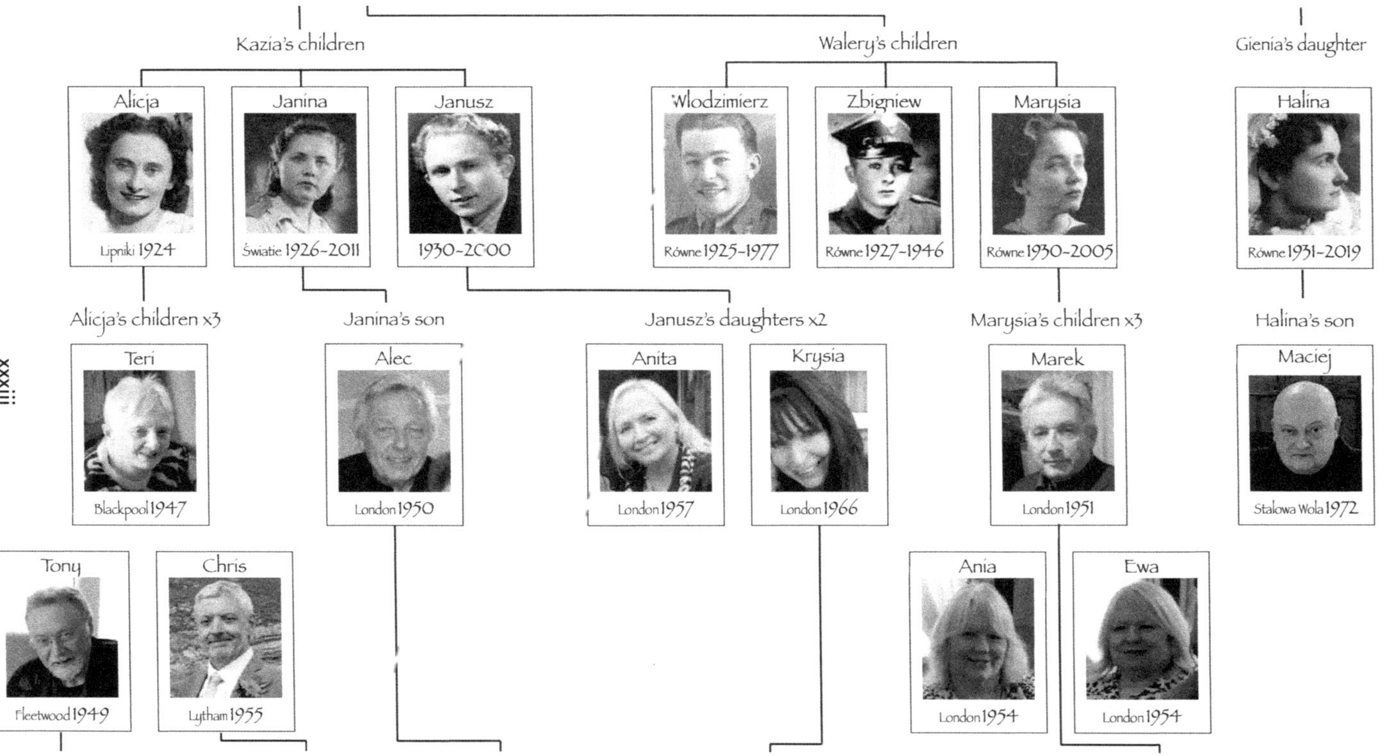

Kazia's children
Walery's children
Gienia's daughter
Alicja
Lipniki 1924
Janina
Światie 1926-2011
Janusz
1930-2000
Włodzimierz
Równe 1925-1977
Zbigniew
Równe 1927-1946
Marysia
Równe 1930-2005
Halina
Równe 1931-2019
Alicja's children x3
Janina's son
Janusz's daughters x2
Marysia's children x3
Halina's son
Teri
Blackpool 1947
Alec
London 1950
Anita
London 1957
Krysia
London 1966
Marek
London 1951
Maciej
Stalowa Wola 1972
Tony
Fleetwood 1949
Chris
Lytham 1955
Ania
London 1954
Ewa
London 1954

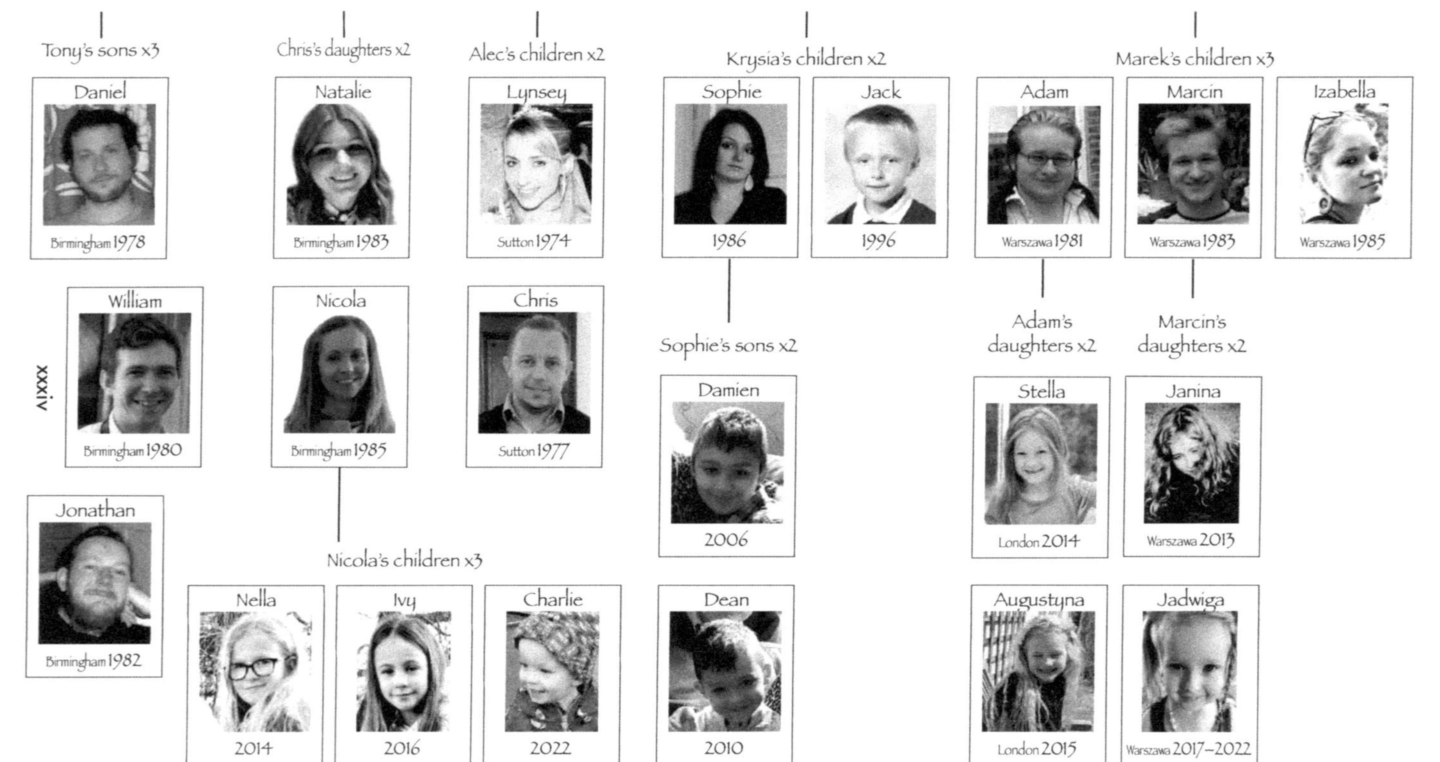
Tony's sons x3
Daniel
Birmingham 1978
William
Birmingham 1980
Jonathan
Birmingham 1982
Chris's daughters x2
Natalie
Birmingham 1983
Nicola
Birmingham 1985
Nicola's children x3
Nella
2014
Ivy
2016
Charlie
2022
Alec's children x2
Lynsey
Sutton 1974
Chris
Sutton 1977
Krysia's children x2
Sophie
1986
Jack
1996
Sophie's sons x2
Damien
2006
Dean
2010
Marek's children x3
Adam
Warszawa 1981
Marcin
Warszawa 1983
Izabella
Warszawa 1985
Adam's daughters x2
Stella
London 2014
Augustyna
London 2015
Marcin's daughters x2
Janina
Warszawa 2013
Jadwiga
Warszawa 2017–2022

CHAPTER 13

# A Brief History of Russia

Ivan the Terrible, Russia's first Tsar five centuries ago, was a tyrant who would require his subjects to refer to themselves as 'your slave' when addressing him. A similar subservience I'm sure the current 'Tsar' Putin exerts on his countrymen to this day.

On the whole, from 882 to 2024, it has been an autocracy, with its secret police, pogroms and purges, torture chambers, many thousands of gulags across its vast plains. These were already the Russian institutions by the time of the Bolshevik revolution in 1917, well before Communism.

The Russian Empire was aggressive, wired into its psyche, expansionism and warmongering. Between 1500 and 1917 it grew at 130sq km on average every day,' its land mass is huge.

Wars in Georgia and Ukraine, threats to Latvia and Poland, stem from what Russians feel is an amputation. Their nationality linked with their severed republics, their empire.

Russia's tyrannical leaders have to continue terrorising their neighboring states to maintain 'Russia's standing in the world,' which Putin fears has been eroded since WW2 and the Cold War. It's the reason for his obsession at reclaiming the many lost republics, his sacred mission, to follow in the footsteps of Stalin, his hero.

*(from an article by Lord Daniel Hannan 2024).*

When Putin invaded Crimea in 2014, in violation of its sovereignty, the West responded with a few harsh words and he rightly concluded that the West was spineless. Come 2022 he thought he could waltz into Ukraine, straight to the capital Kiev but the Ukrainians had resolve and reacted with some force and the West for once showed some purpose

There may have been sanctions imposed on Russia but the tyrant's vaults are filling with gold and diamonds from his 'African Policy,' where Putin's financial interests now lie, $2billion worth of precious metals since 2022 alone.

Helped by Western indifference, Putin takes his slice of the cake to continue funding his agenda for the rest of Europe. He just needs to wait for the West to weaken and he can then follow in the footsteps of Stalin, reclaiming that lost empire.

Germany seems to be the weakest EU link, greed mostly playing a big part in pursuing lucrative deals with Russia and China. Ignoring its debt to its eastern neighbours, 'who it fed into the meat grinder in 1939' It owes them a huge historical debt.' *(Edward Lucas 2024).*

Instead, it refuses to supply the Ukrainians with a potentially pivotal weapon, the Taurus missiles. Be ashamed Germany. East German Angela Merkel, the former Chancellor of Germany, was in thrall to Putin and the German greed, continues, beware Europe!

I cannot ignore the similarity of the most aggressive and violent tactics used by both Stalin and Putin, both bloodthirsty, warmongering, erratic men. They have manipulated the truth to their advantage and Putin has followed closely in the footsteps of Stalin's gruesome purges, with his own poisonous and murderous ones, he has learnt well.

The West needs to wake up and realise that Putin is all boast, lies and propaganda, just like the previous 'rulers' of Russia. Another 'expansionism' was on the lie that 'Ukraine is ruled by Nazis and the people must be saved!'

Stalin used that very term to invade Poland to 'save the Polish people from Hitler' so the Russian fairy tale goes!

Ukrainians are being killed in the tens of thousands, the country demolished, children kidnapped to Russian 'filtration' camps, brainwashed into 'Russian ways' like the Bolsheviks tried to do with the children in the labour camps; their identity swept away. It didn't work with the children of the Polish exiles in the labour camps, certainly not with Ciocia Jasia and Wujek Janusz.

It's a full scale invasion, a refugee crisis, a slaughter and history seems to be repeating itself with the compliance of the West and Poland and Moldovia stand in line as Putin's next likely targets. I still have family in Poland.

Putin has strongly hinted he is not planning to stop if he is victorious in Ukraine, that he is ready for a nuclear war. Yes it may be bluster but in his electioneering circus for a fifth term, he's busy with the propaganda to the Russian majority, completely under his spell.

Dissent crushed by the many comrades who helped in the landslide victory of 87%, his aggressive Police, poisoners, torturers and assassins. The young anti Putin Russians are not fooled but 'choose their words carefully in front of strangers.'

Remind one of Stalinism? All of Europe is at some risk and of the many remaining gulags across the Russian wilderness, I wonder how many are ready and waiting for Polish and other Europeans who are a 'threat to public order'a threat to Putin's evil intentions!

*'to choose one's victims, to prepare one's plans minutely, to slake an implacable vengeance and then go to bed......... There is nothing sweeter in the world' J.V. Stalin*

Stalin, that tyrannical leader with a 70% positive view amongst today's Russians, inflicted a terrible consequence on the Polish people in 1940 and I use my voice to tell that story. Other children of Sybiraks have also added their family stories to the record, we are determined to make this event known.

From Stalin's actions my family and many other Sybiraks, paid an awful penalty all of their lives, unable to return to their homeland, it weighed heavily on my family. Although the positive side is that I was raised in a loving, Polish family swept up in their embrace and culture. Although they lost absolutely everything, they did at least escape communism and had their freedom and family, I know that was some comfort.

My Mother died in early December 2023, just before Wigilia and we spent the first ever Christmas without her. It was a thoughtful, very sad time but celebrated the Polish way as always. She has left a massive gap in our lives, was so loved by her family and we miss her.

Her funeral was a celebration of her life, with family gathered from Poland, Holland, Switzerland, England and as far afield as China and she would have been so very happy to see all her family sharing loving memories, accompanied with of course the obligatory żubrowka, provided by cuzin Alec. Love for her was expressed by us all.

She was almost 100 years old. She didn't give up on life, she was strong to the end, she simply answered the call of the Kresy. A poem by a dear friend will perhaps explain it better than I can.

*Teresa Radomska,*
*proud to be your daughter 2024*

*I also honour the mothers, fathers,grand parents and children*
*left in the Russian tundra, keeping their flame burning bright*

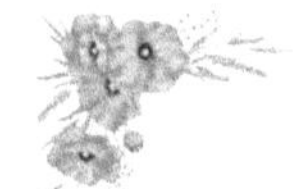

## REST IN PEACE LIL' MOUSE

In the still of the night.
The Snow came
And as if a soul far from home felt its call
A link to childhood winters that stayed
In your deepest heart
You Slipped away
Leaving memories behind

Deep in the night, silent, and soft
Calling to some hidden memory
Of a child who knew distant winter
So different to ours
Snow called you to come.

When the snow came
So long ago a memory torn.
A train ride, to dark forests
Trees to fell for a crouching bear,
While frozen hands, held in prayer
To a god who didn't seem to hear.
Yet heard in the end
The cries of survivors

When the snow came
You once laughed at those
Whose shivering at minus one
Wasn't winter, not knowing
What minus 30 feels like.
But then you had good boots,
Warm clothes and only shivered
at memories

Then the snow came
Quiet as a little mouse
You slipped away
A memory of a young woman
Searching the faces in a host
Searching for one
Reunited, journey on
Let the snow come
Let the snow come

— *Rowan Annette Mills*

***In Loving Memory***
MARIA ALICJA GÓRAL HARTLEY
19th February 1924 – 2nd December 2023

## Author's Notes

Can anyone imagine being woken in the middle of the night by gun toting aggressors breaking into your home? You're stunned, have very little time to absorb what's going on, although those dark clouds had been on the horizon for some weeks!

Your children are terrified and you have to follow, to the letter, the orders screamed at you from the uninvited, aggressive, Soviets.

In this memoir I have outlined an unimaginable experience of horror and survival. Of a Polish family deprived of their liberty and exiled with 1.7millionl of their countrymen by Stalin to the remotest regions of the USSR. A real event, still mostly hidden in the deep vaults of WW2 history.

We have a voice to tell the truth, to bring to light real events. Or, as I've found whilst researching my family story, there are those, who 'modify' events to suit almost any narrative!

Many dishonest voices are trying to hide the truth behind fiction, for their own ends. I've covered this in the sequel to this memoir in ***'Hurricanes of Polish Fury.'***

It's in our power to make a difference, if we choose to and I hope I've been able to do that with the telling of an event of WW2, unknown to very many.

The world of WW2 was one in which it was easier to hide the truth and London and Washington have also obscured the facts of the Polish citizens' exiled to the wastes of Siberia, ever since.

This story came to life because I needed to know what had happened to my family. I knew some of the detail but would have to delve carefully into the horrors they had gone through.

I started the delicate task of prompting those memories of so long ago. I began by talking with the only two surviving members of my family. My Mum (Mamusia) Alicja and my dahlink Aunt (Ciocia) and god mother, Jasia.

My family was just one of very many traumatized by Stalin's invasion of their homeland, on the pretext of saving the Polish nation from the Germans.

Today, a Russian 'Tsar' is doing something similar in the Ukraine, which according to him is in dire need of assistance to rid the country of Nazis!

My Mum and I had many times over the years revisited all that I'd remembered from childhood and onwards. When I had sat with my grandparents Kazia and Adam, listening to what made them laugh and what sometimes made them take a deep breath and go quiet for minutes on end.

Their eyes and thoughts going to what I later found out to be a very distant, isolated and painful place. I'll always remember my Babcia's gaze.

It was often like this when the family got together after they had settled in England. Their meetings were frequent despite the distances between the south and north of England. They needed to physically keep contact and after the many thousands of miles travelled after their escape from Russia, what's a few hundred more! I've never forgotten those get togethers.

Over the years I had made lots of notes and filed them away, which along with memories of many chats, I had to put into some order before I started writing the story of my family's exile to the Arkhangelsk Oblast.

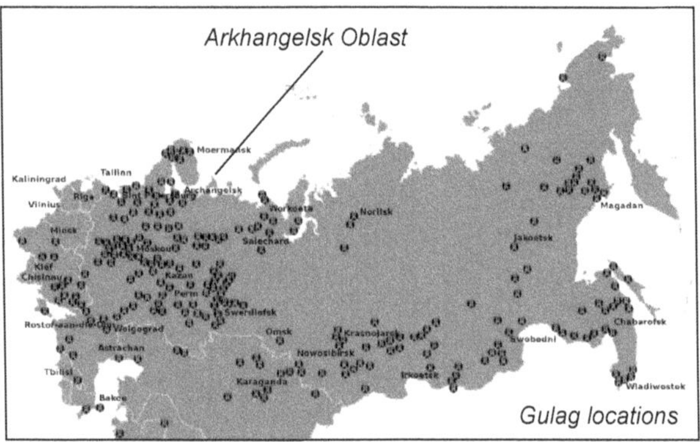

Gulag locations

In 2003, I gave my Mum some writing pads and asked her to make a note of everything she remembered. From the moment the NKVD had charged into their lives with bayonets fixed and arrested them at their home in Równe, in the eastern borderlands of Poland.

I told her that her family, her daughter and sons especially, needed to know their history, it was important, our heritage. My Mum was a little hesitant but I left her with something to think about.

Stalin had decided the Polish were a 'threat to public order' especially those across the eastern borderlands, the military settlers, having fought and won against the Bolsheviks in 1921. They would be a problem in his aim to spread communism to the West through Poland. They had to be removed.

My Mum had thought about our conversation and she started writing and couldn't stop, despite crying each time she went into the events of that particular day, then into all the other days spent in the Russian wilderness. It was so deeply burned into her memory, more suppressed than she had realized.

*Joseph Vissarionovich Stalin*

She knew how important it was to get Poland's long ignored WW2 story on the record. To tell how her beloved country had been invaded not just by the Germans and Russians in 1939 but by the blood thirsty Ukrainian insurgents, the UPA, who began ethnic cleansing the Polish people across the Kresy in 1943.

The eastern borderlands, reclaimed by Poland after WW1, was made up of Byelorussian, Ukrainian, Tatar, Jewish and Lithuanian communities.

*'Who were well disposed towards us but it all changed with Soviet backing.'*

*'Ukrainians, Jews and Bylerussians didn't hide their feelings, joyfully embracing the incoming Soviets for saving them from the Polish capitalists and bourgeoise. Many assimilated into the NKVD and with the Soviets, assisted, with enthusiasm, in the deportations of the Polish settlers.'*

The many thousands in the eastern borderlands who had not been deported, 'were barbarically murdered. Babies nailed to trees, people mutilated, women and children buried alive by the UPA.' (Chapter 11).

*Lipniki, my Mother's birthplace scene of a massacre*

The UPA needed little encouragement, they wanted 'their land' back. Were determined to wipe out any existence of the Polish and anarchy reigned, *'old scores' were being settled.*

*'They had been our neighbours but were the very worst perpetrators of sadism. They committed the most savage massacres of the Polish people in Volhynia and Eastern Galicia.'*

My family would most likely not have escaped this massacre and were perhaps lucky to instead enjoy the hospitality of Stalin! My Babcia's cousin Toscia, however, with her two young children, was a victim of the UPA.

Despite finding it very painful and highly emotional, my Mum put her pen to paper every day. I wondered if I'd put too much pressure on her but my darling Mamusia persevered with the strength she had developed to survive the Labour camps aged only 16.

I sent a copy of the first draft I'd written to her sister Jasia and she was able to recall more detail of those awful times. Of the starvation rations, the constant gnawing hunger and arctic weather conditions .

She would go into her own memory over and over again for me, to bring their story to life. My cousin Alec found his Mum crying over the draft and he read it himself. And I'm so very glad he did.

This reawakened his interest in the family history and since then we have been a very close and productive team. Together exploring our sad but most interesting heritage, putting together this story and the prequel to this, ***'Midnight Train to Siberia.'***

We have had a lot of help from the younger members of the family. It's been a bonus, a considerable help to the older brains of the team! Alec's son Chris and my niece Natalie have helped with designing book covers and Natalie has also done some valuable editing.

Alec's daughter Lynsey has looked into the family archive, on our Dziadek's side, finding new information on our great Grandmother, Konstancja. She got her Dad Alec to do a DNA test. I've also recently done one and am awaiting results.

This is very much a family effort, running through the generations and I'm sure our younger relatives will continue to unearth more detail over the years and add to the story.

We all have Polish heritage, some of us stronger than others, Alec and I especially, who are nearer to the bones of the story.

I hadn't wanted to reopen old wounds but needed to revisit the family past. I wanted to present as truthful an account as possible but I needn't have worried, both Mum and Ciocia although emotional in their telling, were so very helpful.

I wonder if it helped them in some way to offload some of this most traumatic and interesting story. Not just of their suffering but their incredible resolve.

I also realized that a lot of what I had remembered from the days I had sneaked in for a cuddle with my grandparents, and the many visits with them over the years, had stuck.

Those memories had set the pattern for my interest in Poland's WW2 history and I have made many new discoveries on this journey. Mainly through Polish history sites, where members would be searching for information on their family separated or lost in the war.

They would also be looking for some information of what Poland as a country had gone through. There were many personal recollections.

I have uncovered many facts and untruths, as so much of what happened to the Polish deportees and Poland as an Ally, had been buried. Mostly to indulge Stalin.

Reports from Armia Krajowa, Witold Pilecki, Jan Karski and other Polish notables of Hitler's war crimes, were ignored. *The world didn't listen to the warnings.*

Western media, much of it with Communist links (OWI) had covered up anything associated with Stalin. He was the West's Ally!

More of that is covered in the sequel, ***'Hurricanes of Polish Fury.'***

No survivor could avoid the pain of exile to a most remote land, the hard labour and starvation, hostility from their captors. I've met deportees who had buried their feelings so deeply, they couldn't share them with anyone, prisoners of their own most painful memories.

Some had lost a mother, brother and sister and their father in the space of 3 months. Watching your baby sister starve to death on the deportation train left a pain that never went away.

Erasing this from their memories was a means of emotional protection and their lives must have been very difficult to bear. And looking for lost family must have only added to their despair.

No one can walk away from the terror they experienced without scars.

Each family carried the grief of leaving so many behind and of those in unmarked graves.

My Mother remembered those poor souls they couldn't take with them. Emaciated, with no energy to lift themselves off the ground, they wouldn't see another day.

The suffering did not end with their release from the Soviet camps, it continued throughout their lives. She never forgot them, *'the physical pain had healed but the mental pain went on forever.'*

*'We clashed with the Kommandant, with the threat of death many times in the Labour camps. Living in terror of the Bolsheviks and the NKVD on the journeys to Tashkent, but we somehow managed to survive, we tried to forget them, to bury them but they still got into our very beings and became a part of us.'*

*The Labour Camp Security, NKVD*

My Mother had flashbacks throughout her life, it was frozen into her memory. *'It hurts my head'* she would say and she had a nervous breakdown at 39. She had brought up 3 children despite suffering Stalin's terror and I am forever grateful and proud to be her daughter.

I miss her so very much, the ties between us were so strong, she was very special. ***Moja kochana Mama***.

*'It's always there, never goes away, to go without food for days at a time, working in the forests in arctic conditions was so very hard to cope with. I've never forgotten the deaths around me, people died from dysentery, typhus and starvation, the body and spirit were sorely tested.'*

*'It never goes away...'* it followed them throughout their escape over the Russian plains, some 4000km's towards Port Krasnovodsk and freedom. Then eventually onto England and a new life and many changes to overcome.

*'When I came to England I got used to people calling me a bloody foreigner and my children Polish pigs.'*

When it was noticed that my Mother had a foreign accent; when collecting us from school; we also got that tag and my cousins went through the same but our mothers far worse. My Mother made sure her English was near perfect but her accent always gave way to negative comments and behaviour.

*'Yes I was traumatized and sometimes I felt it made me stronger, more able to cope but some days it's in my mind and I can't lose it'.*

I remembered my grandparents were afraid to speak in front of people. My Dziadek would take me to infant school and collect me. On the bus he would say to me, because I used to natter away in this new language I was learning, *'ssssh cicho Tereska ....'* and he'd put his finger to his lips, he didn't want to let people know we were foreign.

Many refugees, who were scattered across the globe, were afraid to speak openly for fear of putting their family back in Communist Poland, in a difficult position, my own family included. 'Phone calls were very 'carefully' held between our family in England and the family in Poland.'

The Communist state kept a careful eye on people who had relatives *'abroad'* and they would be *'invited to have a chat'* with the FSB and were usually asked if they would *'like to share any information'* with them, *'spy for them'* and their apartments and workplaces would be under surveillance, many were bugged.

There was fear of retribution and people didn't start talking openly until the Berlin War fell in 1989 and then the overthrow of Communist rule in 1989-1991 after Gorbachev's loosening of the Soviet yoke on eastern Europe.

This is the story of a most remarkable family, one of so very many, taken by force from the Kresy in 1940. The reason? They were ***'enemies***

***of the state'*** and for that Stalinist label, they were put through a most appalling imprisonment.

They had not committed any crime, yet they had lost absolutely everything. Their property and belongings *'confiscated'* by their *'neighbours'* almost as soon as they had boarded the deportation transport with their captors.

They had withstood the privations of the labour camps and resisted the NKVD. They had never given in despite the hardships, extreme weather conditions and physical labour.

After Yalta 1945, so very many were unable to return to their homeland. Abandoned by the Allies, Poland and eastern Europe had been assigned to Stalin and Communism.

The US and GB had *'agreed future governments of the eastern nations should be friendly to the Soviet regime…'*

Adam my Dziadek had fought in the Polish-Russian war of 1921 which Poland had won. Had he and Kazia gone back to Poland one or both would have been arrested and at best, sent to a gulag. Many who did return were hunted down and went through *'show trials'* by the *'communist lashers of Poland.'* Many were executed, – Stalin's revenge.

*The Communist SB, responsible for many 'show trials' of returning Polish citizens and Resistance members*

The horror and brutality they went through never left them, it also affected the children of survivors, who lived with the impact it had on their family. I think readers may be able to see the impact it has had on me, through reading this and the sequel. How could I avoid it.

I can't hold Stalin to account but I can show how he put a specific number of Polish citizens into the most awful hardship and for some, brutality and how many Polish exiles survived despite him.

This has been a hugely emotional journey for me and many tears have fallen; I do not exaggerate; I have spent years looking into the greater story with help from Polish Facebook history sites, other survivors' testimonies, many other sources of research and of course the family memories.

I recently came across a postcard from my Ciocia, buried in my very own 'archive' which stirred a few memories. She was another valuable source of research. I lived in Streatham with her before finding work off London's Tottenham Court Road.

I was 21, it was my first time away from home and It was a most interesting time as we would chat over supper and really get to know each other. My cousin Alec was courting the lovely Hazel at the time so I didn't see much of him but we've made up for lost time over the years.

What Ciocia and I had in common was an interest in history, especially when history is 'revised' to suit another narrative. It seemed to spur us on and chats got very interesting, putting things right!

I discovered that despite being an Ally of the Grand Alliance the Polish Military was not allowed to celebrate VE Day. The Labour PM Atlee had acquiesced to Stalin's demand that the Polish military would not be allowed to attend.

To deny a most formidable ally this occasion to celebrate Poland's contribution was petty, (refer to sequel) I had never seen Ciocia Jasia so angry.

That really did make me think long and hard about the impact of Russia's control over Poland, on its people, on our family still in Poland. And of course the rest of the eastern bloc and any Government susceptible to Stalin's charms.

Why had Poland been so badly treated? And as I researched Poland and WW2 history I also became aware of the disrespect shown to Poland. Poland was ignored. Today accused by revisionists of even starting WW2, complicit with Germany!

The history of WW2 is deep, it's very easy to hide the truth in its many archives.

Ciocia Jasia also told me of how the family and most refugees, post war entry into England, were treated. Not just by the government and its citizens, but by the media and the Unions.

The Government knew what the peoples of war torn Europe had gone through. The general public however, had little knowledge of their suffering or of Poland's contribution to the war effort.

So much propaganda had been spread and the country was post war, rationing was in place, there was hardship and with an influx of many 'foreigners' times were very difficult.

This reaction can be understood. But not easy for the many refugees who had escaped tyranny and thought they were in a safe, welcoming country!

I usually went to bed with my head buzzing, full of all this information but glad to learn more about my family, what they had gone through. Ciocia had told me a lot more than Mum had been able to and I am forever grateful to her. I could also understand more, from afar, my mother's reluctance to share things. Maybe not wanting to load her trauma onto me.

After many years of researching this period of WW2, I can understand why my aunt was so very angry because many of Poland's war efforts are not acknowledged. Yet like the rest of the family, she somehow managed to put this aside to live a life outside her homeland.

I put all these valuable notes into my 'archive' and sealed the memories to use at a later date. I'd collected so much it was almost overwhelming but it's the basics of this story. From the memories and thoughts of my family and other refugees.

Told by the people who lived it and suffered it. Their personal recollections of a catastrophe they didn't see coming, which was a death sentence for very many. Their memories were a precious resource.

And talking of family, I promised my darling Mum Alicja, only quite recently, that I would finish the family story.

She was 99 and had Alzheimers which is such a cruel way for anyone to spend their later years. She still knew who I was for which I was very thankful. She would squeeze my hand so hard, with those hands strong from labour in the forests of Siberia. She would then kiss my hand and giggle and then we'd snuggle. How I miss those precious moments.

Each time I saw her I would get her book, ***Midnight Train to Siberia*** out, to help jog her memory and we would look at the family photo's. Slowly going through page by page and she would look at me and point to the pictures of the family in Poland, in that book she and her sister Jasia, helped me to write, their story, my heritage.

She would say 'Mama' when recognizing her Mother and 'Tatus' when seeing her father in his Cavalry uniform. She would smile at the pictures of herself on a bicycle in Poland at about 13 years of age.

Laugh at the photo's of her and her sister Jasia, her bother Janusz and cousin Marysia. Happy and free, before their world was shattered by those hostile invaders.

We have many photo's of the family in Poland because the albums were smuggled out by my Babcia Kazia. She protected them over 20,000kms + of journeys from Poland to Russia, to freedom, see Chapter 10. – They are precious.

How did my family survive Russia and then have the mental and physical energy to escape through those many miles to freedom? How did they cope in England post war? Another alien land, so different from their own.

They had made their home in the eastern borderlands of Poland. The land of the Kresy and the great forest of Białowieża that gives the Kresy its magic and mystery.

The Poles displaced by Stalin in 1940 from that region made the Kresy a synonym for the land of their birth.

A beautiful land on my list to visit. I have been to Poland but not yet to the land where my family lived and where my Mother grew up. It's now a part of the Ukraine and currently under attack by the warmongering Putin, in his bid to recover Russia's lost empire.

Białowieża forest is one of the last and largest remaining part of the immense primeval forest that once stretched across the European plain and is home to more than 800 bison. And those bison have a most remarkable claim to fame. I can highly recommend Żubrówka Bison Grass flavoured Wódka.

'With a history spanning centuries this will take your taste buds on an unforgettable journey.' It's a journey we make to raise a glass of this medicinal potion at certain times of the year. It's also a great throat elixir!

I have a deep affinity with my Polish heritage and I will continue on behalf of my darling Mother Alicja and family to finish their story.

The members of my family who were exiled to Siberia have now gone, my Mother Alicja died just before Wigilia 2023. Stalin's shadow is at last laid to rest, for them at least, they are at peace.

*'... they have slipped away leaving memories behind after a train ride to dark forests, trees to fell for a crouching bear, while frozen hands, held in prayer to a God who didn't seem to hear...'*

*Extracts from a poem by Rowan Annette Mills 2024*

And what a heritage they have left us. As a family, to escape imprisonment from Siberia and as a nation, to use their fury and frustration as an Ally, to defeat the German occupier of Europe.

It's also a story of love, courage and resolve. A story to share with many.

This part of the memoir and the sequel ***Hurricanes of Polish Fury***, will illustrate that Stalin did not, ever, break the spirit of my family. Or their dogged determination to escape his clutches, through the thousands of miles travelled in their bid for freedom.

*Teresa Radomska 2024*

## And the story continues in the sequel...

Telling of Poland's role as an ally after the Sikorski-Majeski agreement of 1941, the thoroughly misnamed, *'amnesty.'*

## In Hurricanes of Polish Fury

I tell of the absolute spirit and targetted fury of the Polish forces...

*Hurricane LF363 flying in the markings of 303 Squadron*

It's first operational squadron in 1944 was 309, Ziemia Czerwieńska (land of Czerwień) Squadron. It had a camera fitted and carried out reconnaissance patrols over the North Sea.

The above photograph was donated by Tadeusz Dippel, a friend of my cousin Alec, who has worked diligently with me on our family history.

The Dippel family were victims not just of the Russian invaders but also of the Germans. His Father's pre war partner was murdered at Majdanek Concentration camp and his great aunt survived Ravensbruck Concentration Camp.

Tadeusz's uncle Stefan fought in the Warsaw Uprising and his cousin was also involved as a nurse at the age of only 18. Tadeusz will be interviewed regarding his Uncle Stefan, in July 2024 at the Warsaw Uprising Museum in Poland.

It's a sad but very interesting story of the bravery of the Polish people in WW2. Tadeusz has given us more information on the survival of and sad outcome of some members of his family and I've included that in the sequel... ***Hurricanes of Polish Fury -Chapter 2***

**Read on...**

## Monte Cassino, captured by Polish troops

*'they walked, crawled through Siberia through the whole of Persia to North Africa to turn the tide in El Alamein. They fought from Tobruk through Sicily and into the impregnable mountain fortress and 213 Benedictine monastery that could not be broken, Monte Cassino, which was occupied by a crack division of German paratroopers, the crack division of the Luftwaffe. They fought their way from hilltop to hilltop up to that precipitous mound and planted the red and white flag in the still smoking ruins of Monte Cassino.'*

*Steven Pound MP - Westminster Hall debate 2019*

*My cousin Alec's Dad, Bolesław, was awarded the Monte Cassino Cross. Alec has been a big part of the team behind this and the other memoirs.*

After winning this most bloody campaign, the Polish people, heard that their country had been gifted to Stalin at Yalta. For many of them there was no return to their homeland but Poland held out, they had opened the gateway to Italy.

**Read on how...**

**Poland as an ally** contributed towards the winning of WW2 and is not to this day acknowledged at war memorials as an ally. Yet France is, despite being overwhelmed by the Germans and as the Vichy, collaborated with the Germans.

**How the communist influenced OWI propaganda...** was used to show Polish refugees fleeing from Russia, in a most healthy condition to appease Stalin. Having walked from Russia to Iran with good footwear and clothes and not in the least malnourished or in the skeletal condition the majority of them actually were.

**WW2 history is manipulated by many revisionists to this day**

However, authentic photo's were captured by Lieut. Col. Henry Szymanski, classified until 1952. The Polish refugees were mostly kept isolated to prevent them embarrassing the Soviets and told not to talk to anyone but they insisted on having their photographs taken for the record. Hossain Gattari, has built an archive, compiling a virtual museum of those Polish refugees who reached safety in Iran. It includes my own family.

**How revisionists...**

are portraying Poland as 'starting WW2' and as collaborators and in other negative ways, erasing the past with regard to WW2 history.

How Holocaust survivor Edward Mosberg has stood for the truth, refuting many of the revisionists' claims and those of the Israeli Government.

**How Poland's Govt in exile...**

based in England, supported Poland's Armja Krajowa and other Polish Resistance in exposing to the Allies, the Genocide being conducted by the Germans.

***The world did not listen***

**Poland's D-Day story...**

Polish forces fought on the beaches in Normandy and played a vital role in the operation. In the Falaise bloody battle, they 'trapped the Germans like a cork in a bottle' and 3,000 Polish servicemen died.

**Read on and explore Poland's WW2 history**

**The Battle of Britain** – which Squadron had the most 'kills'

**Enigma** – who really broke the code?

If this has got your interest.

**Read on in the sequel...**

'Hurricanes of Polish Fury'

## Acknowledgements

My most sincere thanks and love go to Alec Dyki, my skilful, lovable and dependable cousin who supported me in many aspects of this and the prequel, the most important parts of our heritage and also to family members for photographs from pre and post WWI Poland, WW2 Persia, Lebanon and England.

Anita de Haan • Janina Misik • Marek, Ania and Ewa Skoczylas

• Kazia and Adam Góral • Alicja Góral Hartley

Book Jacket Design by Alec Dyki & Natalie Lewis

Page layout by Alec Dyki

And very special thanks must go to a very dear friend, the late Patricia Murphy, without her input and encouragement I would have found this most emotional task much harder to bear.

I also gratefully acknowledge the permission granted by Ryszard Grzybowski of the Association of the Families of the Eastern Borderlands to use artwork and poems and personal recollections reproduced in this book and also in the prequel, Midnight Train to Siberia.



I am indebted especially to my family, in particular my Babcia Kazia, Dziadek Adam, Mamusia Alicja, and Ciocia Jasia. Their role in providing me with the facts of their ordeal from 1940 to 1946 has been invaluable in piecing this story together.

## Sources of research

• The Góral and Radomski families personal recollections and archives • Children of Sybiraks • Kresy Family • Kresy Siberia.• Stalin's Ethnic Cleansing • Forgotten Refugees • Silenced Refugees • Silent Heroes of the Forgotten Holocaust • Becky Little, National Geographic • Poland Forever • Wikipedia • Norman Davies • Max Hastings • Christopher R. Browning • Joanna Ostrowska & Marcin Zaremba • Polish Academy of Sciences • Dr Janusz Wróbel IPN, • Michael Checinski, IPN • Prof. Chwalba, Jagielonian Univ. • Dr Kathrine R. Jolluck, Stanford Univ. • Vyacheslav, Volodin, Prof. Daniel Tiles, Krakow Univ. • Jarosław Kaczynski, Polish President 2005-2010 • Prof. Andrzej Paczkowski, Dr Jan Zaryn, IPN • Władyslaw Bartoszewski • Sergey Radchenko • Mateusz Morawiecki, Polish PM • Prof. Szewach • Brendon Dougherty • David Moorhouse • Sergey Andreev • Timothy Snyder • Anne Applebaum • Polishmediaissues • Poland.pl/history • Britishpoles.uk • Polish Truth • Historynotesfrompoland.com • Justiceforpoland • PolishForums.com

www.ingramcontent.com/pod-product-compliance
Ingram Content Group UK Ltd.
Pitfield, Milton Keynes, MK11 3LW, UK
UKHW062255290726
14090UKWH00017B/710